downsizing
THE FEDERAL GOVERNMENT

CHRIS
EDWARDS

downsizing
THE FEDERAL GOVERNMENT

CATO
INSTITUTE
WASHINGTON, D.C.

Library of Congress Cataloging-in-Publication Data

Edwards, Chris (Chris R.)
  Downsizing the federal government / Chris Edwards.
    p. cm.
  Includes bibliographical references and index.
  ISBN 1-930865-82-1 (cloth : alk. paper) — ISBN 1-930865-83-X
(paper : alk. paper)   1. Government spending policy—United
States.   2. Waste in government spending—United States.   3. Budget
deficits—United States.   I. Title.

HJ7537.E33 2005
352.3′67—dc22

                                                    2005054275

Cover design by Jon Meyers.
Printed in the United States of America.

CATO INSTITUTE
1000 Massachusetts Ave., N.W.
Washington, D.C. 20001
www.cato.org

To Karen, Anna, and Sophia

Contents

1. Introduction

The federal government is running large budget deficits, spending too much, and heading toward a financial crisis. Federal spending increased by one-third in President George W. Bush's first four years, with large increases for agriculture, defense, education, health care, and other areas.[1] Those increases have come just as the costs of federal entitlement programs are set to balloon when the baby-boom generation retires. Spending on the three main entitlement programs—Social Security, Medicare, and Medicaid—is expected to double from $1 trillion in 2005 to $2 trillion by 2015.[2]

Where will the money come from? If government spending is not cut, average working families will face huge tax increases that dwarf anything seen in decades. Tax increases would damage the economy and be strongly resisted by the public. As a consequence, policymakers need to begin identifying programs in the federal budget that can be cut, transferred to the states, or privatized.

This book provides policymakers and the public with a detailed guide to federal budget reforms. It proposes eliminating more than 100 agencies and programs to reduce federal spending from 20 to 15 percent of the nation's economy. The country would be better off if the $2.5 trillion federal government were downsized. Cutting the budget would avert the looming federal financial crisis and give Americans a stronger economy and a freer society.

The Temptation to Tax

I came to Washington in 1990 to study economics and learn how the federal government works. My first lesson in government came from watching President George H. W. Bush reverse his famous "read my lips: no new taxes" pledge from the 1988 election campaign. Bush increased federal spending 16 percent in his first two years in office and by 1990 was faced with a slowing economy and a rising deficit.[3] Deficits can be reduced by cutting spending, but the president and his budget adviser, Richard Darman, did not look very hard for programs to cut.[4] At the same time, numerous Republicans were telling Darman privately that taxes should be raised.[5]

What to do? Darman suggested that the administration hold a "budget summit" with the Democrat-controlled Congress. With a summit, the blame for a tax hike could be shared with the other party. The result was the 1990 budget deal, which was a victory for bipartisanship but a loss for American taxpayers.

That pattern has been repeated many times.[6] Federal overspending, high deficits, perhaps a recession, and presto—an excuse for a tax hike. Usually, tax increases are coupled with promises of spending cuts. But such "cuts" are usually just reductions in future spending growth, and even those often fail to materialize. With the 1990 budget deal, the Bush administration claimed that there would be two and a half dollars of spending cuts for each dollar of tax increases.[7] But the cuts to defense were against an inflated baseline, and there were no cuts to nondefense spending.[8] Indeed, nondefense spending increased 15 percent in the two years following the budget summit.[9]

Large budget deficits are likely to be an ongoing part of the fiscal landscape. That could mean damaging budget summits and tax increases in the future unless policymakers start making real spending cuts. George W. Bush has so far broken the pattern of the three previous presidents and resisted tax increases. But he has driven up spending and the deficit just a few years before growing numbers of the elderly will be demanding their promised, but unaffordable, Social Security and Medicare benefits. Unless spending is cut, budget summits and tax hikes will begin looking dangerously attractive as the flood of federal red ink turns into a tidal wave.

A Plan to Cut Spending and Balance the Budget

A Brookings Institution book on the looming federal financial crisis argued that "although tax increases are unpopular with those who favor smaller government, no one has suggested how to achieve balance without them."[10] This book takes that as a challenge and provides a detailed plan to balance the federal budget without tax increases.

I analyzed programs across the entire budget and identified large savings. Chapter 4 provides a detailed list of programs that should be terminated, privatized, or devolved to the states to save $380 billion annually.[11] These cuts could be phased in over 10 years. In addition, I propose changes to Social Security, Medicare, and Medicaid that would create growing savings over time, reaching $270 billion annually by 2015.

These reforms would balance the budget by 2011 and create growing surpluses after that, even with all of the Bush administration's tax cuts in place. The plan would reduce the size of the federal government from 20 percent of gross domestic product in 2005 to 15 percent by 2015.

The book examines the problems of federal programs in detail and provides a structure to help policymakers target the most needed spending cuts. I devote chapters to each of the following types of programs:

- Programs that are wasteful, meaning duplicative, obsolete, mismanaged, ineffective, or subject to high levels of fraud and abuse (Chapter 5)
- Programs that are for the benefit of special interests (Chapter 6)
- Programs that actively damage society, such as by distorting the economy or harming the environment (Chapter 7)
- Programs that should be devolved to state and local governments (Chapter 8)
- Programs that should be privatized (Chapter 9)

Any given program may fall into one or more of those categories. Amtrak and the National Zoo, for example, are both mismanaged and good candidates for privatization. Amtrak's problem is that, as a federal agency, it is denied the flexibility it needs to innovate, cut costs, and earn a profit. At the National Zoo in Washington, bureaucratic mismanagement has led to a series of quality control scandals.[12] Both of those institutions provide useful services and would probably survive, adjust, and even flourish if cut free from the government's yoke.

Other programs ought to be handed back to the states. Highway construction, for example, is properly a state function, and there is no economic or technical reason why federal funding is necessary. Indeed, federal highway money is wasted on low-priority projects in the districts of important members of Congress, while useful projects in congested states go unfunded. The solution is to devolve federal highway spending, and the gasoline taxes that support it, to the states. The states could more efficiently plan their own highway systems, and they could encourage growth in private toll highways to help reduce congestion.

Many federal agencies and programs ought to be terminated because of chronic mismanagement. Good examples include the Army Corps of Engineers, the Bureau of Indian Affairs, the Department of Energy, and the National Aeronautics and Space Administration. Those agencies are not crucial in a time of large budget deficits, and any useful functions they perform could be performed by private businesses and charities.

In the preface to a report by the Senate Committee on Government Affairs in 2001, Sen. Fred Thompson (R-TN) concluded that the federal government has "terrible" management and a "staggering" problem of waste, fraud, and abuse.[13] No sooner does Congress try to patch up one mismanagement scandal when new ones erupt, suggesting that the government is simply too big for Congress to oversee adequately. By downsizing, policymakers could focus on improving performance in a limited range of core government services such as national security.

Public and Private Interests

Mismanagement is only one problem with the federal government. A bigger problem is that it does many things that make average citizens worse off. People who don't follow public policy might assume that there must be "a good reason" for existing programs, in the sense of a rational public purpose. It turns out that for many programs there is not. For example, economists widely agree that farm subsidies are counterproductive and should be repealed. The existence of farm subsidies cannot be explained by economic logic. Instead, subsidies exist because of the political logic of self-interested farm-state politicians and powerful farm lobbying groups, who reap benefits at the expense of average Americans.

During much of the 20th century the "public interest theory of government" held sway. The idea was that policymakers acted with the best interests of the general public in mind. Politicians and bureaucrats like to call themselves "public servants"; thus one might assume that they would act accordingly. The public interest theory of government probably reached its apex in the 1930s. President

Franklin Roosevelt skillfully set up a contrast in the public mind of greedy businessmen on the one hand and a "brains trust" of enlightened Washington officials on the other.

However, experience with a large federal government since the 1930s shows that the public interest theory has little real-world explanatory power. Ill-conceived laws with little public support get enacted all the time. Many federal agencies perform poorly year after year, yet receive steadily growing budgets. Government officials often put career advancement, turf protection, and other personal factors ahead of the public interest.

The view that government officials put the public interest first took a nosedive after Watergate. In academia at about the same time, the public interest theory of government was being unseated by "public choice" theory, which holds that self-interested officials and lobbying groups are the key drivers of government policy.[14] That theory explains the perverse results we often observe in government. Of course, the Founding Fathers were well aware that private interests would try to use government to the detriment of the general welfare. Accordingly, they created a constitutional framework that sought to limit federal power. Unfortunately, that framework was largely discarded in the 20th century—limits on federal power did not seem to be needed because the government was assumed to act in the public interest.

Today, Americans are more skeptical about government. There is also a renewed appreciation that even well-intentioned programs and regulations are poor substitutes for competitive private markets. The large expansion of the federal government between the 1930s and 1970s saw the birth of many failed, even disastrous, programs. Under "urban renewal" policies, for example, the government bulldozed inner-city neighborhoods across the country and warehoused millions of people in hideous, crime-infested high-rises.[15] American cities are still recovering from the damage caused by the urban policies of 50 years ago. The task ahead is to mop up the mess left by all the failed federal interventions of the last century and to resurrect the framework of limited government that the Founders established.

What's Ahead

Chapter 2 examines the size and scope of the federal government and discusses recent increases in federal spending. Chapter 3 examines arguments in favor of downsizing the government. Chapter 4

5

presents a detailed plan to cut the budget by eliminating more than 100 agencies and programs and reducing entitlement spending. Chapters 5 to 9 describe in detail the problems that plague federal programs. Chapter 10 provides suggestions for structural reforms and discusses some reasons for optimism regarding budget restraint. Appendix 1 discusses how the government caused and sustained the Great Depression of the 1930s. Appendix 2 contains a department-by-department discussion of programs and proposed reforms.

Readers may not be convinced about every budget cut proposed here. But I hope they will be more skeptical the next time a politician promises to solve some problem in society by spending more tax-payer money. Given the poor record of the programs examined here, there should be a bigger burden on policymakers to prove that programs fill crucial needs that the private sector cannot meet. The federal government's legacy of failure suggests that policy questions ought to be approached with a strong presumption of laissez faire.

Some readers may argue that I have not given a balanced presentation of the benefits we derive from the federal government. That is true in a sense. James Beck, once a member of Congress and U.S. solicitor general, wrote a similar book about the government in 1932, *Our Wonderland of Bureaucracy*. He said that the purpose of his book was to "remind such Americans as are seriously interested in their governmental system, of some of its defects, and the author cheerfully leaves to the tellers of economic 'bed-time stories' the narration of the glories of federal bureaucracy."[16]

I also leave the "bedtime stories" of how government programs are *supposed to* work to the politicians and lobbying groups. This book focuses on how federal programs *actually* work in the real world.

2. Size and Scope of the Federal Government

A fundamental change in American democracy in the past century has been the massive growth in government at all levels. Federal, state, and local spending has increased from 8 percent of the nation's economy a century ago to 31 percent today. The federal government has grown particularly rapidly, and it has expanded into many areas that were formerly reserved to the states and the people. This chapter looks at the growth of the federal government, the broad scope of its activities, and Washington's culture of spending that has posed a hurdle to reform.

Growth of the Government

Federal spending increased from 2.8 percent of the nation's gross domestic product a century ago to 20.0 percent today. Spending on national defense was at high levels in the middle of the 20th century, but declined relative to GDP in recent decades, as shown in Figure 2.1.[1] Spending on all nondefense programs soared from 1.8 percent of GDP in 1900, to 9.0 percent in 1950, to 16.0 percent today. Much of the added federal spending has been for traditionally state and local activities such as education. But state and local spending has not been displaced. Instead, it has also grown rapidly, particularly since 1950.

The growth of the federal government has been spurred by crises such as the two world wars and the Great Depression. Federal taxing and regulatory powers tend to expand during crises, but the government does not shrink to pre-crisis levels when troubles subside. That has caused a ratcheting up of the size of the government over the decades. During the Great Depression, the government claimed vast new powers to regulate the economy, and it created hundreds of new programs. Federal expansion in the 1930s dealt a severe blow to federalism, which had been a key constraint on government growth during the nation's first 150 years.

7

Figure 2.1
GOVERNMENT SPENDING AS A SHARE OF THE U.S. ECONOMY

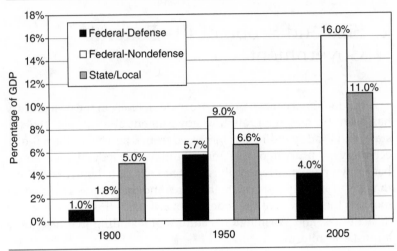

SOURCE: Author's calculations based on data from the U.S. Bureau of the Census and *Budget of the United States Government: Fiscal Year 2006, Historical Tables*. Federal grants to state and local governments are included under federal spending and excluded from state/local spending.

Programs from the 1930s and other eras linger on decades after their failures should have been obvious to policymakers. The folly of farm subsidies, for example, has been recognized for at least seven decades, but they have yet to be repealed.[2] Some agencies become obsolete as society and technology change, but policymakers usually find new activities for them to engage in.

Occasionally, Congress does kill failed regulations and failed programs. But each new crisis provides opportunities for policymakers to demand more powers for the government and added spending. Acting rashly after 9/11, the government took control of the nation's airport security with an army of 45,000 new Transportation Security Administration bureaucrats. Only four years later, it is clear that this intervention was a big failure. The TSA is hobbled by poor performance, has low worker morale, and has made the news for scandalous overspending.[3] The cost to hire TSA airport screeners after 9/11 soared from $104 million to $741 million due mainly to mismanagement.[4] A government study in 2005 found that the five

U.S. airports that still have private screeners did a better job than airports with TSA screeners.[5] Clearly, government is no cure-all, and policymakers need to restrain their impulses to try and instantly "solve" every problem from Washington.

Scope of the Government

The federal government spent about $2,500,000,000,000 in 2005. After taking out the government's core functions of national defense and justice, it still spent $2,000,000,000,000, or roughly $18,000 for every household in the country.[6] Clearly, the federal government has amassed a huge range of spending programs beyond its basic national security responsibilities.

Figure 2.2 shows what the federal government spent the taxpayers' money on in 2005.[7] The "entitlement" programs, including Social Security, Medicare, Medicaid, and "other," account for 54 percent of total spending. (Other entitlements include such programs as unemployment compensation and food stamps.) Those programs are on autopilot, and they grow each year unless Congress passes laws to limit benefits or to limit the number of beneficiaries.

"Discretionary" programs account for 39 percent of federal spending. Funds for those programs are appropriated annually by Congress. Discretionary programs cover a huge array of federal activities including agriculture, commerce, defense, education, energy, environment, foreign aid, housing, labor, science, space, and transportation. Interest represents the remaining 7 percent of the budget.

The government might be able to competently perform a small number of those many functions under active oversight by Congress and the media. But it is a mistake to think that the government can be expanded so greatly and still retain adequate levels of performance. Each new bureau and program stretches thinner the ability of citizens and their representatives to keep track of the government's activities and to correct failures and abuses. This problem has been called "political overloading."

When private businesses expand, they usually enjoy "economies of scale," allowing them to produce more with reduced per unit costs. There are no economies of scale in government. Indeed, as the government expands, coordination problems between the many overlapping bureaus probably make performance worse. Congress

9

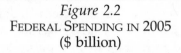

Figure 2.2
FEDERAL SPENDING IN 2005
($ billion)

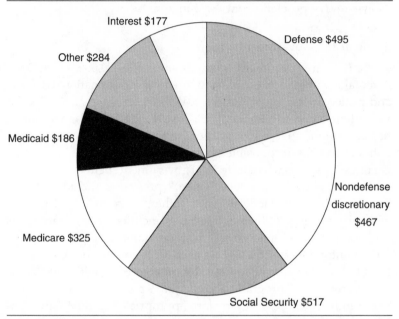

Interest $177

Defense $495

Other $284

Medicaid $186

Nondefense discretionary $467

Medicare $325

Social Security $517

SOURCE: Congressional Budget Office, "An Analysis of the President's Budgetary Proposals for Fiscal Year 2006," March 2005. Data are fiscal year outlays. Medicare is gross of offsetting receipts, which are included under "other." The figure for defense is a broader budget category than the figure for Department of Defense in Tables 2.2 and 4.2.

is too overloaded to do a decent job of ensuring that taxpayer money is spent efficiently in the hundreds of different bureaus and agencies.

Scandal after scandal attests to the fact that Congress is incapable of running a $2.5 trillion organization with a reasonable degree of competence. Certainly, financial management is a mess in many agencies. The Government Accountability Office has not been able to certify the government's financial statements eight years in a row because of weak accounting controls and mismeasurement of assets, liabilities, and costs.[8]

As the federal government has grown, it has infiltrated a vast range of activities that were previously private. Like an octopus, the

Figure 2.3
TENTACLES OF THE FEDERAL GOVERNMENT IN 2005

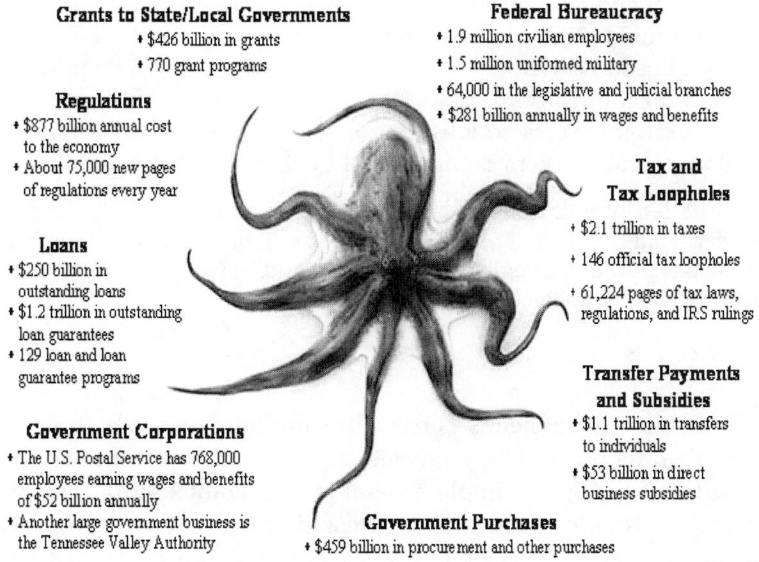

Grants to State/Local Governments
- $426 billion in grants
- 770 grant programs

Regulations
- $877 billion annual cost to the economy
- About 75,000 new pages of regulations every year

Loans
- $250 billion in outstanding loans
- $1.2 trillion in outstanding loan guarantees
- 129 loan and loan guarantee programs

Government Corporations
- The U.S. Postal Service has 768,000 employees earning wages and benefits of $52 billion annually
- Another large government business is the Tennessee Valley Authority

Federal Bureaucracy
- 1.9 million civilian employees
- 1.5 million uniformed military
- 64,000 in the legislative and judicial branches
- $281 billion annually in wages and benefits

Tax and Tax Loopholes
- $2.1 trillion in taxes
- 146 official tax loopholes
- 61,224 pages of tax laws, regulations, and IRS rulings

Transfer Payments and Subsidies
- $1.1 trillion in transfers to individuals
- $53 billion in direct business subsidies

Government Purchases
- $459 billion in procurement and other purchases

SOURCE: Author's compilation based mainly on the *Budget of the United States Government: Fiscal Year 2006.*

government has eight tentacles that reach out to manipulate society, as illustrated in Figure 2.3.[9] Those include direct activities of the bureaucracy, government purchases, loans, grants to state governments, transfer payments, regulations, taxes, and stand-alone federal businesses such as the U.S. Postal Service.[10] Federal spending in 2005 included $1.1 trillion in transfer payments, $0.5 trillion in purchases, $0.4 trillion in grants, and $0.3 trillion in compensation for federal workers.

This book focuses on spending and not taxation and regulation. However, the federal government is increasingly manipulating society through those two tentacles as well. With regard to taxes, the number of pages of federal rules has tripled in the past three decades.[11] With regard to regulations, the employee count of regulatory agencies has more than doubled in three decades.[12]

11

Table 2.1
FEDERAL WORKFORCE INCLUDING SHADOW WORKFORCE

a. Federal civilian workforce	1.9 million
b. Uniformed military personnel	1.5 million
c. U.S. Postal Service	0.8 million
d. Federal contractors	5.2 million
e. Federal grant-created jobs	2.9 million
f. State/local workers doing federal business	4.7 million
Total workers doing federal activities	17.0 million

SOURCE: Paul C. Light, "Fact Sheet on the New True Size of Government," Brookings Institution, September 5, 2003. Items d, e, f are Light's 2002 data. Items a, b, c are updated to 2005.

From the government's perspective, multiple tentacles enable it to expand its power to the greatest extent possible within the constraints it faces. For example, federal loan guarantees grew rapidly in the 1970s as members of Congress discovered that they could reward special interests while side-stepping the constraints on direct spending.[13] Similarly, grants (or "grants-in-aid") to the states have allowed the federal government to circumvent concerns about expansion of its power over state activities. Grants allow federal politicians to become activists in areas such as education, while shoveling cash into state coffers to muffle concerns about federal encroachment.

By using the various tentacles, the federal government leverages its 1.9 million civilian employees to gain broad control over society. For example, federal procurement turns private-sector workers into government-directed agents. Federal grants turn state and local workers into tools of the federal government. One scholar set out to determine how many people were in the federal government's "shadow workforce," meaning all those people who perform government-directed work.[14] The total federal workforce is 17 million, including 1.9 million in the civil service, 1.5 million in the uniformed military, 0.8 million in the USPS, 5.2 million contractors, 2.9 million employed through grants to private organizations, and 4.7 million employed through grants to state and local governments, as shown in Table 2.1.[15]

Republicans and the Culture of Spending

There are occasional revolts against the sprawling and grasping federal octopus. The most recent revolt was in 1994 when the Republicans took control of Congress for the first time in 40 years. They promised to end deficit spending, terminate programs, and give power back to the states and people. Unfortunately, they generally did not follow through on those promises.[16]

The Republicans did slow federal spending growth in their first few years in power, but budget restraint was abandoned by the late 1990s. It is true that the Republicans faced a president of the other party, who also abandoned restraint. But as Sen. Tom Coburn (R-OK) concluded on his experience in the House in the 1990s, "Washington turns outsiders into insiders," and the Republicans started behaving just like the big-spending Democrats had when they were in power.[17]

Under a Republican Congress during the past decade, most federal departments have enjoyed large increases in their budgets, as shown in Table 2.2. The fastest growing departments since 1995 have been Homeland Security, Education, Justice, Health and Human Services, and State. Aside from interest, total federal spending increased 79 percent in the last decade. By contrast, the consumer price index, which measures inflation, increased just 28 percent.

Figure 2.4 shows some of the ups and downs in major categories of spending since 1980, measured in constant dollars. Defense spending peaked in the mid-1980s, fell at the end of the Cold War, but has risen again in recent years. Social Security overtook defense to become the largest federal program in 1993, and its rapid growth is expected to continue for years to come. Medicare and Medicaid have grown rapidly as a result of both expansions in coverage and high medical inflation.

For Republicans, a remarkable embrace of Big Government has been in the area of nondefense discretionary programs. This budget category includes much of the wasteful spending that fiscal conservatives have long criticized, such as business subsidies. Figure 2.4 shows that real nondefense discretionary spending was cut back in the early 1980s, expanded in the early 1990s, trimmed in the mid-1990s, and then has been increased rapidly in recent years. In current (or actual) dollars, this category of spending was roughly constant at near $270 billion in the mid-1990s.[18] But in 1999 spending began to explode, reaching $467 billion by 2005.

Table 2.2
FEDERAL SPENDING BY DEPARTMENT OR AGENCY
($ billion)

Department or Agency	1995	2005	Increase
Homeland Security	9.4	33.3	254%
Education	31.2	71.0	127%
Justice	10.1	21.2	109%
Health and Human Services	303.1	585.8	93%
State	6.3	11.9	90%
Commerce	3.4	6.3	85%
Veterans Affairs	37.8	68.0	80%
Defense	259.5	444.1	71%
Agriculture	56.6	94.9	68%
Transportation	35.1	58.2	66%
Defense retirement	28.0	43.5	55%
Social Security Administration	361.4	559.0	55%
Labor	32.8	50.0	53%
Civil service retirement & related	41.3	61.0	48%
Housing and Urban Development	29.0	42.6	47%
International aid programs	11.1	14.8	33%
Corps of Engineers	3.7	4.9	32%
Interior	7.5	9.4	26%
Energy	17.6	22.2	26%
Environmental Protection Agency	6.4	7.9	23%
NASA	13.4	15.7	17%
Other items	(20.9)	75.7	
Total spending on programs	1,283.8	2,301.4	79%
Net interest	232.0	178.0	−23%
Total federal spending	1,515.8	2,479.4	64%

SOURCE: *Budget of the United States Government: Fiscal Year 2006, Historical Tables*. Data are fiscal year outlays. Social Security Administration includes Supplemental Security Income.

Part of the recent spending explosion is a consequence of the Republicans reversing their position on federalism, the idea that most government functions are properly the responsibility of the states and cities. Republicans used to favor moving federal activities such as education, housing, and transportation back to state jurisdiction or to the private sector. Many Republicans in the 1980s and

Figure 2.4
REAL FEDERAL SPENDING BY BUDGET CATEGORY

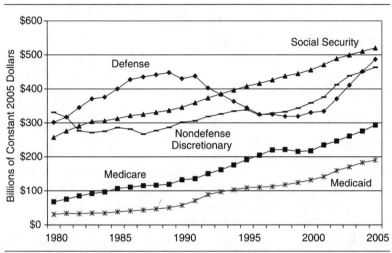

SOURCE: Author's calculations based on *Budget of the United States Government: Fiscal Year 2006, Historical Tables*. Data are fiscal year outlays. Medicare is net of offsetting receipts.

1990s, for example, supported abolishing the Department of Education. But that department's spending has exploded from $36 billion in 2001 to $71 billion by 2005.[19]

What happened to the Republican reformers who came into office in 1994 determined to downsize the government? Some continued to fight for spending cuts throughout the 1990s, but the Republican leadership gave up the battle as early as 1996 when it became obsessed with winning reelection. Senate Majority Leader Bob Dole (R-KS) and House Speaker Newt Gingrich (R-GA) had little, if any, interest in cutting spending. Dole ran for president in 1996 and did not want to rock the boat. Gingrich was determined to retain the majority in the 1996 congressional elections, which would cement his historic political achievement.

Some fiscal conservatives, such as House Budget Committee chairman John Kasich (R-OH), did push for spending cuts, but most Republicans came under the grip of Washington's culture of spending. That is confirmed by National Taxpayers Union data on the number of bills introduced in Congress that would increase or

15

decrease spending.[20] In the 104th Congress (1995–96), House and Senate members introduced two bills to increase spending for each bill that they introduced to cut spending. But by the 108th Congress (2003–04), the pro-spending bias of Congress had become much worse. In the House, there were 1,343 bills introduced to increase spending but just 63 to reduce it, for a ratio of 21 to 1. In the Senate, there were 1,040 bills to increase spending and just 35 to reduce it, for a ratio of 30 to 1.

Studies have also examined the voting patterns of particular members of Congress over time. Those studies generally find that the longer politicians are in office, the more they spend. One NTU analysis looked at the budget effects of all bills introduced by the 30 Republican freshmen elected in 1994 who are still in Congress today.[21] This group was very reform minded, and it led the charge to cut spending when it first entered Congress. The NTU analysis found that in the mid-1990s most members in this group sponsored legislation that would cut spending on net. But in recent years, all but 2 of the 30 members have legislative agendas that would increase net spending.

Box 2.1 examines the reasons why most incoming members of Congress get turned into big spenders over time. One factor is that congressional hearings are heavily stacked in favor of pro-spending witnesses. Policymakers usually only hear why spending on particular programs should be increased, and they rarely hear testimony in favor of cutting or terminating programs.

To take one example, a March 15, 2005, hearing of the Senate Agriculture, Nutrition, and Forestry Committee examined funding of school nutrition programs.[22] The hearing had five witnesses. The first witness was Sen. Elizabeth Dole (R-NC), who lent her support to increased funding of those programs. The next two witnesses were from the School Nutrition Association, a lobbying group that supports the programs. The final two witnesses were school administrators from Texas and Georgia. They also offered support. There were no witnesses who favored restraint, and certainly none who questioned whether the federal government ought to be in the school lunch business at all.

Hearings do not in themselves determine policy, but they are an important source of information for politicians and the media. Interestingly, the slanted witness phenomenon has been a problem

Box 2.1
Washington's Culture of Spending

In a 1991 book political scientist James L. Payne described the culture of overspending that permeates Washington.[1] In the 1994 elections, Republicans took control of Congress for the first time in four decades and promised that they would change that culture and cut spending. The 1994 "Contract with America" said that the Republicans would put an end to "government that is too big, too intrusive, and too easy with the public's money."[2]

A decade later, it is clear that the entrenched spending culture in Washington defeated the reformist principles of the incoming Republicans. Payne's analysis, which is the basis of the following points, helps explain the GOP's failure to follow through on spending reforms.

- **Pro-Spending Environment**. Members of Congress are bombarded from every angle with requests for added spending. This occurs in visits from constituents, at receptions, at policy forums, in fundraising phone calls, in meetings with lobbyists and other members, and in articles in the media. While constituents also tell members that they favor tax cuts and balanced budgets, few people have a personal interest in telling politicians to cut spending on particular programs.

- **One-Sided Congressional Hearings**. Congressional hearings examining particular programs are typically dominated by witnesses favoring more spending. Witnesses usually include federal program administrators, state officials who rely on federal funding, members of Congress who favor programs, recipients of program benefits, and lobbyists from organizations that support programs.

  Unlike court proceedings where a balance of views is presented, congressional hearings do not present policymakers with both the pros and cons of programs. Hearings

(continued next page)

Box 2.1 *continued*

are often just cheering sessions to promote program expansion. The prestige of committee members depends on programs within their jurisdiction being seen in a positive light. They usually have no interest in inviting dissenting witnesses, especially ones who would question the basic worth of programs. To appreciate the problem, one can examine hearing testimony on the websites of most House and Senate committees, such as those covering agriculture, education, and health care.

- **Presumption of Government Efficacy.** Members of Congress usually hear only that their favored programs "work." They hear from program beneficiaries, from experts who support programs, and from federal administrators. Members hear about the number of jobs created and the great things that could be done with more money. They do not hear about the damage caused by the taxes needed to fund programs.

  To many legislators, the power to spend is a powerful tool that *ought* to be able to solve problems. During election campaigns, politicians are encouraged to make promises that they will use this great tool to help people. When they listen to politicians, the public receives the message that any problem can be solved if only Congress could spend a bit more on it.

- **Philanthropic Fallacy.** Members of Congress enjoy helping their constituents. The various groups that ask them for funding seem like they have worthy causes. Legislators often have personal family reasons for promoting spending on particular issues.[3] The legislators' impulse to help is reinforced when they receive thanks from program beneficiaries, when they receive awards from interest groups, and when they are toasted at gala dinners for their support. Members begin to think of themselves as private philanthropists generously spending their own money.

Legislators cannot see the beneficial activities that would have been pursued by taxpayers if they had been able to keep their money. Nor do legislators perceive the negative effects of higher taxes on the economy. Legislators usually don't seek out any critical analyses of programs to get a balanced view. They mainly interact with program supporters who laud their selfless "public service."

Senate appropriations committee member Ted Stevens of Alaska is typical. He often appears at gala Washington dinners to accept awards for "his support" of federal arts spending, public television, and other activities to which he channels taxpayer money.[4] For example, the Corporation for Public Broadcasting gave the senator its "most prestigious honor" in 2003 for his steadfast support of "public broadcasting on behalf of our nation."[5]

Sen. Mike DeWine (R-OH) lists no fewer than 75 awards on his webpage for "public service" on behalf of "our children," "our young people," and others.[6] He touts his awards for "leadership in advancing regional economic development," "dedication to improving highway safety," and "work to improve mental health care for all Americans." Unfortunately, such puffery goes to the heads of most politicians, and they spend little time considering where the money for such spending programs comes from.

- **Manifest and Latent Perspectives**. Payne theorizes that some people have a "manifest" approach to policy. They are drawn to try and solve immediate and visible problems, and they have a emotional urge to right wrongs as quickly as possible. Other people are more cautious and take a "latent" approach. They think about the long-term and less-visible effects of actions. Politicians of the former mindset look at the immediate benefits to recipients of more spending. Politicians of the latter mindset consider

(continued next page)

Box 2.1 *continued*

secondary effects, such as the effects of higher taxes, increased deficits, and problems caused by the spending. Most people drawn into careers as politicians probably view public policy from a manifest perspective. Politicians are not randomly selected from the population; they are self-selected. They are people who want to further a cause, and they become unswerving advocates for programs. They forget that they are supposed to uphold the Constitution and dispassionately balance the claims of advocates of spending with broader concerns such as tax levels.

The overspending phenomenon in Washington is not caused simply by the desire of politicians to "buy votes" back home. If federal politicians had lifetime terms, there would probably still be an overspending problem. On the other hand, if term limits were imposed on Congress, the culture of spending would not get as entrenched because legislators would spend shorter periods of time in Washington. Term limits and other institutional reforms are discussed in Chapter 10. But the first step to limiting the budget bloat is to understand that politicians enjoy spending and they come to believe in it.

1. James L. Payne, *The Culture of Spending: Why Congress Lives beyond Our Means* (San Francisco: Institute for Contemporary Studies, 1991).
2. Ed Gillespie and Bob Schellhas, eds., *Contract with America: The Bold Plan by Rep. Newt Gingrich, Rep. Dick Armey and the House Republicans to Change the Nation* (New York: Times Books, 1994), p. 7.
3. For an example, see Jeffrey Birnbaum, "Personal Loss Changes Business as Usual," *Washington Post*, May 30, 2005 p. E1.
4. For example, Senator Stevens received the Creative Coalition's "Capitol Hill Spotlight Award" on March 13, 2005, at a gala dinner in Washington for "his support" of the arts.
5. Corporation for Public Broadcasting, press release, February 25, 2003, www.cpb/programs/pr.php?prn=310.
6. See Biography: Chronology at http://dewine.senate.gov. Accessed June 2005.

for decades. In a 1952 book, Sen. Paul Douglas (D-IL), a reform-minded liberal, complained about appropriations subcommittee hearings: "Almost invariably, witnesses testifying before these subcommittees represent agencies defending the budget requests or pressure groups demanding larger expenditures."[23]

The overspending problem in Congress is often portrayed simply as politicians wanting to secure "pork" projects for their districts in order to gain votes. But with reelection rates in the House at about 98 percent in recent years, vote buying does not seem to be the key source of the problem.

The bigger problem is that politicians *want to* spend because they come to believe in it after being surrounded by Washington's pro-spending culture. Aside from hearings, members of Congress receive pro-spending messages from constituents needing favors, lobbying groups, local politicians from their home states, media commentators, congressional aides, and federal administrators. Also, committees tend to be stacked with self-selected members who support the particular programs that the committees oversee.[24] Unfortunately, the costs of federal spending are harder to understand and less visible to politicians.

If frugal-minded members ask for cuts to programs they will make enemies in Congress, they will be scolded in the media for being uncaring, and they will be targeted for defeat by lobbying groups. Members who oppose spending that important members of their own party want will be ostracized and may be disciplined by party leaders. Ultimately, members of Congress are social creatures who do not want to make enemies, so it is easier to go along with the system. Staunch House conservative Sue Myrick (R-NC) recently lamented that support for big spending "is just the way you get along here."[25]

An ongoing problem for reform-minded Republicans is that their leaders show no personal restraint with regard to the budget. House Speaker Dennis Hastert, for example, is a champion at bringing pork, or special interest, spending back home to Illinois. As the *Washington Post* noted, Hastert "makes a habit of helping Illinois-based corporations," such as Boeing, Caterpillar, and United Airlines.[26] Even in the wake of the recent Boeing defense procurement scandal, Hastert continues to twist arms to keep Pentagon money flowing to the company.[27] Hastert's pork spending has included trying to get United a $1.6 billion loan guarantee and adding $250,000 to a defense bill for a candy company in his hometown to study chewing gum.[28] In May 2005, the *Washington Post* did a special report on how Hastert has slipped tens of millions of dollars of special projects into legislation for his hometown.[29] Why should rank-and-file Republicans restrain their own appetites for pork spending when they see that their leader is the chief porker?

The executive branch also plays a key role in spending growth. The basic operating principle for bureaucrats is to increase their annual budget allocations. As an agency's budget grows, bureaucrats gain clout, prestige, and promotions. Bureaucrats see their job as selling the public and members of Congress on the fabulous things that their programs are doing for the country. Federal agencies pump out streams of press releases and glossy publications full of high-minded rhetoric. Officials exaggerate problems in society that their agencies are then charged with solving.[30] Cabinet secretaries spend their time giving speeches about how their spending programs are helping America. Under President Bush, federal agencies have even paid private pundits to tout their programs, and agencies have created prepackaged policy stories that have appeared on television as "news."[31]

Bureaucrats are also skilled at playing budget defense. They can work against the president's budget office on proposed restraint. They can get news stories and opinion articles placed to suggest that cuts would be a disaster. They can use the "Washington monument" strategy, which offers up the most visible and sensitive programs as the ones to be hit under any restraint plan. Also, powerful federal unions are quick to denounce any scaling back of federal agencies.

This is the culture in Washington that sustains big spending. The spending culture is a big hurdle to downsizing the government, but it can be changed. The president could task cabinet secretaries to come up with cuts in their departments. Congressional hearings could be opened to alternative views. House members might see their job as protecting the taxpayer, which was the historic role of the lower chamber. Politicians might view running deficits as immoral, as they did in decades past. The spending culture can be changed, and some of the structural reforms discussed in Chapter 10 can help. But Americans need to demand change for it to happen. They need to demand a broader and deeper revolution than was delivered in 1994.

3. Why Downsize?

In considering the proper size and scope of the federal government, policymakers should take a number of factors into account. First, they should recognize that most existing programs are not authorized by the U.S. Constitution, as they involve activities that were meant to be left to the states and the people. Second, today's vast array of programs has overloaded the ability of policymakers to competently oversee the executive branch, let alone focus on priorities such as national security. Third, the rising costs of programs for the elderly dictate that large cuts be made throughout the budget. Fourth, the costs imposed by the government on the economy are large, and the returns from many of its activities are negative. Those reasons to downsize the government are discussed in turn.

Respecting the Constitution

The Constitution established a federal government of limited powers. Those powers are enumerated largely in Article I, section 8, which allows for spending on such limited functions as national security, establishing courts, coining money, and providing for an open national economy.[1]

Despite the straightforward limitations created by the Constitution, the Supreme Court has accepted looser readings of those limits over time, especially since the 1930s. Today, federal spending is directed into virtually any area that suits the whims of Congress. The government funds a wide range of activities that violate the letter and spirit of the Constitution, as the modern Court fails to enforce the original limits on federal power.

The Constitution's Commerce Clause is said to provide a justification for many of today's programs. Article 1, section 8, states, "The Congress shall have power . . . to regulate commerce . . . among the several states." The clause was meant primarily to ensure the free flow of interstate commerce and to bar states from erecting trade barriers.[2] But that original meaning was turned on its head by Supreme Court rulings in the 20th century that allowed the federal government to expand its power over anything that has even a remote connection to interstate commerce. Instead of acting as a brake on state power as originally intended, the clause has been used to expand federal power over a vast array of activities. Much of today's huge federal regulatory structure exists because of the Court's excessively broad reading of the Commerce Clause.

Occasionally, the Supreme Court puts some limits on the abuse of the Commerce Clause. In the *United States v. Lopez* decision of 1995, the Court ruled that Congress exceeded its authority when it outlawed the possession of handguns near schools.[3] In defending the law, the federal government argued that it had authority to pass it under the Commerce Clause. But the Court's ruling acknowledged for the first time in nearly 60 years that there are limits to the commerce power. The ruling has been followed by others that have revived federalism, at least in a limited way.

However, in the 2005 *Gonzales v. Raich* decision regarding medical marijuana, the Court reversed that recent trend and allowed expanded federal power. In his dissent in *Raich*, Justice Clarence Thomas expressed dismay at the majority's expansionist view of the commerce power: "If Congress can regulate this under the Commerce Clause, then it can regulate virtually anything, and the federal government is no longer one of limited and enumerated powers."[4]

The General Welfare Clause of Article I, section 8, is also said to provide a justification for much federal spending. Just about every lobbying group in Washington argues that their favored program is for the general welfare. But the clause does not create an independent power for Congress to spend. Instead, it was "meant to serve as a brake on the power of Congress to tax and spend in furtherance of its enumerated powers or ends: the spending that attended the exercise of an enumerated power had to be for the general welfare, not for the welfare of particular parties or sections of the nation."[5] If the General Welfare Clause meant that Congress could simply spend money on whatever it wanted, we would have a government of unlimited powers, nullifying the whole idea of constitutional government. Unfortunately, that is essentially what happens today, aided by expansive interpretations of the clause by the Supreme Court.

Members of Congress should start taking seriously their oaths to uphold the Constitution. Too often Congress ignores the Constitution or inserts boilerplate language into legislation to claim authority. Instead, when a questionable program comes before them, members of Congress should ask whether there is constitutional authority for it, and vote against it if they believe it violates the fundamental law of the land.

Many policymakers think that respecting constitutional limits is not practical in today's world. However, the tight limitations on federal power laid down by the Constitution's Framers were the embodiment of their practical experience with governments. The Framers knew that it would be destructive to have too much power concentrated in the national government. They turned out to be correct.

Consider the watershed years of the 1930s, when policymakers decided that they could jettison the constitutional wisdom of generations. During President Franklin Roosevelt's first term, the Supreme Court knocked down New Deal programs that had claimed unprecedented powers for the federal government. The justices believed that the Constitution meant what it said, and that federal powers were defined and limited. The Court rejected expansionist views of the Commerce and General Welfare Clauses, and they took the Tenth Amendment seriously.

In striking down a New Deal scheme for centralized economic planning in 1935, Chief Justice Charles Evans Hughes stated: "It is not the province of the Court to consider the economic advantages or disadvantages of such a centralized system. It is sufficient to say that the Federal Constitution does not provide for it."[6] In striking down an interventionist agriculture law in 1936, Justice Owen Roberts writing for the Court majority stated, "The question is not what power the federal government ought to have, but what powers, in fact, have been given by the people."[7]

However, President Roosevelt thought that he knew better, and in 1937 he bullied the justices with his infamous Court-packing scheme. After this episode, the Court changed its tune and allowed most of FDR's interventionist schemes to stand. In 1937 it eviscerated the doctrine of enumerated powers. A year later it decided that some freedoms guaranteed in the Constitution were "nonfundamental," and could be pushed aside to give the government more power.[8]

FDR and the new Court majority figured that, notwithstanding the restraints imposed by the Constitution, the government needed new powers to fix the Depression. The ends justified the means.

However, the progressive or socialist economic policies of the New Deal turned out to be a huge blunder that prolonged the Depression, as discussed in Appendix 1. Few economists today would support the New Deal policies of industry cartels, high prices, monopoly unionization, subsidies, and sky-high marginal tax rates. It is true that hindsight is 20/20, but the Roosevelt administration was stumbling in the dark with its economic interventions. With constitutional constraints relaxed, the New Deal schemes used Americans like they were guinea pigs in failed laboratory experiments.

The wisdom of the Constitution's Framers in restricting such federal activism was proven correct. Federal intervention did not fix the Depression; it made it worse. Politicians should be more humble about their ability to use coercive government to improve on the free economy and voluntary society. Today, as in the 1930s, too many politicians let their daydreams run amok. They should recognize that constitutional constraints on federal power were put there for good, practical reasons.

Less Is More

As the federal government has expanded into state, local, and private activities, it has been distracted from its basic constitutional duties. The litany of failures in the security and intelligence agencies leading up to 9/11 sadly drove this home. Those agencies had misallocated their resources, they ignored clues on terrorist threats, and they did not adequately communicate threat information to each other. For their part, policymakers paid far too little attention to the ongoing failings of the security bureaucracies.

The government failures leading up to 9/11 have been discussed widely. The CIA was mismanaged, and it underinvested in human intelligence.[9] The State Department had extremely lax procedures for issuing foreign visas.[10] U.S. border control was not up to the task of screening for terrorists. The Federal Aviation Administration received 52 intelligence reports regarding Bin Laden and Al Qaeda in the six months leading up to 9/11, some of which discussed hijackings and air suicide missions, but the agency did not pay enough attention to them.[11] The FBI severely mismanaged its internal information flow. Even more than three years after 9/11, the inspector general of the Justice Department said that the FBI was still "significantly hampered" in its ability to fight terrorism because of its failure to replace antiquated computer systems.[12]

Although federal agencies failed, the ultimate failure was in Congress and the White House. Policymakers were too distracted by other issues during the past decade to focus on the rising threat of terrorism. The distraction was brought home on the day that New York and Washington were attacked. President Bush was in Florida promoting his policies to expand federal powers over the nation's schools. Schools are traditionally and constitutionally a state and local activity, yet recent presidents have unwisely spent much of their valuable time acting as if they were local school board officials.

A major bipartisan report on federalism in 1981 warned that the increasing federal takeover of state and local functions was causing "a growing overload of major decisionmaking institutions."[13] That problem is even worse today. Top federal officials today spend much of their time dealing with narrow and local issues rather than truly national ones.

Consider that the Bush White House at the highest levels was spending substantial time and effort in the months before 9/11 helping out Enron Corporation on an investment in India that had gone bad.[14] When the *Washington Post* reported this in 2002, the administration argued that it was simply trying to guard taxpayer interests in the $640 million in federal loans that had been given to Enron for the project.[15] But the government should not be putting taxpayer money into such risky private schemes in the first place. Sadly, this is typical of the special interest minutiae that top administration officials and members of Congress spend much of their time dealing with.

Even after 9/11, policymakers have been slow to deal with basic national security problems. Consider that a year and a half after 9/11, the GAO reported that the government had a dozen different terrorist "watch lists" in nine different agencies that were complex, inefficient, and not comparable.[16] Fixes were promised, but agency infighting has prevented much progress. In 2004 the inspector general of the Department of Homeland Security lambasted the government for failing to fix the watch list problem.[17] In 2005 the GAO reported that the problem had still not been fixed.[18]

Members of Congress spend little time on agency oversight to fix these problems because of their busy schedules. They deal with dozens of policy issues unrelated to the federal government's proper functions. They also spend a huge amount of time seeking money and support from special interest lobbyists who have issues before Congress that are properly state, local, and private activities.

Even members of Congress on the defense and intelligence committees spend too little time on national security issues. The *Washington Post* reported in 2004 that most members of the House and Senate intelligence committees had been too busy on other activities to have read crucial terrorism reports or to hold oversight hearings to rectify problems in the intelligence agencies.[19] A former chief counsel of the Senate Intelligence Committee has confirmed that very few senators bother to view secure intelligence documents.[20] Tim Roemer, a member of the September 11 Commission and former member of Congress, also conceded that members who are supposed to be overseeing intelligence are usually too busy dealing with other issues.[21]

The American people deserve better than that. They would be better off if the size, scope, and complexity of the federal government were reduced and policymakers focused on delivering a limited range of high-quality core services such as national security. The federal government has become like a bloated conglomerate corporation that is involved in so many activities that the top executives are distracted from their core mission. Modernist architects argued that "less is more" in building design. The same is true in government design. Many poorly performing corporations have shed extraneous activities in recent years and refocused on "core competencies." The federal government should do the same.

The Explosion of Spending on the Elderly

The number of retirees will grow rapidly in coming years as the large baby-boom generation retires and elderly life expectancies continue to increase. These changes will create severe strains on the budget because Congress has made generous promises to future retirees without any plan to pay for them. *Washington Post* columnist Robert Samuelson noted that the aging of America combined with those overgenerous promises "could trigger an economic and political death spiral."[22]

28

Figure 3.1
GROWTH IN U.S. POPULATION BY AGE GROUP
(percentage increase from 2005 to year indicated)

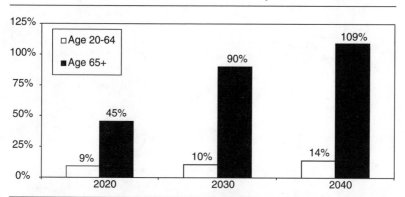

SOURCE: Author's calculations based on *2005 Annual Report of the Board of Trustees of the Federal Old-Age and Survivors Insurance and Disability Insurance Trust Funds*, p. 77.

Demographic projections illustrate the basic problem. By 2040 the number of Americans aged 65 and older is expected to have more than doubled, but the number of working-age Americans will have increased just 14 percent, as shown in Figure 3.1.[23] Under current rules, Social Security benefits for the growing number of elderly are paid for by payroll taxes on the stagnant number of workers. The program is not sustainable as currently structured.

Medicare is even more unsustainable. The program faces the same unfavorable demographics, but it is also strained by high-cost inflation in the health care industry. Rapid growth in Medicaid also adds to the federal financial crisis. Medicaid spending is expected to grow at 8 percent annually during the next decade and will represent a growing share of GDP unless reformed.[24] About one-third of Medicaid benefits go to the elderly.

Without cuts to those and other programs, the tax threat faced by young Americans will be huge. Consider Social Security and Medicare Part A, which are funded by the 15.3 percent federal payroll tax. The Social Security Board of Trustees estimates that the cost of these two programs as a share of workers' taxable wages will rise from 14.2 percent in 2005 to 24.6 percent in 2040.[25] Thus, unless

29

Figure 3.2

FEDERAL SPENDING UNDER A BUSINESS-AS-USUAL POLICY

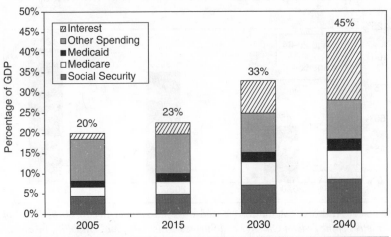

SOURCE: Government Accountability Office, "21st Century Challenges: Reexamining the Base of the Federal Government," GAO-05-325SP, February 2005. Revenues assumed to be unchanged from the 2005 level. Medicare is net of offsetting receipts.

reforms are made, taxes to pay for those programs will consume a 73 percent greater share of wages by 2040.

The problem is even worse than that. As tax rates rise, the tax base shrinks as productive efforts fall and tax avoidance rises. To get the money it would need to pay for rising benefits, the government would have to hike taxes even higher than 24.6 percent. Harvard's Martin Feldstein estimates that rather than a 9 percentage point increase in payroll taxes (I estimated about 10 percentage points), a 14 percentage point hike would be needed to make up for the shrinking tax base.[26] Thus, to fund unreformed Social Security and Medicare Part A benefits, the government would need to hike the federal payroll tax to about 30 percent by 2040. That would be a crushing blow to working Americans, who would have to pay this tax in addition to all the other federal and state taxes they pay.

The Government Accountability Office has projected a long-range business-as-usual scenario for the budget, shown in Figure 3.2.[27] The projections assume that entitlement programs are not reformed and

30

Figure 3.3
FEDERAL TAXPAYERS' FINANCIAL EXPOSURE

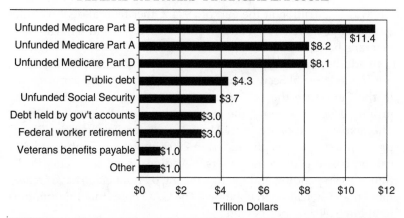

Unfunded Medicare Part B — $11.4
Unfunded Medicare Part A — $8.2
Unfunded Medicare Part D — $8.1
Public debt — $4.3
Unfunded Social Security — $3.7
Debt held by gov't accounts — $3.0
Federal worker retirement — $3.0
Veterans benefits payable — $1.0
Other — $1.0

Trillion Dollars

SOURCE: Government Accountability Office, "Fiscal Year 2004 U.S. Government Financial Statements," GAO-05-284T, February 9, 2005. Social Security and Medicare figures are based on 75-year net present values. "Debt held by government accounts" includes the Social Security and Medicare Trust Funds.

that other programs and taxes stay the same size as today relative to GDP. In this scenario, federal spending would grow from 20 percent of GDP today to a staggering 45 percent of GDP by 2040. Given that state and local spending is more than 10 percent of GDP, well over half of the U.S. economy would be consumed by governments.

The GAO projection assumes that a key source of spending growth would be interest costs on the growing federal debt. But even aside from interest costs, federal spending increases would be huge. Federal noninterest spending would rise from 18.5 percent of GDP today to 28.0 percent by 2040 if no reforms were made. That means that the cost of federal programs as a share of American incomes would increase 51 percent. To put this into perspective, the average U.S. household currently pays more than $20,000 per year in federal taxes. A government cost increase of 51 percent would be like raising taxes on every household by more than $10,000.

Without major reforms, these figures suggest a bleak fiscal future awaiting young Americans. The young face a huge amount of liabilities that the government has built up over the years. Figure 3.3

shows GAO data on the government's debt and its unfunded promises.[28] The government's public debt from accumulated annual deficits was $4.3 trillion at the end of 2004. Other federal debt includes $3.0 trillion in federal worker retirement costs and $1 trillion in veterans benefits owed.

In addition to that debt, taxpayers face the costs of promised, but not funded, Social Security and Medicare benefits. The costs shown in the figure are the net costs in present value over 75 years of promised benefits above the tax revenues available to fund them. The taxpayer exposure from Medicare is massive. Just the Part D prescription drug benefit added in 2003 imposes an unfunded $8.1 trillion cost on future taxpayers.[29] Adding up all the items in the figure, overspending and overpromising by politicians have created more than $40 trillion in liabilities. The GAO notes that this amounts to about $140,000 per person.

The burdens on future taxpayers can be reduced by cuts to both entitlement and discretionary programs in the budget, as proposed in Chapter 4. Reforms to Social Security, Medicare, Medicaid, and numerous discretionary programs are discussed in Appendix 2. The cuts proposed here will seem radical to some policymakers, but they will seem less so in coming years when rising waves of red ink are crashing into the federal budget.

If cutbacks are not begun soon, we will be in for a "war between the generations" as young workers battle against the growing demands of the elderly. If policymakers give in to the elderly lobby and increase taxes to pay for rising elderly benefits, the whole economy will suffer from reduced growth, which in turn will make benefits even harder to sustain. The sooner reforms are begun, the better chance we have of averting an economic death spiral.

The Cost of Government

To support its huge array of programs, the federal government extracts more than $2 trillion in taxes from families and businesses each year. That extraction comes at a large cost. Every dollar the government spends is one dollar less for the private sector to spend. For individuals, the more tax money they hand over to government, the less they have to spend on food, clothing, and other needs. For businesses, the more they are taxed, the less they have available to spend on research, investment, and hiring.

The resources needed to produce government goods are drawn from the private sector and cannot be used to produce goods for private markets. Thus, the engineers working on a $1 billion defense contract might otherwise have been working for technology companies producing goods for consumers. Politicians and defense companies could be expected to tout the jobs created by such a contract, but the $1 billion of private activities that would otherwise have taken place is overlooked.

Indeed, there would be substantially more than $1 billion of private activities displaced by such a government program. Every added dollar of federal spending costs the private sector more than a dollar because taxes create "deadweight losses." These are the costs caused by distortions to working, investment, entrepreneurship, and other productive activities. Consider a worker who is starting a side business to earn extra income. If the government raises tax rates and dissuades this budding entrepreneur, the nation loses the added production and the new ideas that would have been added to the economy.

How big are the deadweight losses from taxation?[30] The Congressional Budget Office says that "typical estimates of the economic cost of a dollar of tax revenue range from 20 cents to 60 cents over and above the revenue raised."[31] Thus, to take the midpoint estimate of 40 cents, government programs would need to create benefits at least 40 percent greater than their explicit tax cost to make any economic sense. Studies by Harvard's Martin Feldstein have found that deadweight losses are even larger than that. He concludes that "the deadweight burden caused by incremental taxation . . . may exceed one dollar per dollar of revenue raised, making the cost of incremental governmental spending more than two dollars for each dollar of government spending."[32] Thus, $1 billion of added defense spending would cost the private economy more than $2 billion.

It is doubtful that most federal programs create benefits large enough to offset the damage they cause to the private sector. Consider the effects of farm subsidy programs, which will pay out about $26 billion this year. First, the subsidies add $26 billion to the farm economy, but they destroy $26 billion of activity elsewhere as resources are shifted away from other industries. Second, the extraction of taxes to pay for the subsidies creates deadweight losses of as much as $26 billion if Feldstein is correct. Third, the government spending itself causes further damage. For example, farm subsidies are thought to harm the environment by causing excessive use of fertilizers and overuse of marginal farmland.

The government essentially uses a "leaky bucket" whenever it takes action because of damage caused on both the tax and spending sides. Michael Boskin, former chairman of the President's Council of Economic Advisers, explains: "The cost to the economy of each additional tax dollar is about $1.40 to $1.50. Now that tax dollar . . . is put into a bucket. Some of it leaks out in overhead, waste, and so on. In a well-managed program, the government may spend 80 or 90 cents of that dollar on achieving its goals. Inefficient programs would be much lower, $.30 or $.40 on the dollar."[33]

Despite the high costs of government activity, the government does perform some very useful functions for society. Economists call those functions "public goods." Such goods create broad benefits that outweigh the costs, but they are underprovided by the private sector.[34] Public goods have the characteristics of "nonrivalry" and "nonexcludability." Nonrivalry means that one person's benefit from the good is not reduced as others consume more of it. Nonexcludability means that once a good is provided, it is difficult to exclude anyone from consuming it. National defense is a classic public good. We all benefit from it simultaneously, and once it is provided people cannot be excluded from it whether they helped pay for it or not.

These two features of public goods make private provision difficult. Because defense spending is nonexcludable, voluntary funding would fall short as people waited for their neighbors to pay the cost. Since some level of defense spending is a high-value activity and private provision is doubtful, a "market failure" occurs. When market failures occur, government provision may be appropriate.

Under the traditional public interest theory of government, policymakers would respond to market failures with efficient programs that had outcomes superior to those of laissez faire. The problem is that the government itself is prone to failure in at least three basic ways. First, policymakers often misdiagnose problems, and they are too quick to intervene when no real market failure has occurred. Second, government "solutions" to problems are often mismanaged and wasteful, and they sometimes make problems worse. Third, policymakers have political reasons for intervening in markets that have nothing to do with fixing real market failures or improving the general welfare. Politicians look for sexy issues on which to intervene in order to grab headlines, and they look to help special interest supporters and narrow groups of voters in their districts.[35]

Voters often go along with the activist plans of politicians because they are subject to a "halo effect" regarding government. Psychologists say that we sometimes allow the positive traits of people to obscure their less attractive features. With the government, people regard its basic functions, such as criminal justice, as so crucial that it creates a positive halo over government in general. Government officials do everything they can to reinforce that halo with grand sounding promises and slogans. The government halo is particularly strong in democracies because leaders express stirringly optimistic sentiments such as President Abraham Lincoln's "government of the people, by the people, for the people."

For this reason and others, the public often ends up supporting a government that is beyond its optimal size. Figure 3.4 provides a representation of this idea. On the left-hand side, the government delivers key public goods such as crime reduction and enforcement of contracts. These create a high rate of return, and per capita income initially rises with the size of government. People notice that with a modest contribution of tax dollars, the streets are safer and commerce thrives. The government gets a positive halo.

As government expands further, it engages in less and less productive activities. The marginal return from government growth falls and then turns negative. On the right-hand side, incomes fall as the government expands, but the halo effect convinces some people that larger government is beneficial. Today, the government has expanded far beyond the optimal point that maximizes the nation's well-being. The proposed cuts in the next chapter are to programs that I believe are on the right-hand side of Figure 3.4. Cutting them would increase incomes and make society better off.

Former Supreme Court Justice Oliver Wendell Holmes Jr. famously said that "taxes are what we pay for civilized society."[36] That comment is sometimes invoked to suggest that government should be as big as or bigger than it already is. But Holmes made his observation in 1927 when federal, state, and local taxes represented just 10 percent of the U.S. economy. Those taxes mainly supported basic functions such as justice and national defense, which are indeed

Figure 3.4
THE SIZE OF THE GOVERNMENT AND AVERAGE INCOME

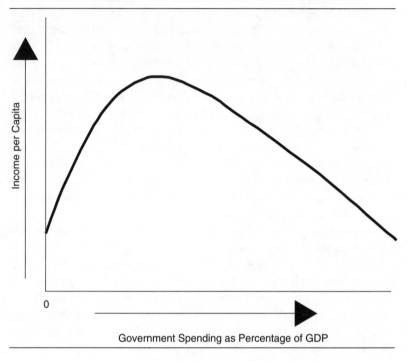

Income per Capita

0

Government Spending as Percentage of GDP

prices of a civilized society. Today, taxes represent a share of the economy that is three times larger, and they fund many activities that undercut private civil society. Much of the federal government today is a burden on civilized society, not a benefit.

4. A Plan to Cut Spending and Balance the Budget

This chapter details a plan to cut federal spending, balance the budget, and avert a federal financial crisis. The plan would cut spending on a wide range of mainly discretionary programs by $380 billion annually.[1] In addition, the plan would reduce growth in the major entitlement programs—Social Security, Medicare, and Medicaid—to create savings reaching $270 billion annually by 2015. These reforms would cut the size of government, increase individual freedom, and spur economic growth as resources flowed to higher-value private uses.

Discretionary Spending Cuts

Discretionary spending encompasses a large range of activities including defense, education, energy, housing, space, and transportation. Table 4.1 summarizes the types of activities that should be terminated, privatized, or devolved to the states as follows:

- Activities that are mismanaged, obsolete, and ineffective, such as NASA
- Activities that subsidize special interests and make no economic or moral sense, such as farm subsidies
- Activities that damage the economy, curtail freedom, create negative social effects, or harm the environment
- Activities that are properly state and local functions, such as highway spending
- Activities that should be left to the private sector and carried out by individuals, businesses, and charities

Building from this structure, Table 4.2 lists more than 100 programs and agencies that should be cut to create $380 billion in annual savings.[2] The proposed cuts are from nearly every federal department. Appendix 2 provides a discussion of most of these programs and agencies.

Table 4.1
FEDERAL PROGRAMS: PROBLEMS AND REFORM SOLUTIONS

Problem	Reform Solution
1. Wasteful (fraud/abuse, duplicative, obsolete, mismanaged, ineffective)	Terminate, devolve, or privatize
2. Special interest spending	Terminate
3. Actively damaging	Terminate
4. State and local function	Terminate or devolve
5. Private function	Terminate or privatize

The table indicates why each program should be eliminated and provides a recommended reform solution. For example, on the one hand, it probably makes sense to privatize Amtrak as an ongoing entity rather than to simply close it down. On the other hand, foreign aid programs could be simply terminated and foreign aid left to private charity groups. Multiple reform options are marked in some cases because different reforms may be suitable for different parts of some agencies. Ultimately, it would be up to entrepreneurs, consumers, and private philanthropists to determine whether formerly government activities were worth sustaining in the business and nonprofit sectors.

Numerous information sources were used to select the programs in the table. The Government Accountability Office, an arm of Congress, provides a steady stream of analyses of wasteful and ineffective programs. The *Washington Post* and *Washington Times* have stories every week about scandals and failures in federal agencies. Many programs listed here were targeted for cuts in the mid-1990s by the Republican Congress. In 1995 the House passed a plan to eliminate more than 200 programs and agencies. Unfortunately, few of those cuts were signed into law.[3]

Entitlement Spending Cuts

In addition to these cuts, federal entitlement programs should be reformed.[4] Table 4.3 includes four reforms that would create annual savings reaching $270 billion by 2015.[5] Appendix 2 has a detailed discussion of these reforms, but in brief they would do the following:

• Reduce the growth in Social Security by indexing initial benefits to changes in prices instead of wages.

Table 4.2
PROPOSED FEDERAL BUDGET CUTS

	2005 Spending ($ million)	Problem					Reform Solution		
		Wasteful	Special Interest Spending	Actively Damaging	State/Local Function	Private Function	Terminate	Devolve to States	Privatize
Department of Agriculture									
Economic Research Service	$73	X					X		
Agricultural Statistics Service	$133						X		X
Agricultural Research Service	$1,227	X	X			X	X		X
Coop. State Research and Ext. Service	$1,090	X	X		X	X		X	
Agricultural Marketing Service	$1,246	X	X			X	X		
Risk Management Agency	$3,366		X			X	X		
Farm Service Agency	$26,237		X	X			X		X
Rural Development	$1,047	X	X				X		
Rural Housing Service	$1,255	X	X				X		
Rural Business Cooperative Service	$134	X	X			X	X		
Rural Utilities Service	$136	X	X			X	X		
Foreign Agricultural Service	$1,529	X	X			X	X		
Forest Service: State and Private	$482		X		X	X		X	
Forest Service: Land Acquisition	$153	X				X	X		
Total proposed cuts	$38,108								
Total department outlays	$94,912								
Department of Commerce									
Economic Development Administration	$392	X	X		X		X		
International Trade Administration	$370	X	X				X		
Minority Business Development	$23	X	X				X		
Pacific salmon state grants	$83			X	X				
Fisheries Loans and Marketing	$21			X	X	X			

(continued next page)

Table 4.2
Proposed Federal Budget Cuts (*continued*)

	2005 Spending ($ million)	Problem					Reform Solution		
		Wasteful	Special Interest Spending	Actively Damaging	State/Local Function	Private Function	Terminate	Devolve to States	Privatize
Department of Commerce (cont.)									
Technology Administration	$6	X					X		
Advanced Technology Program	$144		X			X	X		
Manufacturing Extension Partnership	$117		X			X	X		X
Various NIST programs	$448					X	X		X
Total proposed cuts	$1,604								
Total department outlays	$6,278								
Department of Defense									
Cut in half troop levels in Europe/Asia	$20,000	X					X		
Cut low-priority weapon systems	$10,000	X					X		
Close excess military bases	$6,000	X					X		
Foreign Military Financing	$4,899	X					X		
International Military Training	$95	X					X		
Total proposed cuts	$40,994								
Total department outlays	$444,068								
Department of Education									
Elementary and Secondary Education	$23,241	X		X	X		X	X	X
Innovation and Improvement	$754				X		X	X	
Safe and Drug-Free Schools	$484	X			X		X		
English Language Acquisition	$840				X	X	X		
Special Education and Rehab.	$13,747				X	X	X	X	
Vocational and Adult Education	$2,030		X			X	X		X

40

Program	Amount								
Postsecondary Education	$2,408		X					X	X
Student Aid	$26,212	X	X					X	X
Education Sciences	$632					X		X	
Other	$605					X			X
Total proposed cuts	**$70,953**								
Total department outlays	**$70,953**								
Department of Energy									
General Science	$3,558			X				X	X
Energy Supply	$820			X				X	X
Fossil Energy Research and Clean Coal	$615			X				X	X
Energy Conservation	$874			X				X	X
Strategic Petroleum Reserve	$169							X	X
Energy Information Administration	$83							X	X
Power Marketing Administrations	$179						X		X
Total proposed cuts	**$6,298**								
Total department outlays	**$22,178**								
Department of Health and Human Services									
Medicare [Increase premiums and deductibles (see Table 4.3). Add savings accounts.]	$12,679							X	X
Medicaid [Convert program to a block grant and cap spending growth (see Table 4.3).]	$3,191							X	X
Nat. Institutes of Health: Applied R&D	$354							X	X
Substance Abuse and Mental Health	$18,099					X		X	X
Health Care Research and Quality				X					
Temp. Assistance for Needy Families	$4,142							X	X
State Payments for Family Support	$2,115							X	
Low-Income Home Energy Assistance			X					X	

(continued next page)

41

Table 4.2
Proposed Federal Budget Cuts (continued)

	2005 Spending ($ million)	Problem					Reform Solution		
		Wasteful	Special Interest Spending	Actively Damaging	State/Local Function	Private Function	Terminate	Devolve to States	Privatize
Department of Health and Human Services (cont.)									
Promoting Safe and Stable Families	$395					X	X		
Child Care Entitlement Grants	$2,718				X			X	
Child Care and Development Grants	$2,099				X			X	
Social Services Grants	$1,764				X			X	
Foster Care and Adoption Grants	$6,474				X			X	
Head Start	$6,843	X			X			X	
Community Services Grants	$631	X					X		
Health Professions Education	$416	X	X			X	X		
Administration on Aging	$1,367	X					X		
Total proposed cuts	$63,287								
Total department outlays	$585,772								
Department of Homeland Security									
State and Local Programs	$2,796				X			X	
Firefighter Assistance Grants	$551				X			X	
Transportation Security: Airports	$2,700	X		X		X			
Coast Guard—Boat Safety Grants	$46					X	X		X
Total proposed cuts	$6,093								
Total department outlays	$33,259								
Department of Housing and Urban Development									
Low-Income Housing Assistance	$22,874	X		X		X	X		
Public Housing subsidies	$8,465	X		X		X	X		X

Program	Amount						
Community Development Block Grants	$5,373	X		X		X	X
Home Investment Partnership Program	$1,650	X		X		X	X
Homeless Assistance Grants	$1,300		X			X	X
Other Community Planning programs	$359		X			X	X
Assisted Housing programs	$601		X			X	X
Administration	$1,068			X		X	
Other	$924			X			
Total proposed cuts	$42,614						
Total department outlays	$42,614						
Department of the Interior							
Bureau of Reclamation	$1,221	X	X	X		X	X
State and Tribal Wildlife Grants	$61		X			X	X
Land Acquisition Programs	$45			X		X	X
Sport Fish Restoration Fund	$342	X	X			X	
Bureau of Indian Affairs	$2,404			X		X	X
Total proposed cuts	$4,073						
Total department outlays	$9,433						
Department of Justice							
Antitrust Division	$114				X	X	
State and Local Assistance	$1,094	X			X	X	X
Weed and Seed Program	$37		X			X	
Community Oriented Policing Services	$575	X				X	X
Juvenile Justice Programs	$244	X				X	X
Total proposed cuts	$2,064						
Total department outlays	$21,171						

(continued next page)

Table 4.2
PROPOSED FEDERAL BUDGET CUTS (continued)

		Problem					Reform Solution		
	2005 Spending ($ million)	Wasteful	Special Interest Spending	Actively Damaging	State/Local Function	Private Function	Terminate	Devolve to States	Privatize
Department of Labor									
Employment and Training Admin.	$5,237	X	X			X	X		
Welfare to Work	$6					X	X		
Community Service for Seniors	$436	X			X	X	X		
Trade Adjustment Assistance	$1,097	X	X				X		
International Labor Affairs	$93	X					X		
Total proposed cuts	$6,869								
Total department outlays	$50,034								
Social Security	Cut growth in future benefits (see Table 4.3). Add savings accounts.								
Department of State									
Education and Cultural Exchanges	$351	X	X			X	X		
United Nations	$362	X					X		
Inter-American Organizations	$130	X					X		
OECD	$67	X					X		
International Narcotics Control	$520	X					X		
Andean Counterdrug Initiative	$722	X		X					
Total proposed cuts	$2,152								
Total department outlays	$11,934								
Department of Transportation									
Essential Air Service	$74	X	X			X	X		
FAA-Air Traffic Control	$2,814	X		X		X			X

Item	Amount	1	2	3	4	5	6	7
FAA-Grants to Airports	$3,041				X	X		X
FAA-Facilities and Equipment	$2,867				X	X		X
Federal Highway Administration	$32,950				X		X	X
Federal Transit Administration	$8,420				X		X	
Maritime Administration	$411			X	X			X
Amtrak	$1,259				X			
Total proposed cuts	**$51,836**							
Total department outlays	**$58,215**							
Other Agencies and Activities								
Agency for International Development	$3,688			X	X			
Appalachian, Delta, Denali Comm.	$94			X	X			
Army Corps of Engineers	$4,891			X	X	X		X
Cargo Preference	$563			X	X			
Corporation for Nat. and Comm. Service	$923				X	X		
Corporation for Public Broadcasting	$466				X	X	X	
Davis-Bacon Act	$1,000					X	X	
EPA: State Grants	$3,592				X	X	X	
EEOC	$327				X	X		
Export-Import Bank	$0			X	X	X		X
Federal Trade Commission: Antitrust	$89			X	X			
International Assistance: Economic	$3,523			X	X	X		
International Assistance: Multilateral	$1,913			X	X			
International Trade Commission	$60				X			
Legal Services Corporation	$331			X	X			
Millennium Challenge Corporation	$450			X	X			
NASA	$15,719			X	X			X

(continued next page)

Table 4.2
Proposed Federal Budget Cuts (continued)

Other Agencies and Activities (cont.)	2005 Spending ($ million)	Problem					Reform Solution		
		Wasteful	Special Interest Spending	Actively Damaging	State/Local Function	Private Function	Terminate	Devolve to States	Privatize
National Endowment for the Arts	$121	X	X				X		
National Endowment for the Humanities	$133	X	X				X		
National Labor Relations Board	$250					X	X		
National Mediation Board	$12					X	X		
Neighborhood Reinvestment Corp.	$114				X		X		
OPIC	$0	X		X		X			X
Peace Corps	$326	X	X				X		
Presidio Trust	$46				X			X	
Public Accounting Oversight Board	$130					X	X		
Service Contract Act	$1,000	X	X	X			X		
Small Business Administration	$3,036	X	X			X	X		
Tennessee Valley Authority	$0	X		X		X			X
Trade and Development Agency	$57	X				X	X		
U.S. Postal Service subsidies	$568	X				X	X		X
Total proposed cuts	$43,422								
Grand total spending cuts	**$380,367**								

Source: Author's analysis. Spending figures are outlays for fiscal year 2005 from the *Budget of the United States Government: Fiscal Year 2006.*

Note: "Wasteful" programs are those that are duplicative, obsolete, mismanaged, ineffective, or have high levels of fraud and abuse.

Table 4.3
PROPOSED REDUCTIONS TO ENTITLEMENT PROGRAMS

Proposal	Annual Savings in 2015 ($ billion)
1. Change indexing of growth in Social Security benefits from wages to prices	$33
2. Increase Medicare Part B premiums to cover 50% of program costs	$59
3. Increase and conform deductibles for Medicare Parts A and B and medigap policies	$18
4. Convert Medicaid to a block grant. Limit growth to inflation.	$160
Total annual savings in 2015 compared to current baseline projections	$270

SOURCES: Items 1, 2, and 3 are author's estimates based on data in CBO, "Budget Options," February 2005. Item 4 is the author's estimate working from the CBO baseline projection. All options are assumed to be enacted in 2006. See Appendix 2 for details.

- Increase premiums for Medicare Part B. Part B premiums were originally supposed to cover 50 percent of program costs, but they cover just 25 percent today. The proposal would increase premiums to 50 percent of costs.
- Increase and conform the deductibles and cost sharing for Medicare Part A, Medicare Part B, and medigap plans.
- Turn Medicaid into a block grant and limit growth. Medicaid funding is split between the federal and state governments, a structure that encourages overspending by the states. Medicaid is expected to grow at 7.7 percent annually during the next decade.[6] This option would turn Medicaid into a block grant and limit the growth in federal grants to inflation, as measured by the consumer price index. The CPI is projected to grow at 2.2 percent annually during the next decade.[7]

10-Year Budget Projections

Figure 4.1 shows a 10-year projection of federal spending under a business-as-usual scenario and under the reform plan proposed here.[8] The reform plan includes the cuts proposed in Tables 4.2 and

Figure 4.1
PROJECTED FEDERAL REVENUES AND SPENDING

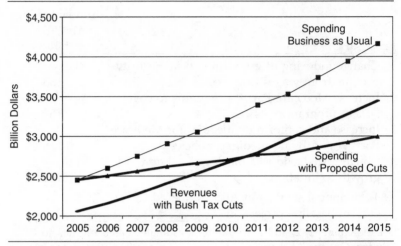

SOURCE: Author's estimates based on projections in CBO, "An Analysis of the President's Budgetary Proposals for Fiscal Year 2006," March 2005. Data are fiscal year outlays. The "Business-as-Usual" scenario is the CBO baseline but with discretionary spending rising at the GDP growth rate.

4.3.[9] The projections assume that the cuts from Table 4.2 would be phased in over 10 years. Note that because of projected growth in these programs, the $380 billion of cuts would be valued at $450 billion by 2015.[10]

The figure also shows a projection of federal revenues, based on the Congressional Budget Office forecast of March 2005.[11] The projection assumes that all of President Bush's tax cuts of recent years are made permanent and that the alternative minimum tax is reformed. It also assumes the elimination of the federal gasoline tax, which currently raises about $40 billion annually. The gas tax funds federal highway and transit programs, which would be devolved to the states under this plan. Note that even with these tax cut assumptions, federal revenues would still be expected to rise steadily in coming years because of growth in the economy.

If the reform plan were enacted, Figure 4.1 shows that the budget would be balanced by 2011, and there would be growing surpluses after that. By 2015, federal spending would be 28 percent lower than

Figure 4.2
PROJECTED FEDERAL REVENUES AND SPENDING, PERCENTAGE OF GDP

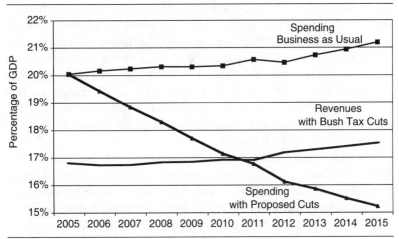

SOURCE: Author's estimates based on projections in CBO, "An Analysis of the President's Budgetary Proposals for Fiscal Year 2006," March 2005. Data are fiscal year outlays. The "Business-as-Usual" scenario is the CBO baseline but with discretionary spending rising at the GDP growth rate.

it would be under a business-as-usual scenario and 21 percent lower than under CBO's "baseline" projection. The business-as-usual scenario reflects the CBO's baseline but assumes that discretionary spending grows with GDP, not inflation as under the baseline.[12]

With the president's tax cuts in place, alternative minimum tax (ATM) reform, and gas tax repeal, federal revenues are expected to increase from $2.1 trillion in 2005 to $3.4 trillion by 2015. Under the reform plan, spending would increase from $2.5 trillion in 2005 to $3.0 trillion by 2015, and large surpluses would be generated. Under the business-as-usual scenario, spending would increase to $4.2 trillion in 2015, and huge deficits would be created. (Under the CBO baseline, spending would be $3.8 trillion in 2015.)[13]

Figure 4.2 includes the same revenue and spending projections, but measured as a percentage of GDP. Revenues are expected to rise from 16.8 percent of GDP in 2005 to 17.5 percent by 2015. Under the reform plan, spending would fall from 20.0 percent of GDP in

49

2005 to 15.2 percent by 2015. Under the business-as-usual scenario, spending would rise to 21.2 percent of GDP by 2015.

The budget savings generated under the spending reform plan could be used to cut taxes or reduce the federal debt. Alternately, the savings could be used to fund transition to a Social Security system based on personal accounts, as discussed in Appendix 2. Diverting a portion of payroll taxes into personal accounts would increase budget deficits in the short term. But the spending cuts proposed here would offset that effect and help bring the budget into balance. Also note that, as personal accounts were built up, traditional Social Security benefits would be cut to reduce the government's long-term liabilities.

The cuts included in this plan are not all the budget reforms that should be pursued. Management overhead in federal agencies should be cut. Government procurement should be reformed to end cost overruns. Additional grant programs for the states should be cut. Most important, further long-term reforms should be made to Social Security, Medicare, and Medicaid, as discussed in Appendix 2. Nonetheless, these cuts provide policymakers with a menu of high-priority targets. If enacted, they would avert a financial crisis and shrink government in a responsible way while increasing economic freedom and spurring growth.

5. Wasteful Programs

People tend not to spend other people's money as carefully as they spend their own. That is clear from the mismanagement, duplication, obsolescence, and ineffectiveness of many programs in the federal budget. For federal policymakers, it is more pleasant to add new programs and expand existing ones than it is to weed out low-priority programs and cut costs. The result is the uncontrolled waste in federal agencies that is the focus of this chapter.

Causes of Waste

In the private sector, individual companies become bloated and mismanaged, but competitive markets ensure that they eventually go bankrupt or get taken over and restructured. About 10 percent of U.S. companies go out of business each year, and corporate executives get ousted all the time.[1] Failures get eliminated in the private sector, and poor performance gets punished. By contrast, many federal agencies are inefficient and perform poorly year after year, and yet they survive and grow. Here are some of the reasons for this wastefulness:

- Poorly performing federal agencies do not go bankrupt, and thus there is no built-in mechanism to eliminate failures.
- Government managers face no profit incentive, giving them little reason to reduce costs. Indeed, without profits to worry about, managers favor budget and staffing increases to boost their power and prestige.
- Without the profit motive, there is little incentive for government workers to innovate and produce better services.
- The output of much government work is hard to measure, making it difficult to set performance goals for managers and workers.
- Even if performance could be measured, federal pay is generally tied to longevity, not performance.

- Disciplining federal workers is difficult, and they are virtually never fired, as discussed below, resulting in agencies carrying heavy loads of poor performers.
- To prevent corruption, governments need complex and costly regulations and paperwork to carry out routine functions such as procurement.
- Because of the frequent turnover of political appointees, many agencies experience continual changes in their missions.
- Congress imposes extra costs on agencies in carrying out their duties, such as resisting closure of unneeded offices in the districts of important members.
- Agencies get influenced or "captured" by special interest groups that steer policies toward satisfying narrow goals rather than broad public interest goals.
- Agencies have the incentive to play up problems in society as crises in order to rally public support for budget increases.
- The large size and overlapping activities of federal agencies make coordination of related functions very difficult. Sadly, we saw the results of this problem with the failures of U.S. intelligence agencies to effectively communicate with each other prior to September 11, 2001.

Those sorts of government idiosyncrasies have been observed for decades.[2] In his 1952 book, Sen. Paul Douglas identified reasons for the "elephantiasis" of federal bureaucracies.[3] He noted that (1) agencies have no incentive for cost control, (2) managers come to believe that their agencies are vitally important and deserve larger budgets, (3) managers' egos and salaries expand as their budgets and staff expand, and (4) it is almost impossible to fire "deadwood" employees.

Can federal management reforms fix these sorts of problems? That has been tried many times. President George W. Bush has a "management agenda" to make government work better. Former vice president Albert Gore had a "reinventing government" plan to fix the bureaucracy. President Ronald Reagan appointed the Grace Commission to reduce waste. President Jimmy Carter proposed budget and civil service reforms to create a leaner government. Going back further, President Herbert Hoover tried to reorganize the executive branch to eliminate duplication and waste.[4] And President Taft appointed the Committee on Economy and Efficiency in Government in 1910 for the same reason.[5]

No doubt those were all useful exercises, but the government never seems to recover from its fundamental bureaucratic illnesses. Consider one recent indicator of federal performance: the Government Accountability Office list of activities that are at high risk for waste and abuse.[6] The GAO's original list of 14 activities in 1990 grew to 25 activities by 2005. Some activities were improved and taken off the list, but a greater number were added. Some items, such as NASA contracting, have been on the list for 15 years despite repeated calls for reform.

Consider also that despite recent efforts to reinvent government, the bureaucracy is more top-heavy than ever. A study by Paul Light of the Brookings Institution found that the number of different federal executive titles (such as "principal associate deputy undersecretary") rose from 33 in 1992 to 64 by 2004.[7] Light argues that the plethora of high-ranking federal executives means that information must flow through an excessive number of offices before decisions are made. He also thinks that the rising number of layers in the bureaucracy has made it harder to hold anyone responsible for actions because many people are involved in each decision. In recent years, American businesses have become leaner and adopted flatter managements, but the federal government is as "bureaucratic" as ever.

However, federal inefficiency is not caused just by the bureaucracy itself. Congress is also a key culprit. Congress micromanages federal agencies, limits the flexibility of managers, and imposes added costs on agencies for narrow political gain. Congress encourages waste because *costs are benefits to politicians*. The termination of an obsolete program might be good for the country, but it will be resisted by members of Congress whose districts are affected. For example, NASA's operations are full of duplications at its facilities across the country, and the agency sustains many white elephant projects only because they are in the districts of important members of Congress.[8]

In the defense budget, parochial interests inflate costs a number of ways. Failed weapons systems are supported long after they should have been canceled because a few politicians want to keep the money from contracts flowing to their districts. Also, the development and production of weapons are inefficiently spread across

53

as many states as possible to maximize support. The $70 billion F/A-22 fighter program provides an example. The *Washington Post* noted that the F/A-22 "is an economic engine, with 1,000 suppliers—and many jobs—in 42 states guaranteeing solid support in Congress."[9]

An Iraq spending bill in 2005 provides another example. It contained language slipped in by Senate Appropriations Committee chairman Thad Cochran (R-MS) to prevent the Pentagon from selecting a single shipbuilder for the new DD(X) destroyer.[10] That will ensure that the shipyard in Cochran's home state gets work, but it will likely increase overall costs for American taxpayers.

The upshot is that reforms to the bureaucracy, such as President Bush's initiatives, can produce only limited improvements. Government failure and waste are deep-seated in the basic functioning of both Congress and the executive branch. Instead of having their management reformed, chronically wasteful and poorly performing agencies and programs should be terminated outright. The following sections can help to target cuts by identifying five types of wasteful programs: those that are (1) subject to excessive fraud and abuse, (2) duplicative, (3) obsolete, (4) mismanaged, and (5) ineffective.

Fraud and Abuse

Government investigators and private watchdog groups uncover fraud and abuse in the federal budget on a regular basis. There are three common problems: ineligible individuals and businesses receiving benefits, bureaucrats who abuse the public trust, and members of Congress who abuse their privileges for private or political gain.

In the first type of problem, fraud artists are attracted to the government because there are billions of dollars in contracts and grants to take advantage of. Here are some examples uncovered by the GAO and other investigators in recent years:

- **Medicare**. Erroneous and fraudulent payments to Medicare providers cost $20 billion annually.[11] The program is vulnerable to an array of different scams such as inflated billings, claims for phantom patients and phantom procedures, and billings for services that are not supposed to be covered. The fraud goes on year after year and Medicare administrators are unwilling or unable to stop it. Experts are predicting that the huge new

Medicare prescription drug plan will be particularly susceptible to fraud and abuse.[12]

- **Medicaid.** As with Medicare, inflated billings and bogus claims under Medicaid waste billions of dollars each year. The GAO found $1 billion of fraud in California's portion of Medicaid alone.[13] After a year-long investigation, the *New York Times* reported in 2005 that from 10 to 40 percent of the state's annual Medicaid budget of $45 billion may be siphoned off in fraud and abuse.[14] The paper found that outrageously bold rip-offs have proliferated due to the indifference of New York and federal policymakers.
- **Medicaid Nursing Home Benefits.** These benefits are supposed to be for the poor, but financial consultants help higher-income seniors hide their assets in order to qualify. This scam imposes $10 billion in extra costs on taxpayers each year.[15]
- **Post-9/11 Grants.** Much of an $8 billion federal program to help repair damaged New York offices near Ground Zero ended up going to build luxury condos and to projects outside Lower Manhattan.[16]
- **Post-9/11 Grants.** A federal program to hand out free air conditioners to New Yorkers affected by the collapse of the World Trade Center ballooned in cost from $15 million to $100 million because of management failures and bogus claims.[17]
- **Housing Subsidies.** Overpayments in federal rental housing subsidies cost $2 billion each year.[18]
- **Head Start.** This $7 billion program is rife with misuse of funds.[19]
- **Social Security.** Social Security pays out about $1 billion in fraudulent disability benefits each year.[20]
- **Farm Subsidies.** The Department of Agriculture pays out millions of dollars—perhaps as much as half a billion dollars—of improper farm subsidies each year.[21]
- **Food Stamps.** This program pays out about $1 billion annually in erroneous and fraudulent benefits, although problems have been reduced in recent years.[22]
- **Federal Emergency Management Agency.** FEMA has a reputation for being sloppy with its disaster aid.[23] It tends to hand out money indiscriminately after hurricanes and other disasters, and it loses millions of dollars to fraud because of its poor management.

- **Earned Income Tax Credit**. Almost one-third of EITC payments—about $9 billion annually—are erroneous or fraudulent.[24]

It seems that just about every federal hand-out program has a big fraud problem.[25] People can be quite resourceful in their abuse of the taxpayer. An interesting case was a Department of Housing and Urban Development program for police officers. Officers were encouraged to move into troubled neighborhoods by the offer of houses at discount prices. But the program was suspended after it was discovered that officers were buying the subsidized houses, but then renting them out rather than moving in, thus making a profit at the taxpayers' expense.[26]

Federal grant programs are often the target of fraud and abuse. In one case in 2004, a Washington, D.C., anti-poverty organization was found using grant money to purchase a fishing boat, sports tickets, luxury automobiles, and other personal use items for its executives. Regarding this scam, the *Washington Post* editorialized that "it's an old but nauseating story: anti-poverty workers advancing their interests at the poor's expense."[27]

Congress occasionally looks into these problems and promises reforms. But fraud generates a Catch-22 for legislators who support government programs. On the one hand, fraud is clearly a waste of taxpayer money and should be stopped. On the other hand, minimizing fraud to acceptable levels requires heavy bureaucratic rules and enforcement, which cost money and reduce program efficiency. The EITC is a good example. A high error and fraud rate had plagued the program, so the government created a special "EITC compliance initiative," which costs taxpayers about $200 million per year.[28] That is a big bureaucratic expense just to police a single program.

The second type of fraud and abuse problem involves federal bureaucrats. A recent example is the scandal over a $23 billion Pentagon contract to lease tanker airplanes from Boeing. The deal involved Air Force procurement officials and members of Congress currying favor with Boeing and pushing through an inflated contract.[29] The Pentagon's inspector general concluded that the deal broke federal contracting rules and would have wasted up to $2.5 billion of taxpayer money. It was widely known in the Air Force that the proposed deal was a wasteful giveaway to the company.[30] The deal ended in a public relations disaster for Boeing, and a number of government officials were forced to resign and one went to prison. Presumably such corrupt relationships are not uncommon, given that the government spends more than $400 billion annually on procurement.

The third type of abuse involves members of Congress who use the government to line their pockets or to buy electoral support. A *Los Angeles Times* investigation found that former Senate Appropriations Committee chairman Ted Stevens (R-AK) has become a millionaire by using his legislative power to channel federal contracts to business partners in his home state.[31] In one deal, Stevens steered a $450 million military housing contract to an Anchorage businessman. The businessman, in turn, helpfully turned a $50,000 investment by Stevens into a $750,000 windfall for the senator six years later.[32]

Another example of abuse engineered by Senator Stevens involves Alaska Native Corporations. Because of rule changes slipped in by Stevens, those shadowy businesses based in his state are allowed to circumvent normal federal procurement rules and win no-bid contracts. The result of such loopholes is that taxpayers do not get value for their money. For example, in 2002 a half billion dollar contract for scanning machines at U.S. border crossings was given to a native corporation with little experience in the technology, instead of to established leaders in the field who were not allowed to bid.[33]

It is sad that members of Congress are willing to do favors for special interests that jeopardize the nation's security, but that is how Washington works. The only lasting solution is to cut the government's size and scope. With a smaller government, members of Congress would have less money to steer toward dubious projects. At the same time, citizens, watchdog groups, and the media could pay closer attention to the problems in core programs that really matter, such as border security.

Duplicative Programs

Different federal programs often have overlapping objectives. The GAO reports that there are 50 different programs for the homeless in eight different federal agencies, 23 programs for housing aid in four agencies, 26 programs for food and nutrition aid in six agencies, and 44 programs for employment and training services in nine agencies.[34]

The Senate Committee on Government Affairs also examined federal duplication.[35] It found 27 different programs for teen pregnancy, 130 programs for at-risk youth, 19 programs for prevention of substance abuse, 17 agencies that monitor international trade agreements, 10 agencies that are involved in export promotion, and 342 programs for economic development. A recent study by the Federal Home Loan Bank of Des Moines found an astounding 1,399 federal programs that served rural America, of which 337 were "key" programs for rural areas.[36]

One reason why such duplication occurs is that politicians and bureaucrats have their fingers in the wind to discern the sexy issue of the day, whether it is "environment," "exports," "jobs," "children," or "homeland security." When an issue is hot, every department is quick to erect a new program to score a larger budget allocation. For example, the Small Business Administration has cashed in on the popularity of anti-drug programs with the creation of a Drug-Free Workplace grant program for small businesses. At least nine other federal departments are on the anti-drug gravy train.[37]

Program duplication often occurs when it becomes clear that a government program simply does not work. In that case, politicians create a new program to tackle the problem. However, to avoid bureaucratic turf fights and offending special interests, policymakers usually leave old programs in place to spin their wheels.

A good example is the Bush administration's Millennium Challenge Corporation, a multi-billion-dollar foreign aid agency that was recently added on top of the half dozen existing federal aid agencies.[38] Millennium Challenge was created because it is widely recognized that traditional foreign aid is a failure. Steven Radelet, a foreign aid expert and former Treasury official, testified to Congress: "The U.S. foreign aid system, particularly USAID, is bogged down under heavy bureaucracy, overly restrictive legislative burdens, and conflicting objectives."[39] Indeed, much of the foreign aid budget goes down a black hole because many recipient countries have corrupt and incompetent governments.[40] Millennium Challenge is supposed to deliver foreign aid in a new way, but taxpayers are stuck funding all the old aid agencies as well.

Congress gets much of the blame for federal duplication. It resists consolidation of any program that might adversely impact an important member's district. A striking example involved the Navy's recent efforts to trim the number of U.S. aircraft carriers down from 12 to 11. Sensing that the aged USS *John F. Kennedy* based in Jacksonville might be the one cut, Florida's congressional leaders slipped language into a defense bill in 2005 that required that the Navy maintain its full fleet of 12 carriers.[41] That sort of parochial politics is not just wasteful; it also reduces military effectiveness when it misallocates resources within the Pentagon's budget.

Obsolete Programs

Federal programs have an unfortunate tendency to linger decades after the problems they were designed to solve have disappeared. Economic growth, technological changes, and entrepreneurial innovations often mitigate the social ills that programs tried to solve. For example, the rise of cable television undercuts the traditional justification for subsidies to the Public Broadcasting System. PBS is supposed to be an educational alternative to the four main commercial TV networks. But today there are dozens of cable channels, including numerous educational ones.

Federal loan programs provide another example of obsolescence. The government has loan and loan guarantee programs for farmers, small businesses, housing developers, students, and other favored groups. But those programs make less sense all the time because of the increasing sophistication of financial markets. Better credit information, better management of risks, and financial deregulation have reduced the need for federal loan programs.[42] For example, federal loan programs for small businesses make no sense today— if they ever did—after the explosion in private venture capital and angel financing in recent decades.[43]

Some government agencies start off with some energy and new ideas, but over time they stagnate and fossilize. Paul Light, an expert on the federal bureaucracy, noted of the three-year-old Transportation Security Agency: "As memories of 9/11 have faded, TSA has begun to look like any other federal agency. It has lived an entire bureaucratic life in quick time, moving from urgency toward complacency in just three short years."[44]

John Stuart Mill noted this evolution of government bureaucracies in his 1861 book on representative government: "The disease which afflicts bureaucratic governments . . . is routine . . . whatever becomes a routine loses its vital principle, and having no longer a mind acting within it, goes on revolving mechanically, though the work it is intended to do remains undone."[45]

Mill's description fits many federal agencies. Consider NASA. The space agency began its life with high ambition and was initially able to attract the best and brightest. But over time, the entrepreneurial types left, routine took over, and the rot set in. In the 1960s NASA played a role in winning the Cold War by ensuring that the United States was the leader in space. But NASA is now obsolete. It has foundered with poor management, cost overruns, and unclear goals. Its manned space flight program, in particular, makes little sense.

In recent decades, private businesses, such as communications satellite firms, have gained a foothold in space. In 2004 Burt Rutan put the world's first privately financed astronaut into space with an innovative spaceship design and a small $20 million budget. Entrepreneurs such as Virgin Group founder Richard Branson are planning for space tourism flights to begin later in the decade.

In the 1990s the government cut off funding for NASA's Search for Extraterrestrial Intelligence project, which uses radio telescopes to search for life on other planets. Private funders have stepped in to create a SETI Institute, and the project is now thriving. The *Washington Post* recently observed that Silicon Valley techies have infused the project

> with money and unconventional technical ideas, bringing a new respect and energy to the organization. Some argue that being cast away by the federal government was the best thing that could have happened to SETI, that it has become stronger and more innovative in the private sector than it ever could have as part of a public bureaucracy.[46]

The rest of NASA ought to be terminated or privatized as well. Unfortunately, NASA funding is sustained by politics. As President Bush was beginning his reelection effort in 2004, the White House cast about for an uplifting initiative. They came up with a nutty scheme to send a manned space mission to Mars called "Vision for Space Exploration." The public has not asked for a Mars mission, NASA would probably bungle it, and the costs of such a mission would be astronomical over the next couple of decades—just as the costs of programs for the elderly are exploding. Unfortunately, politics won the day because House Majority Leader Tom Delay (R-TX) pushed the funding through Congress because his district—home of the Johnson Space Center—would be a big winner.[47]

Defenders of federal programs often suggest that even if federal programs are old and decrepit there are no private alternatives available. But in many cases it is the existence of government programs and regulations that prevents entrepreneurs from providing an alternative. For example, NASA has discouraged private competition, and the threat of regulation has been a hurdle to the private space industry.[48]

Low-income housing provides another example of government hurdles. Developers are dissuaded from constructing low-income housing by rent controls, costly construction standards, and other regulations.[49] In other cases, federal law simply bars competition with the government. It is illegal to compete against the U.S. Postal Service on first class mail, for example. In sum, entrepreneurs could provide many services that the government currently provides if the government would just get out of the way.

To end obsolete government activities and give entrepreneurs a chance, all federal programs and regulations should be "sunsetted."[50] That means terminating them after a fixed period of time, perhaps 10 years, unless Congress affirmatively reauthorizes them. An expert commission could be set up to examine programs on a rotating basis and make recommendations to retain or kill each program prior to its sunset date. About 20 states have some sort of sunset process, and legislation for federal sunsetting has been introduced in Congress.

Sunset legislation is needed because Congress rarely prunes unnecessary programs. By contrast, private companies are routinely put out of business, or "sunset," by new and better firms. For example, Montgomery Ward was sunset by consumers when more efficient retailers, such as Target, arrived on the scene. As noted, about 10 percent of U.S. firms go out of business each year because of mismanagement, obsolete products, and other reasons.[51] Other data show that more than half of new businesses disappear within four years of being established.[52] The federal government needs some parallel method of eliminating programs when they fail or become obsolete.

Mismanaged Programs

Federal mismanagement runs wide and deep. Some common problems in federal agencies are poor financial controls and bungled technology projects. At many agencies, mismanagement continues year after year despite criticism by the GAO and other watchdogs. Mismanagement is not just a problem from the taxpayers' perspective; it also prevents the government from effectively performing its proper duties in areas such as defense and border security.

The following are some examples of serious management failures in recent years:

- **Department of Defense.** The GAO says that the Pentagon's financial management problems are "pervasive, complex, long-standing, and deeply rooted in virtually all business operations throughout the department."[53] The Pentagon loses track of assets, wastes billions of dollars on poor management of its excessive inventory, keeps unreliable budget data, lowballs project costs, and makes billions of dollars in overpayments to contractors. A GAO investigation in 2005 found that the Pentagon spent at least $400 million over two years on new boots, tents, and other items at the same time it was discarding identical products as excess.[54] Of the $33 billion of inventory that the Pentagon marked as excess over three years, $4 billion was in excellent condition and often in unopened packages. Of 68,000 first-class plane tickets purchased by the DoD in one recent year, 73 percent were not justified.[55] The Pentagon promises to fix such problems, but such waste has been going on for years, and Congress has never bothered to really crack down.
- **Border Security.** In April 2005 the *Washington Post* reported that a $239 million system that monitored U.S. borders "has been hobbled for years by defective equipment that was poorly installed, and by lax oversight by government officials who failed to properly supervise the project's contractor."[56] One ex–Border Patrol chief said, "The contractor sold us a bill of goods and no one in the Border Patrol and INS was watching . . . all these failures placed Americans in danger."[57] After a 2005 hearing the *Post* reported that members of Congress denounced the system "as a scandal and an embarrassment, citing defective equipment, rampant overcharging by contractors, and a failure

... by government officials to properly oversee it."[58]

In May 2005 the *New York Times* reported that much of the $4.5 billion worth of new border security equipment purchased by the government since 9/11 will have to be replaced because it is ineffective and unreliable.[59] For example, despite $3.2 billion spent on airport screening equipment, the *Times* reports that "the likelihood of detecting a hidden weapon or bomb has not significantly changed since the government took over airport screening operations in 2003."[60] In another recent management failure, dozens of Border Patrol agents in Arizona participated in a kickback scheme under which local landlords paid off agents for their business.[61] Top officials ignored the abuse for years, yet in the end only low-level workers were disciplined in the case.

- **FBI**. The Federal Bureau of Investigation has been severely criticized for its poor management during the 1990s, which prevented it from possibly averting the 9/11 disaster. William Odom, a retired Army lieutenant general, argued in the *Washington Post* in 2005 that "of all the failures that allowed Al Qaeda's attacks on Sept. 11, 2001, to succeed, those of the FBI are the most egregious."[62] Indeed, Odom argues that the FBI's history is "saturated with disgraceful failures" of its intelligence operatives.[63] It seems that all the clues needed to prevent Al Qaeda's destructive activities were available to the FBI in the aftermath of the 1993 World Trade Center bombing, and that the agency could have prevented further attacks if it had pieced the clues together.[64] In a June 2005 report, the Justice Department's inspector general found that the FBI failed to detect the 9/11 plot because of "widespread and longstanding deficiencies" in agency management.[65]

- **Department of Energy**. Laboratories overseen by DOE, including Los Alamos, Oak Ridge, Sandia, and Lawrence Livermore, were mismanaged for years with ongoing security lapses. The GAO began reporting on those problems at least 20 years ago, but few reforms were made. Then a major scandal erupted in the late 1990s when it was revealed that China may have been stealing design information on nuclear weapons from the labs.[66] A 1999 House of Representatives report concluded: "Despite repeated PRC thefts of the most sophisticated U.S. nuclear weapons technology, security at our national nuclear weapons laboratories does not meet even minimal standards."[67] A high-level administration panel investigating the scandals condemned the DOE as a "dysfunctional bureaucracy" where "organizational disarray, managerial neglect, and a culture of arrogance . . . conspired to create an espionage scandal waiting to happen."[68]

- **NASA**. The official report on the *Columbia* disaster in 2003 found that NASA suffers from ineffective leadership, flawed analyses, and a reactive and complacent approach to safety. It noted that the mistakes made on *Columbia* were "not isolated failures, but are indicative of systematic flaws" in the agency.[69] The 1986 *Challenger* disaster was also traced to flawed NASA management. NASA's poor management also manifests itself in the large cost overruns of the International Space Station. The project's estimated cost has skyrocketed from $17 billion in 1995 to $30 billion today, and the station is years behind schedule.[70] The GAO has repeatedly criticized NASA's financial management.[71]

- **Bureau of Indian Affairs**. In what has been called the "Indian Enron," the BIA has mismanaged billions of dollars in Indian trust funds.[72] Former special trustees of the BIA have given scathing congressional testimony about the agency's inability to clean up the mess. Trustee Thomas Slonaker testified that officials are unwilling to follow the law and do not "hold people accountable for their actions."[73] Trustee Paul Homan testified that the "vast majority of upper and middle management at the BIA were incompetent," yet no senior managers have been removed.[74] In 2004 a court-appointed investigator charged the government with obstructing his probe into federal corruption related to the trust funds.[75]

- **Army Corps of Engineers**. This $5 billion agency has long falsified its economic analyses to justify large white elephant construction projects.[76] The agency has poured billions of dollars into unneeded and environmentally damaging projects in the districts of important members of Congress. In 2000 it was discovered that the agency's top managers manipulated studies to lend support to a wasteful $1 billion Mississippi River project.[77] A similar scandal erupted over a $311 million project to dredge the Delaware River.[78] In this case, local refineries were the main beneficiaries of the project. The Army Corps has had these problems for decades. In his 1952 book, Sen. Paul Douglas observed that the Army Corps "have never been restrained in estimating the benefits which will result from their projects and whose estimates in recent years have greatly underestimated the costs."[79] As discussed in Appendix 2, the solution is to privatize the Army Corps.

A management problem that plagues just about every federal department is cost overruns on construction projects and procurement.[80] Cost overruns occur on military weapons systems, energy projects, highway projects, and computer upgrades. Table 5.1 summarizes the cost overruns on a variety of federal projects in recent years. The table compares the original estimated cost when the projects got the go-ahead with the most recent comparable cost estimate. The data in the table come from the sources noted here.

- **Transportation.** Large, sometimes massive, cost overruns are commonplace in federally funded transportation projects.[81] In 1994 Virginia officials claimed that the Springfield interchange project would cost $241 million. The estimated cost of the ongoing project has now soared to $676 million.[82] The cost of New York's Penn Station redevelopment has more than doubled, and the project is years behind schedule.[83] The GAO found that half of the federal highway projects it examined in recent years had cost overruns of more than 25 percent.[84] Denver residents agreed to construction of a new $1.7 billion international airport in a 1989 referendum. By the time the airport was opened in 1995 the cost had mushroomed to $4.8 billion.[85]
- **Boston's Big Dig.** The most infamous transportation cost overrun is Boston's "Big Dig," or Central Artery project. In 1985 government officials claimed that the Big Dig would cost $2.6 billion and would be completed by 1998. The cost has ballooned to $14.6 billion and the project is now expected to be finished in 2005.[86] (The federal share of the cost is $8.5 billion.) The Big Dig has been grossly mismanaged, as revealed by a *Boston Globe* investigation.[87] The state government bailed out bungling Big Dig contractors 3,200 times instead of demanding accountability. Contractors were essentially rewarded for delays and overruns with added cash and guaranteed profits. As a final insult

Table 5.1
FEDERAL GOVERNMENT COST OVERRUNS
(defense items in constant dollars; other figures in
current dollars)

Project	Estimated Cost and Date of Estimate	
	Original	Latest or Actual
Transportation		
Boston "Big Dig"	$2.6b (1985)	$14.6b (2005)
Virginia Springfield interchange	$241m (1994)	$676m (2005)
Kennedy Center parking lot	$28m (1998)	$88m (2003)
Air traffic control modernization	$8.9b (1998–2004)	$14.6b (2005)
Denver International Airport	$1.7b (1989)	$4.8b (1995)
Seattle light rail system	$1.7b (1996)	$2.6b (2000)
Energy		
Yucca mountain radioactive waste	$6.3b (1992)	$8.4b (2001)
Hanford nuclear fuels site	$715m (1995)	$1.6b (2001)
Idaho Falls nuclear fuels site	$124m (1998)	$273m (2001)
National ignition laser facility	$2.1b (1995)	$3.3b (2001)
Weldon Springs remedial action	$358m (1989)	$905m (2001)
Defense (per unit in 2003 dollars)		
Global Hawk surveillance plane	$86m (2001)	$123m (2004)
F/A-22 Raptor fighter	$117m (1992)	$254m (2002)
V-22 Osprey aircraft	$36m (1987)	$93m (2001)
RAH-66 Comanche helicopter	$33m (2000)	$53m (2002)
CH-47F cargo helicopter	$9m (1998)	$18m (2002)
SBIRS satellite system	$825m (1998)	$1.6b (2002)
Patriot advanced missile	$5m (1995)	$10m (2002)
EX-171 guided munition	$45,000b (1997)	$150,000b (2002)
Entitlement Programs		
Medicare drug bill, first 10 years	$400b (2003)	$534b (2004)
Medicare Part A, cost in 1990	$9b (1965)	$67b (1990)
Medicare, home care, cost in 1993	$4b (1988)	$10b (1993)
Medicaid special hospital subsidy	$100m (1987)	$11b (1992)
1996 farm subsidy law (over 7 years)	$47b (1996)	$118b (2002)
Other		
Capitol Hill visitor center	$265m (2001)	$559m (2005)
Kennedy Center Opera House	$18.3m (1995)	$22.2m (2003)
Kennedy Center Concert Hall	$15.1m (1995)	$21.3m (1997)
Washington, DC, baseball stadium	$435m (2004)	up to $614m (2004)
International space station	$17b (1995)	$30b (2002)
FBI Trilogy computer system	$477m (2000)	$600m (2004)
Pentagon secret spy satellite	$5b (n/a)	$9.5b (2004)
Pentagon laser anti-missile system	$1b (1996)	$2b (2004)

SOURCES: Compilation by author based mainly on GAO reports and *Washington Post* stories. See endnotes for detailed references. Figures in $ million (m) or $ billion (b).

to taxpayers, hundreds of leaks were found in the project in 2004, which are expected to cost taxpayers tens of millions of further dollars to fix.

- **Air Traffic Control.** A review in 2005 of Federal Aviation Administration projects designed to upgrade the nation's air traffic control found that the combined costs of 16 projects had risen from $8.9 billion to $14.6 billion.[88] For example, a computer system called STARS has jumped in cost from $940 million to $2.8 billion, and it is seven years behind schedule.[89] The Department of Transportation's inspector general notes that the expensive project is "facing obsolescence" even before it is completed.[90]

- **Energy.** The Department of Energy's performance on big contracting projects is abysmal. Table 5.1 includes a sample of projects examined by the GAO.[91] The agency tracked 80 major energy projects begun between the mid-1970s and mid-1990s.[92] It found that 31 were terminated prior to completion, causing billions of dollars in losses. Most of the rest were either overbudget or behind schedule. A GAO review in 2003 found that little had changed.[93] Energy Department contracting has been on GAO's watch list for waste, fraud, and abuse since 1990. Billions of dollars have been wasted on megaprojects, such as the $2 billion spent on the canceled Superconducting Super Collider in Texas.

- **Defense.** Table 5.1 includes a sampling of cost overruns in weapons systems.[94] When weapons systems are conceived, there is a tendency for the Pentagon and other project supporters to low-ball the costs and squeeze as many projects into the procurement pipeline as possible. Then, after projects are begun, they are very hard to kill because weapons contractors skillfully spread out the work across plants and subcontractors in many states and congressional districts.

- **Technology Projects.** Big cost overruns are routine on federal technology projects.[95] For example, the Department of Veterans Affairs scrapped a $472 million computer upgrade project in 2004 as a total failure.[96] The agency had already spent $265 million on the project, which is a complete loss to taxpayers. In 2005 the Treasury Department's inspector general found that $43 million spent to install Treasury's new $173 million personnel system was wasted.[97]

The FBI has chronic failures in its technology projects. The $600 million Trilogy project to update the FBI's computer systems was nearing completion in 2004, but it was $123 million overbudget and 21 months late.[98] The FBI abandoned a part of the upgrade, a $170 million system called Virtual Case File, after $100 million had been spent.[99] VCF would have been used to help agents share terrorist threat data.

- **Around Washington.** It is hard for members of Congress not to be aware of the chronic problem of federal cost overruns, given the plethora of examples right under their noses in Washington. The cost of the new Capitol Hill Visitors Center has jumped from $265 million to $559 million, and the project is years behind schedule.[100] The cost of a new Kennedy Center parking lot has jumped to $88 million from the original estimate of $28 million in 1998.[101] And the GAO reported in 2005 that renovations to the Kennedy Center's Opera House were 21 percent overbudget, and its Concert Hall was 41 percent overbudget.[102] The cost of the proposed new D.C. baseball stadium has jumped from the $435 million that the mayor used to sell the project to as much as $614 million.[103]

In a recent study for the National Bureau of Economic Research, two economists compared actual costs with originally estimated costs of a sample of large government projects dating back to the Erie Canal begun in 1817.[104] They found a pattern of large cost overruns, with the problem getting worse in recent decades. Some of the cost overruns they calculated were the Erie Canal (46 percent overbudget), the Panama Canal (106 percent), Hoover Dam (12 percent), Louisiana Superdome (366 percent), and the 1970s renovation of Yankee Stadium (317 percent).

Cost overruns are the typical pattern on federal entitlement programs as well. The government usually low-balls its estimates of the costs of entitlements in order to get initial approval. Legislators put supposed benefit limits into bills to hold cost estimates down on paper. But such limits do not work, are evaded, or are later repealed. When costs soar and programs do not work, politicians hold hearings to cast blame elsewhere, such as on drug firms or hospitals. When Medicare Part A was enacted in 1965, costs were projected to rise to $9 billion by 1990, but actual costs reached $67 billion.[105] When the Medicaid special hospitals subsidy was added in 1987, the annual costs were projected at $100 million. By 1992 costs had risen to $11 billion annually.

Soon after the ink was dry on the 2003 Medicare prescription drug bill, the Bush administration informed the public that the cost would be $534 billion, one-third more than the $400 billion that had been promised. Subsequent investigations revealed that Medicare's chief cost analyst knew about the higher costs months before the legislation was enacted, but he was threatened with termination if he made that knowledge public.[106]

Clearly, there is a strong incentive for supporters of projects in Congress, the bureaucracy, and lobbying groups to low-ball initial cost estimates. Consider the recent scandal that saw Air Force officials trying to push through an inflated contract for Boeing tanker planes. A government report on the scandal notes an Air Force official saying that "numbers were contorted a lot of different ways to sell the program."[107] This strategy of manipulating numbers has also been common, for example, in Army Corps of Engineers projects.

A 2002 study by Danish economists looked at 258 government transportation projects in the United States and abroad. They found that cost overruns are routine and that they stem from government deceit, not honest errors.[108] Nine of 10 projects they examined had cost overruns, with an average overrun of 28 percent. The study concluded that lying, or intentional deception, by public officials was the source of the problem: "Project promoters routinely ignore, hide, or otherwise leave out important project costs and risks in order to make total costs appear low."[109] This is called a "salami" strategy, whereby project costs are revealed to taxpayers one slice at a time in the hope that the project is too far along to turn back when the true costs are revealed.

An added problem with federal-state projects, such as highway construction, is that the states have few incentives to manage funds wisely knowing that federal taxpayers are footing much of the bill. When cost overruns occur, federal officials point fingers at state officials. State officials, in turn, point their fingers at poor contractor performance, as occurred with the Big Dig.

However, the ultimate culpability for cost overruns is with Congress. Members who secure projects for their districts have little, if any, interest in cost efficiencies. As noted, costs are benefits to politicians. What counts to members of Congress are the amounts of federal cash and the number of government-funded jobs brought home to their state or district. If highway projects or space stations are overbudget, it simply means more federal jobs in the hometowns of legislators.

The only real and lasting solution to those problems is to move funding of highways, airports, space flight, and as many other activities as possible to the private sector, as discussed in Chapter 9.

Ineffective Programs

Many federal programs do not solve the problems that they were set up to solve. That results from a combination of bureaucratic failings and the fact that many problems in society are simply not amenable to government "solutions." Foreign aid for economic development is a good example. Much of the aid budget gets consumed by layers of management including federal workers, U.S. contractors, subcontractors, foreign bureaucrats, and their expenses such as hotels, office space, plane flights, meals, and report writing. Even the aid that actually reaches the ground in foreign countries has no positive effect when recipient countries do not have stability, the rule of law, or market economies. Indeed, spending can create perverse incentives that undermine program goals. For example, if foreign aid helps sustain corrupt foreign governments, it stalls economic reforms that would create lasting progress.

Another example of perverse incentives is Housing and Urban Development's Section 8 housing program, which provides rent vouchers to poor families. Vouchers are supposed to allow recipients to spread out widely and integrate into middle-class neighborhoods. But the program creates incentives that promote the concentration of poor families.[110] Also, the program is supposed to subsidize poor tenants, but it ends up profiting the landlords who specialize in the bureaucratic complexities of owning Section 8 apartments.[111] Housing subsidies also create long-term dependence, as did the old welfare system that was replaced in 1996. HUD Secretary Alphonso Jackson testified to Congress in 2005, "There is little incentive for families to seek housing outside of the voucher program; in fact, there is a disincentive to make positive life decisions."[112]

Many federal programs accomplish little of value, and one sus-pects that the bureaucrats in charge know it. Their strategy is to obfuscate their program goals in order to cover up their ineffective-ness. Consider the opaque goals of one program discussed in the federal budget: "The Rural Strategic Investment Program will pro-vide rural communities with flexible resources to develop compre-hensive, collaborative, and locally-based strategic planning pro-cesses; and will implement innovative community and economic development strategies that optimize regional competitive advan-tages."[113] If the bureaucrats in charge of this program write some memos, hold meetings, and file a few reports, who can say that these goals were not met?

One good strategy for bureaucrats in charge of useless programs is to describe their goals with fancy pie-in-the-sky language. Con-sider this mission statement of the Department of Agriculture's Eco-nomic and Community Systems program:

> Research, education and extension can be redesigned and targeted to further enrich diverse human capacity to build prosperity for sustainable communities. ECS encourages a whole systems approach. From inner city to farmland cross-roads, locally geared, "people-focused" programs will result in families, farms, businesses, and community-based organi-zations linking to one another and will ensure that people share tools and strategies for community discovery of issues, needs and resources. It will also result in effective delivery of place-based, community-led solutions that are needed to balance trends toward globalization of information and the economy.[114]

That statement contains no actual content. Other program descrip-tions reveal the underlying wastefulness of the bureaucracy. Con-sider this description from the federal budget:

> The Hydrogen R&D Interagency Task Force, established by OSTP shortly after the President's announcement of the Hydrogen Fuel Initiative, serves as the mechanism for collab-oration among the nine Federal agencies that fund hydrogen-related R&D. In 2003, the task force gathered information and provided guidance for agency research directions. In 2004, the task force will complete an interagency 10-year plan that will improve coordination of agency efforts, accelerate

progress toward the goals of the initiative, and foster collaboration between the Federal Government and the private sector, state agencies, and other stakeholders. The DOE-led International Partnership for the Hydrogen Economy coordinates hydrogen research between the U.S. and other participating governments.[115]

The paragraph exposes a number of classic bureaucratic crutches. Funding for hydrogen research is spread out across nine agencies, which guarantees that many taxpayer dollars will be spent simply to coordinate the different efforts. The paragraph uses the warm and fuzzy phrase "foster collaboration" but does not mention the inevitable turf wars that will break out between the various "stakeholders." Phrases such as "task force" and "accelerate progress" sound good, but how accelerated can the work be when the government is giving itself 10 years to get results? Indeed, the government was off to a slow start: 2003 was spent "gathering information," and 2004 was spent simply drafting a plan.

To the Bush administration's credit, it is attempting to sort through the federal budget in a structured way and score each program's effectiveness. The president's budget office has so far evaluated 607 separate programs. The results reveal that federal performance is mixed at best, even by the government's own standards. The budget office rated only 41 percent of federal programs as "effective" or "moderately effective."[116] The administration has also created a "management scorecard," which grades each department on various parameters. The scorecard has shown improvements over time, but by 2005 there were still only 41 of 130 items that were considered successfully achieved.[117]

Those Bush management reforms build on procedures established under the Government Performance and Results Act of 1993. That act required federal agencies to prepare strategic plans on a regular basis. Agencies now have to put down on paper what their goals are and whether they have reached them. That sounds like something that agencies should have always done, but in the past many agencies made no attempt to account for their performance. Despite those modest reforms, the GAO concludes that "few agencies adequately show the results that they are getting with the taxpayer dollars they spend."[118]

Reforming the Bureaucracy

In addition to scoring the performance of federal programs, the Bush administration has pursued some structural changes to the bureaucracy. In the wake of 9/11, the national security and intelligence agencies were reorganized. A new Department of Homeland Security has been created. Workforce rules have been reformed for 110,000 DHS employees and are being reformed for the 750,000-person Pentagon. A new position of director of national intelligence (DNI) has been created.

There is debate about whether the new federal security and intelligence bureaucracies will work any better than the old ones. When created, it was not clear what the mission and structure of the DNI would be. Also, the DHS has been hobbled by bureaucratic infighting and a demoralized staff in its first few years of existence.[119] The *Washington Post* detailed the agency's hugely wasteful procurement spending in a series of articles in 2005.[120]

One key problem is that portions of DHS's massive structure are overseen by 79 separate congressional committees and subcommittees. The *Washington Post* called this fragmented congressional oversight "sheer lunacy."[121] The official 9/11 commission report in 2004 called congressional oversight of intelligence "dysfunctional."[122] Unfortunately, turf-protecting committee chairmen have refused to allow a consolidation of intelligence oversight.

Nonetheless, an area of clear progress by the Bush administration has been the creation of more flexible workforce rules in these agencies. New rules for the DHS and Pentagon limit union power, tie pay raises to good performance, streamline appeals of disciplinary actions, and allow managers more freedom to reassign people.[123]

Those sorts of reforms should be applied throughout the federal government. Under the rigid workforce rules that are in place for most federal agencies, workers get virtually automatic pay raises based on longevity, bad workers are rarely disciplined or fired, and morale in most agencies is low. One survey of 100,000 federal workers in 2002 found that only 43 percent held their agency's leaders "in high regard."[124]

Those sorts of views are common in surveys of federal workers by the government's Office of Personnel Management and Merit Systems Protection Board. An OPM survey of almost 150,000 federal workers in 2004 found that only 37 percent thought that their

Table 5.2
FEDERAL WORKERS FIRED FOR POOR PERFORMANCE

Department	Annual Average Number			Share of Workforce,
	1980s	1990s	2000s	2000s
Agriculture	22	21	24	0.02%
Commerce	3	9	14	0.04%
Education	2	1	1	0.03%
Energy	2	3	4	0.02%
HHS	40	11	13	0.02%
HUD	4	2	1	0.01%
Interior	12	18	25	0.04%
Justice	5	17	33	0.03%
Labor	4	4	6	0.04%
State	1	0	0	0.00%
Transportation	21	20	6	0.01%
Treasury	26	27	25	0.02%
Veterans	42	49	48	0.02%
Other	23	26	51	0.02%
Nondefense	205	206	254	0.02%
Defense	152	225	290	0.04%
Total	356	431	544	0.03%

SOURCE: Author's calculations based on Office of Personnel Management data. The 1980s include 1984 to 1989. The 2000s include 2000–2004.

agency's leaders "generate high levels of motivation and commitment," and only 34 percent thought that "promotions in my work unit are based on merit."[125] The survey found that only slightly more than one-quarter thought that sufficient steps are taken to deal with poor employees.[126] The OPM has concluded that "the federal white-collar pay system sends and reinforces the message that performance does not matter."[127]

A key factor that impedes effective federal management is the inability to fire poorly performing workers. OPM data reveal that the firing rate for poor performers in the federal government is stunningly low at just 0.03 percent (about 1 in 3,000) per year.[128] Among nondefense workers, just 0.02 percent (1 in 5,000) is fired annually. Table 5.2 shows that fewer than 600 civilian federal workers are fired for poor performance in a typical year. Federal firing rates have been low for decades, although they have risen somewhat in recent years.[129]

The lack of firing in many agencies is remarkable. Since 9/11, numerous commentators have observed that few if any employees in the intelligence agencies have been fired for mistakes leading up to that tragic day. The *Washington Post* noted:

> Despite sharp critiques from the president's commission and the Senate intelligence committee, no major reprimand or penalty has been announced publicly in connection with the intelligence failures, though investigations are still underway at the CIA. George J. Tenet resigned as CIA director but was later awarded the Medal of Freedom by Bush.[130]

Consider that the 30,000-person State Department fired just seven employees for poor performance in two decades. Yet that agency has had numerous high-profile cases of mismanagement, including cases of mishandling secret documents, extreme sloppiness in handing out visitor visas before 9/11, and letting Russian spies bug a meeting room down the hall from the secretary's office during the Clinton administration.

The federal firing rate needs to be increased substantially. Available evidence indicates that firing rates in the private sector are much higher than in the federal government. No private-sector data exist to compare directly with federal data, but for the broader category of "involuntary separations," the federal rate is just one-fourth the private-sector rate.[131] Certainly, top corporate executives frequently get fired if their performance falls short. One survey found that 37 percent of departing CEOs at the largest U.S. companies had been fired instead of leaving voluntarily.[132]

Private-sector firing is probably below the optimal as well because firms are under threat of wrongful discharge lawsuits. Laws vary across states, but only five adhere to "employment at will," which allows broad freedom to dismiss workers.[133] Since workers are free to "fire" their employers at any time, employment at will is a balanced approach that should be the rule in both the private and government sectors.

While some procedures are in place to fire poorly performing federal workers, most managers shy away from it because it involves a huge time commitment. The Bush administration has said that it takes 18 months or longer to fire a federal employee. The OPM notes that federal managers need to put in "heroic" efforts to overcome obstacles to removal of an employee.[134] According to OPM, managers think that "procedures dealing with poor performance are too complicated, time consuming, or onerous; they do not get higher management support; and they perceive their decisions will be reversed or that they will be falsely accused of discrimination in their actions."[135] Indeed, federal workers lodge discrimination complaints at 10 times the rate of nonfederal workers.[136]

Rather than discipline or fire bad workers, federal managers try to move them into other offices like hot potatoes. Managers who are stuck with bad workers often give them good reviews so as not to rock the boat. The Merit Systems Protection Board notes that there is an ingrained federal culture to score virtually all workers highly in annual reviews.[137] A *Washington Post* analysis found that almost two-thirds of federal civilian employees receive annual merit bonuses.[138] Excessive bonuses and false high performance scores create a hurdle for agencies that wish to terminate workers.[139]

Further protections for bad workers come from abuse of federal "whistle-blower" rules. For example, in 2002 the number-two official at the Bureau of Indian Affairs was fired after being put under two federal probes for influence peddling. But he fought his ouster by filing for whistle-blower protection.[140]

Increasing the firing rate would be an important reform because retention of bad employees damages an agency's morale. Bad employees waste the time and efforts of better workers. Good federal employees would welcome more firing because it would reduce the frustrations of dealing with coworkers who do little work. Most federal workers think that poor performers are not dealt with adequately.[141] One survey of federal workers found that 23 percent thought that their coworkers were "not up to par."[142]

The poor performance of federal executives is also a big problem. Indeed, it is even more important to remove bad executives and managers because they can cause the most talented workers to quit. There is certainly a lack of executive accountability when scandals erupt. Usually, when investigators are finally able to box a federal executive in a corner with evidence of failures, the executive goes in front of the television cameras and says, "I take full responsibility." But then he or she doesn't quit!

Consider the prisoner abuse scandals in Iraq. More than 100 low-level military personnel had charges brought against them or were court-martialed, but only one senior military leader was disciplined, and none fired.[143] U.S. army commanders failed to properly supervise their subordinates, they handed down unclear and even illegal policies, and they ignored signs of abuse, but they got off the hook.[144] The *Washington Post* called this lack of accountability "disgraceful for the American political system."[145] Fairness and improved performance require that firing should be increased at all levels in the federal government.

Increased firing is just one of many needed reforms to the federal bureaucracy. Another idea is to make executive pay raises contingent on good agency performance, perhaps as defined by receiving a good grade on the administration's "management scorecard." Executives in agencies that fail performance tests should have their salaries frozen. Ultimately, however, better management can improve government performance only so much. A more fundamental reform is to move as many federal activities as possible back to the states and the private sector.

6. Special Interest Spending

In theory, federal policymakers have the broad public interest in mind when they consider budget issues. But that is not how Washington works in practice. Many federal programs are sustained by special interests that convince legislators to take from the many and give to the few. Subsidies are often directed to small groups of individuals and businesses, but the costs are distributed broadly across the nation's 110 million households. The federal government is not so much an institution that helps the needy as one that helps organized groups at the expense of average working taxpayers.

Concentrated Benefits and Diffuse Costs

Recipients of federal handouts are usually represented by organized groups that lobby for their cause. Those groups have a big incentive to keep the federal gravy train rolling. By contrast, average citizens do not have a strong motivation to try and block particular programs. People may think that a program is unjustified, but they will not pay much attention if it is only one of hundreds of federal activities that cost them tax dollars.

When average citizens do speak out against particular programs, they are usually outgunned. For one thing, they are at an informational disadvantage because of the specialized nature of most federal programs. Special interest groups are usually the top experts on programs and they are skilled at generating media support for them. To further strengthen their position, lobbying groups usually cloak their narrow private interests in public interest clothing.

Another problem is that program supporters in Congress, lobbying groups, and federal agencies rarely admit that a program is wasteful or ineffective. After all, their careers, pride, and reputations are on the line. It is very difficult for outsiders to challenge program supporters and prove that programs do not have the large benefits that the inside experts claim for them.

Table 6.1
Majority Voting Does Not Ensure That a Project's Benefits
Outweigh Costs

Legislator	Vote	Benefits Received by Constituents	Taxes Paid by Constituents
Frist	Yea	$12	$10
Stevens	Yea	$12	$10
Domenici	Yea	$12	$10
Rockefeller	Nay	$2	$10
Kennedy	Nay	$2	$10
Total	Pass	$40	$50

The result is that Congress often passes special interest legislation in which the costs to society outweigh the benefits. Table 6.1 shows how this happens. The table assumes that legislators vote in the narrow interests of their districts. The hypothetical project shown creates benefits of $40 and costs taxpayers $50, and thus is a loser to the nation overall. Nonetheless, the project is able to gain a majority vote and it passes. The project's benefits are more concentrated than its costs, and that is the key to finding a political winner in Washington.

Logrolling

Congress operates as a complex web of vote trading, or logrolling, which further strengthens the pro-spending bias of the institution. Table 6.2 shows that because of logrolling, projects that are net losers to society can pass even if they have only minority support. Because projects X and Y would fail with stand-alone votes, Frist, Stevens, and Domenici enter an agreement for mutual support of the two projects. That is, they logroll. The result is that the two projects get approved, even though each imposes net costs on society and each benefits only a minority of voters.

The existence of logrolling means that spending programs that make no economic sense and have only minimal support get enacted all the time. "Pork" spending is one conspicuous manifestation of the problem. It usually involves very narrowly targeted spending in just one state or congressional district, as discussed in Box 6.1.

Former representative Joe Scarborough of Florida has described the logrolling that led to the passage of the bloated 2002 farm bill,

Table 6.2
LOGROLLING ALLOWS PASSAGE OF SUBSIDIES THAT BENEFIT MINORITIES OF CONSTITUENTS

		Project A			Project B	
Legislator	Vote	Benefits Received by Constituents	Taxes Paid by Constituents	Vote	Benefits Received by Constituents	Taxes Paid by Constituents
Frist	Yea	$15	$10	Yea	$8	$10
Stevens	Yea	$15	$10	Yea	$8	$10
Domenici	Yea	$4	$10	Yea	$20	$10
Rockefeller	Nay	$3	$10	Nay	$2	$10
Kennedy	Nay	$3	$10	Nay	$2	$10
Total	Pass	$40	$50	Pass	$40	$50

which he calls the "largest corporate welfare scam in history."[1] Dairy subsidies had the support of members from Maine, Pennsylvania, and Vermont. Peanut subsidies had the support of members from Virginia, Alabama, and Georgia. Sugar subsidies had support from the Florida delegation. The logrolling continued for cotton, wheat, wool, mohair, and other products. Scarborough concludes, "Standing alone, not one of these corporate welfare measures could survive the bright light of public scrutiny."[2]

Unless congressional leaders use party discipline to impose restraint, logrolling exacerbates the overspending problem in Congress. In recent years, Republican leaders have allowed an "every man for himself" ethos to permeate Congress, giving members free rein to trade spending favors with each other and to grab all the money they can for their narrow causes. Members with safe seats often raise excess campaign money from special interests, which they can offer to other members in return for their support on bills.[3] Committee chairpersons routinely buy votes in support of fiscally irresponsible bills by handing out taxpayer dollars for earmarked projects in the districts of committee members.

Mavericks who raise objections to special interest projects favored by other members often get punished by committee chairpersons and party leadership. Most members give in to temptation, go along with the system, and grab as much spending for their states as they can. Members begin to view "Christmas tree" bills that are loaded with narrow giveaways as fruitful "bipartisan cooperation." But

---

Box 6.1
Pork: A Microcosm of the Overspending Problem

"Pork" generally refers to wasteful government spending. More specifically, it means special interest projects that are slipped into bills by individual legislators for their state or district. Pork spending has increased dramatically during the past decade.

Pork is tracked by Citizens Against Government Waste, a watchdog group that grew out of Ronald Reagan's waste-cutting Grace Commission in the 1980s. CAGW estimates that the number of pork projects in federal spending bills increased from fewer than 2,000 annually in the mid-1990s to almost 14,000 in 2005, as shown in Figure 6.1.[1] Republicans, elected to the congressional majority in 1994, promised to cut wasteful spending, but pork has exploded under their control. In past decades, the "Kings of Pork" were mainly Democrats such as Sen. Robert Byrd of West Virginia and former representatives Tom Bevill of Alabama and Jamie Whitten of Mississippi.[2] But in recent years, the leading pork spenders are Republicans such as Sen. Ted Stevens and Rep. Don Young of Alaska, and Sens. Trent Lott and Thad Cochran of Mississippi.

The rise in pork spending parallels the increase in budget "earmarks." Earmarks and pork are similar concepts, and the phrases are often used interchangeably. Earmarked spending is money set aside by legislators for specific highways, museums, universities, and other projects in particular congressional districts. Earmarks can be inserted into spending bills, or they can be added quietly to committee reports and managers' statements that accompany spending bills. Either way, earmarks skirt normal rules for federal grants that require competitive bidding or expert review. Thus, if the government had $100 million to spend on bioterrorism research, the money might go to laboratories in the districts of important politicians, not to labs chosen by federal scientists. One consequence of earmarks is that research labs, highways, and other installations

---

across the country bear the names of the biggest wastrels who have sat in Congress, such as the Thad Cochran Research, Technology, and Economic Development Park in Starkville, Mississippi. As former representative Joe Scarborough noted, Americans get stuck paying the bills for the "million-dollar vanity name plates" on earmarked projects.[3]

The Congressional Research Service found that the number of earmarks increased from 4,155 in 1994 to 10,631 by 2002, and the cost increased from $29 billion to $47 billion.[4] Earmarking has increased in nearly all areas of the budget, with rapid increases in defense, education, health and human services, housing, and transportation. Federal research money is also increasingly going to earmarked projects.[5] Rising defense earmarks are diverting money away from the priorities established by Pentagon experts.

Taxpayers for Common Sense, a watchdog group, reports that the number of earmarks reached a record 15,584 for fiscal 2005, including 11,772 in a November 2004 omnibus spending bill.[6] The group called the omnibus an "embarrassment" that Congress should be "ashamed of."[7] They are right, but despite a near quadrupling of earmarks since 1994, members of Congress do not seem the least bit ashamed. Indeed, Majority Leader Tom DeLay (R-TX) and others defend earmarks.[8] Grabbing as many earmarks as possible has become a consuming occupation for many congressional offices, crowding out all other policy activities.[9]

Earmarking (or pork spending) is a corruption of the budget process and, as Sen. Tom Coburn (R-OK) notes, "carries with it the hidden cost of perpetuating a culture of fiscal irresponsibility. When politicians fund pork projects they sacrifice the authority to seek cuts in any other programs."[10] Earmarks are a microcosm of problems in the overall budget. The vast majority of earmarks are projects that are properly the responsibility of state and local governments or the private sector. Consider

(continued next page)

Box 6.1 *continued*

the following sampling of earmarks from the 2005 omnibus bill:[11]

1. $350,000 for the Rock and Roll Hall of Fame in Cleveland
2. $250,000 for the Country Music Hall of Fame in Nashville
3. $150,000 for the Grammy Foundation
4. $250,000 for an Alaska statehood celebration
5. $25,000 for a mariachi music course in a Nevada school district
6. $250,000 for sidewalk repairs in Boca Raton, Florida
7. $1.4 million for upgrades at Ted Stevens International Airport in Alaska
8. $218,000 to the Port of Brookings Harbor, Oregon, for construction of a seafood processing plant
9. $100,000 to the City of Rochester, New York, for a film festival

Projects 1 to 3 give taxpayer money to private groups that should be funding their own activities. The music industry is fat with multimillionaires who could support the shrines in their honor in Cleveland and Nashville. Rep. Jeff Flake (R-AZ), one of the few fiscal conservatives in Congress, noted, "I love music and I've got nothing against music appreciation, but why should taxpayers fund an organization comprised of millionaire singers, producers, and executives?"[12]

Projects 4 to 6 are classic examples of items that state and local governments should be funding locally. Unfortunately, as earmarking has grown, state and local officials are spending more and more time in Washington asking for handouts. Lobbying firms now approach state and local governments, universities, and other groups to hire them to shake the money tree in Washington.

Projects 7 to 9 ought to be left to the private sector. I have no idea whether upgrades to an airport in Alaska are needed, but neither does the U.S. Congress. Only Alaska's airport users can judge that. As discussed in Chapter 9, airports in America ought to be privatized as they have been in other countries. Seafood plants and film festivals are just about the last thing that federal taxpayers ought to be paying for.

What can be done about out-of-control pork spending and earmarks? A good first step would be to shine a brighter light on earmarks before legislation passes. The name of the requesting member of Congress ought to be listed beside each earmark in proposed legislation. Also, all letters sent by members of Congress to the appropriation committees requesting particular projects should be made available on the House and Senate websites.

More substantive budget process reforms are also needed. Omnibus spending bills should be dissuaded or banned. Congress is supposed to consider and pass each of the 13 annual appropriations bills separately. That allows for more scrutiny by members, watchdog groups, and the media, and it allows the president to veto individual bills. Currently, appropriators wait until the last minute, bundle a bunch of bills together as an omnibus bill, throw in hundreds of last-minute earmarks, and ram the package through Congress hoping that no one reads it before passage.

Of course, Congress will not give up its wasteful ways easily. Members enjoy spending money, especially on their own states and districts. Reforms will happen only if voters get angry that their tax money is being wasted and begin throwing the big spenders out of office. It is surprising that they are not doing so already, given that soaring pork is a neon sign advertising the corruption and irresponsibility of Congress.

---

1. Citizens Against Government Waste has seven criteria for "pork." Pork includes projects that are (1) requested by only one chamber of Congress, (2) not specifically authorized, (3) not competitively awarded, (4) not requested by the president, (5) not the subject of congressional hearings, (6) of benefit to only a narrow special interest, and (7) funded at levels greatly exceeding

(continued next page)

Box 6.1 *continued*

the president's request. Spending is pork if it meets at least one of those seven criteria, but most pork satisfies two or more. See www.cagw.org.

2. A recent obituary of Tom Bevill said that he was called "King of Pork" for his success in getting cash for his Alabama House district between 1967 and 1997. The district is littered with projects bearing his name including a chair at a law school, a technology center, and a science research building at a university. See Louie Estrada, "Rep. Tom Bevill, 84; Alabama Democrat," *Washington Post*, March 31, 2005, p. B7.

3. Joe Scarborough, *Rome Wasn't Burnt in a Day* (New York: HarperCollins, 2004), p. 114.

4. The Congressional Research Service data were detailed in John Cochran and Andrew Taylor, "Earmarks: The Booming Way to Bring Home the Bacon," *Congressional Quarterly*, February 7, 2004, p. 324.

5. American Association for the Advancement of Science, "R&D Earmarks Top $2 Billion in 2005," December 7, 2004, www.aaas.org/spp/rd/earm05c.htm.

6. Keith Ashdown, "Omnibus Spending Bill Breaks the Bank," Taxpayers for Common Sense, news release, November 22, 2004, www.taxpayer.net. Also, e-mail from Austin Clemens of Taxpayers for Common Sense, May 13, 2005.

7. Keith Ashdown, "A National Embarrassment," Taxpayers for Common Sense, December 6, 2004.

8. See Cochran and Taylor. Also, consider that the second-ranking House Democrat, Steny Hoyer of Maryland, was asked whether Congress would end pork barrel spending, and he said, "I hope not . . . pork barrel is in the eye of the beholder." Easy for him to say because he has used his rank to become a champion pork barreller for his district at the expense of the rest of the country. Amit R. Paley, "For Hoyer's Constituents, It's All about Saving Bases," *Washington Post*, October 28, 2004, p. B4. See also Brian Friel, "Defending Pork," *National Journal*, May 8, 2004, p. 1404.

9. Cochran and Taylor.

10. Tom A. Coburn, *Breach of Trust: How Washington Turns Outsiders into Insiders* (Nashville: WND Books, 2003), p. 177.

11. See CAGW "Pig Book" at www.cagw.org.

12. U.S. Congress, Office of Jeff Flake, "Congress Funded $150,000 for Grammy Foundation," news release, February 14, 2005.

---

really, such bills just represent the results of selfish politicking and damage the overall economy.

Federal Spending and the Poor

Some citizens and policymakers reflexively support bigger government because they think that it helps the poor. However, most

Figure 6.1
NUMBER OF "PORK" PROJECTS IN FEDERAL SPENDING BILLS

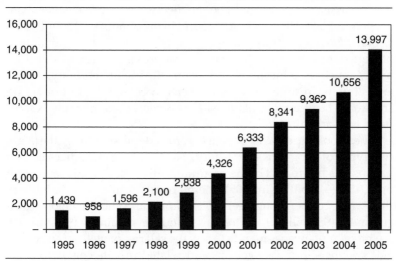

SOURCE: Citizens Against Government Waste, www.cagw.org. Fiscal years.

federal programs transfer resources from middle-class families to other middle-class families. Only a small share of spending is directed at those truly in need. Whether or not programs for the poor are a good idea, downsizing the federal government can proceed without substantially affecting them.

Vito Tanzi, formerly a top International Monetary Fund economist, has examined the distributional effects of the modern welfare state:

> There is a great deal of evidence that much of public spending "benefits" the middle classes. At the same time much of the "burden" imposed by the government in the form of taxes falls also on the middle classes . . . the government taxes the middle classes with one hand and subsidizes them with the other. As a consequence of this "fiscal churning" the government creates disincentives on the side of taxation and on the side of spending. It is evident that this fiscal churning has no, or little, truly distributive role. It significantly reduces the economic freedom of the citizens affected and, probably, the rate of growth over the long run.[4]

87

Tanzi argues that "all the theoretical reasons advanced by economists to justify the role of the state in the economy, including the need to assist the poor, could be satisfied with a much smaller share of spending of GDP than is now found in most industrial countries."[5] Looking at data for a large sample of countries, he finds no advantage of bigger governments in terms of improving "human development," such as educational achievement, infant mortality, or life expectancy. In other words, bigger governments do not create smarter or healthier populations. *The Economist* has concluded essentially the same thing.[6]

When looking at who benefits from federal spending, there are two types of programs to consider. The first type subsidizes certain groups as a byproduct of the program's mission. Consider spending on NASA ($16 billion in 2005), energy research subsidies ($6 billion), the Army Corps of Engineers ($5 billion), and the Pentagon's procurement ($80 billion) and research and development ($66 billion). Taxpayer money goes mainly to pay the salaries of well-off engineers and scientists in those agencies and related private contractors.

More generally, government bureaus are full of high-paid administrators, economists, lawyers, and others whose paper-pushing activities come at the expense of average taxpayers. Even in anti-poverty programs, a substantial share of budget costs is the salaries of well-paid managers and consultants in the federal agencies and in the private aid groups that they fund. It is no coincidence that the suburbs of Washington, D.C., include some of the very wealthiest counties in the country.

The other type of federal spending is transfer programs, which take taxpayer money and give it to certain groups of beneficiaries. The two largest transfer programs, Social Security and Medicare, provide benefits to people aged 65 and older, a group that has higher average wealth and a lower poverty rate than other U.S. families. Features of these two programs are biased against the poor. For one thing, the poor tend to have shorter life spans than others, and thus receive fewer years of retirement and health care benefits. With regard to Medicare, another factor is that well-off beneficiaries of the program tend to incur higher annual expenses than poor beneficiaries.

Social Security and Medicare do not tilt in favor of the poor as much as many people think, and they may even have a slight regressive impact overall. One 1997 study by Mark McClellan and Jonathan

Skinner for the National Bureau of Economic Research concluded that "Medicare has led to net transfers from the poor to the wealthy."[7] A 2000 study by Julia Lynn Coronado, Don Fullerton, and Thomas Glass for NBER found that Social Security is not progressive and may even be regressive depending on the assumptions used in the analysis.[8]

Some federal transfer programs clearly tilt the benefits toward the well-off. Farm subsidies are a good example. Cash subsidies of $26 billion will be paid out in 2005 to farmers producing rice, wheat, soybeans, and other crops. Government data show that farm households have higher-than-average incomes, and their incomes have risen strongly in recent years.[9] Much of the farm subsidy payout goes to wealthy individuals and agribusinesses. Farm subsidy recipients include Fortune 500 companies, members of Congress, and millionaires such as David Rockefeller and Ted Turner.[10]

College loan programs benefit people who will earn higher-than-average incomes during their careers. In part, college subsidy programs tax blue-collar workers to fund law students who will be earning six-figure salaries. Some policymakers support student loan programs because they think that college is a "public good" that would be underprovided in a free market. But that is probably not the case. People have a strong incentive to maximize their own education because education credentials lead to higher earnings. Studies show that people with college degrees will earn, on average, 75 percent more during their lifetimes than those with just high school diplomas.[11] That would seem to provide a big incentive for people to save or borrow in private markets to pay their own way through college.

What is the distributional impact of overall federal spending? That is a complex question, and there has been no definitive assessment.[12] An analysis by the CBO for 1990 looked at spending in 10 major transfer programs including Social Security, Medicare, Medicaid, farm subsidies, and six other programs that accounted for about half of all noninterest federal spending.[13] The study found that spending across income groups was roughly proportional to the number of families in each group, but with a very slight skew toward families at the bottom. For example, those with incomes of less than $10,000 accounted for 18 percent of all families and received 20 percent of federal spending. At the top end, those with incomes above $75,000 accounted for 8 percent of families and received 7 percent of federal spending.

In sum, while federal politicians often profess to be working for the benefit of the poor and downtrodden, the reality is different. The primary beneficiaries of the bloated federal budget are insiders, organized groups, and the politically connected, at the expense of average working taxpayers.

Corporate Welfare

One particularly egregious type of special interest spending is "corporate welfare," or business subsidies. The federal government spends about $90 billion annually on corporate welfare.[14] That includes cash payments to businesses and subsidized loans, insurance, research, and marketing support. The U.S. Departments of Agriculture, Commerce, Energy, Health and Human Services, and Transportation are big dispensers of corporate welfare.

Corporate welfare often props up businesses that are failing in the marketplace. But that makes no sense because companies with second-rate products and poor managers should be allowed to fail because they are a drag on the economy. Corporate welfare that supports companies that are profitable makes no sense either because such companies do not need taxpayer help.

Consider government subsidies for commercial services. The $125 million Market Access Program gives taxpayer money to food producers in support of their foreign advertising campaigns.[15] Surely the business interests getting subsidies from this program, shown in Table 6.3, could pay their own way. Wealthy wine producers can afford to market their own products; they don't need the $4.1 million of taxpayer money going to the Wine Institute. To free funds for foreign advertising, the Wine Institute could cut its president's salary of $595,000.[16]

Or consider the subsidies provided by the Department of Agriculture's Risk Management Agency. The RMA describes its mission as helping farmers "manage their business risks through effective, market-based risk management solutions."[17] If the RMA's services really are "market-based," then subsidies are not needed and the agency may as well be privatized. Wall Street offers a huge array of "risk management solutions" that businesses in other industries purchase without subsidy. Farm businesses should do the same.

Table 6.3
Your Tax Dollars at Work: Market Access Program Subsidies, 2004

Alaska Seafood Marketing Institute	$2,969,653	Distilled Spirits Council	$62,276
American Forest & Paper Association	$7,147,112	Florida Department of Citrus	$4,776,799
American Peanut Council	$1,265,673	Food Export USA Northeast	$5,578,103
American Seafood Institute	$94,354	Ginseng Board of Wisconsin	$5,418
American Sheep Industry Association	$285,358	Hawaii Papaya Industry Association	$9,435
American Soybean Association	$4,230,302	Hop Growers of America	$90,448
Association of Brewers	$101,607	Intertribal Agriculture Council	$415,415
Almond Board of California	$1,515,075	Mid-America Int. Agri-Trade Council	$7,145,583
California Agricultural Export Council	$1,014,110	Mohair Council of America	$67,114
California Asparagus Commission	$237,383	Nat. Assoc. of State Dep. of Agriculture	$1,587,075
California Cling Peach Advisory Board	$344,917	National Confectioners Association	$1,205,523
California Kiwifruit Commission	$125,814	National Dry Bean Council	$519,638
California Pistachio Commission	$892,327	National Honey Board	$116,285
California Prune Board	$2,162,873	National Potato Promotion Board	$2,705,406
California Strawberry Commission	$627,309	National Renderers Association	$364,691
California Table Grape Commission	$2,276,479	National Sunflower Association	$867,957
California/Florida Tomato Commissions	$548,825	Nat. Watermelon Promotion Board	$133,952
California Tree Fruit Agreement	$1,571,463	New York Wine and Grape Fnd.	$181,007
California Walnut Commission	$2,971,836	North American Export Grain Assoc.	$95,022
Cherry Marketing Institute	$135,420	Northwest Wine Promotion Coalition	$465,848
Cotton Council International	$9,899,373	Organic Trade Association	$250,063
Cranberry Marketing Committee	$745,726	Pear Bureau Northwest	$1,688,041

(continued next page)

Table 6.3
Your Tax Dollars at Work: Market Access Program Subsidies, 2004 *(continued)*

Pet Food Institute	$912,048	U.S. Livestock Genetics Export, Inc.	$909,483
Raisin Administrative Committee	$1,988,790	U.S. Meat Export Federation	$10,674,318
Southern U.S. Trade Assoc.	$4,951,225	U.S. Wheat Associates	$2,507,098
Sunkist Growers, Inc.	$1,996,471	USA Dry Pea and Lentil Council	$461,235
Texas Produce Export Association	$73,239	USA Poultry and Egg Export Council	$3,167,558
The Catfish Institute	$305,895	USA Rice Federation	$2,972,700
The Popcorn Board	$258,792	WA State Fruit Commission	$884,823
U.S. Apple Association	$376,931	Washington Apple Commission	$2,565,044
U.S. Dairy Export Council	$2,661,598	Welch's Food	$590,557
U.S. Grains Council	$5,036,065	Western U.S. Agricultural Trade Assoc.	$7,063,750
U.S. Highbush Blueberry Council	$96,509	Wine Institute	$4,101,783
		Total	$125,000,000

SOURCE: U.S. Department of Agriculture, "USDA Announces Funds to Promote U.S. Food and Agricultural Products Overseas," news release, June 17, 2004.

There is no economic reason why taxpayers should foot the bill for RMA's $3.4 billion budget and support its 530 employees.

Federal business subsidies often promote risky and wasteful projects. As one example, two federal agencies provided loans of more than $1 billion to Enron Corporation for dubious overseas projects in the 1990s.[18] At the time, Enron was perfectly capable of gaining private financing for any projects it had that were sound. But many of Enron's foreign projects were losers, and the company might not have pursued them if it had not received subsidies. As it turned out, taxpayers lost their "investment" in Enron's foreign projects when the company collapsed in scandal.

Business subsidies often help some U.S. businesses at the expense of others. As one particular example, the federal Community Adjustment and Investment Program handed out $500,000 to a manufacturer of metal storage lockers in 2003.[19] The purpose of the handout was to allow the company to relocate its Pennsylvania and Mississippi plants to North Carolina. Such handouts are a burden on taxpayers, and they are unfair to the states and businesses that do not receive them.

Similarly, U.S. trade barriers attempt to help some businesses and states, but they impose pain on others. Consider federal import quotas on sugar, which have resulted in U.S. sugar prices being more than two times higher than the world price. That damages both U.S. consumers and U.S. candy companies, which have been moving their production abroad in recent years to avoid the high prices.[20] Chicago, the nation's candy manufacturing capital, has been hit hard, with companies moving to Mexico and elsewhere. In 2002, Kraft moved its 600-worker LifeSavers factory from Michigan to Canada, where there is sugar at half the price of U.S. sugar.[21]

Sugar quotas create benefits of about $30,000 per grower, and growers have become wealthy because the import restrictions give them monopoly power. The controls cost about $2 billion annually in higher prices, or about $20 per U.S. household. The sugar subsidy is a classic example of the government conferring concentrated benefits on the favored few, while creating widely dispersed costs for average households.

Aside from making no economic sense, corporate welfare leads to favoritism and corruption in government. One scandal that came to light in 2002 involved the Maritime Administration's Title XI loan guarantee program for U.S. shipbuilders. A company called American Classic Voyages received a $1.1 billion loan guarantee from the program to buy two cruise ships to be built in Sen. Trent Lott's (R-MS) hometown.[22] Before the ships were completed, the company went bankrupt and left federal taxpayers with a $200 million tab. Perhaps such programs are begun with the intent of neutrally "helping" the U.S. economy, but they usually end up descending into such wasteful cronyism.

The Bush administration's record on business subsidies has been mixed at best. It has sought cuts to some technology and export subsidies but has sought increases in other areas, such as energy subsidies. For example, the Bush administration is spending $1.2 billion over five years on hydrogen car research. The administration should have learned a lesson from the Clinton administration, which dished out $1.5 billion to U.S. automakers for hybrid cars with little success. Meanwhile unsubsidized Honda and Toyota were years ahead of the U.S. firms in bringing hybrids to market. The National Academy of Sciences thinks that hydrogen cars will not replace traditional cars for decades to come, so the Bush subsidies are like flushing taxpayer money down the drain.[23]

Can corporate welfare by cut? Occasionally, some politicians push for cuts to subsidies, as did the former chairman of the House Budget Committee John Kasich (R-OH) in the 1990s. Cutting corporate welfare is popular with budget experts on both the political left and right. An easy first reform step would be to increase budget transparency. Because corporate welfare is doled out by dozens of agencies, it is difficult for taxpayers to find out how much money each company is receiving. The federal budget should provide a detailed cross-agency listing of companies and the total they receive in federal handouts.

A second step would be to establish a corporate welfare cutting commission, akin to the successful military base closing commissions of the 1990s. The commission would draw up a list of cuts and present it to Congress, which would be required to vote on the cuts as a package without amendment. To make the vote a political winner, all budget savings from ending business subsidies could be directed to immediate tax cuts for American families.

7. Actively Damaging Programs

Prior chapters discussed federal programs that are wasteful or targeted to special interests. Such programs make Americans worse off because of the harm caused by the taxes needed to fund them. But many federal programs cause harm above and beyond the costs of funding them. This chapter looks at how programs and regulations can damage the economy, restrict individual freedom, create negative social effects, and harm the environment.

Economic Damage

Many federal agencies damage the economy beyond the cost of the taxes needed to fund them. Agencies impose regulations, trade restraints, price controls, and other restrictions on markets. The direct budget costs of federal regulatory agencies are $39 billion annually.[1] But the costs to the economy of imposing federal regulations have been estimated at $877 billion annually.[2] Regulations are costly because they restrict consumer choices, make production more expensive, and stifle innovation.

Of course, governments need to impose some regulations, some basic rules of the game. Many regulations create benefits. But in many cases, the benefits fall far short of the costs. That is apparently the case, for example, in the health care industry. A two-year study by a team at Duke University found that regulations on the U.S. health care industry create annual costs of $339 billion.[3] At the same time, health care regulations create benefits of $170 billion. That leaves a net cost to society of $169 billion, according to the study.

In theory, federal policymakers could use the best scientific and economic analyses available and impose only those regulations that created net benefits to society. But the government does not work in such a neutral and public interested fashion. Many decisions on regulations and interventions are driven by private interests, not by enlightened policymaking.

The rules on international trade provide a good example. Economists have long noted that trade protections, such as tariffs and quotas, benefit particular industries but damage the U.S. economy as a whole. U.S. trade protections are estimated to cost American consumers more than $100 billion annually.[4] Some of those losses represent gains to protected businesses, but the overall economy loses out, on net.

U.S. "antidumping" laws illustrate how trade protection benefits the few at the expense of the many.[5] Those laws impose tariffs on imported goods that are sold in the United States at prices that are too low. It seems suspicious that our government is concerned about this, given that low prices benefit us all as consumers. Even more suspicious is that the tariffs collected on the "dumped" products are paid directly to the U.S. companies that file complaints against foreign goods. That results in U.S. firms having strong incentives to file complaints whenever foreign competitors offer American consumers better prices. The antidumping laws are ideally structured to reward narrow business interests while imposing costs on millions of average families.

However, suppose that such economic interventions made sense in theory and that policymakers acted in the broad public interest. There would still be the problem that the government does not have enough information to intervene in markets successfully. With the antidumping laws, enforcement is supposed to be based on a scientific analysis of foreign prices, production costs, profit margins, and other data to determine whether products are being dumped. But such information is often not available, and government bureaucrats essentially just make the data up. Indeed, the government's math in antidumping cases is remarkably convoluted, as it was for a shrimp-dumping case in 2004.[6]

The same themes are illustrated by federal antitrust policy. The costs of running the antitrust bureaucracies in the Department of Justice and the Federal Trade Commission are about $200 million annually. But the economic harm caused by antitrust laws is likely much higher than that. As with the antidumping laws, enforcement of antitrust is mainly driven by businesses that are trying to attack their competitors through Washington. For example, the long-running Microsoft antitrust case was driven by other technology companies that resented Microsoft's success.

As with the antidumping rules, the enforcement of antitrust law is not scientifically sound. Antitrust enforcers are supposed to intervene to prevent corporate mergers that are harmful. But antitrust bureaucrats cannot really know this, and their activities are little more than guesswork. Every industry is different and constantly changing, and experts are in frequent disagreement about particular cases. Antitrust interventions are hit-or-miss at best, and a century of experience shows that they are largely miss.

Two Brookings Institution scholars examined antitrust policy in the last century in detail. They found "little empirical evidence that past interventions have provided much direct benefit to consumers or significantly deterred anticompetitive behavior."[7] Indeed, the authors discuss numerous big cases in which the government got it wrong and pursued actions that damaged the economy. Their analysis makes it clear that after a century of trying, antitrust enforcers still have no clear rules to determine when intervening in markets might be a good idea.

Monopolies are virtually unknown in today's competitive marketplace, except for government monopolies such as the post office. Yet the antitrust bureaucrats in the Department of Justice and the Federal Trade Commission keep dreaming up false monopoly problems to go after as "make-work" projects for themselves.[8] They do that by defining "monopoly" to their advantage. In one recent case the DOJ intervened to try and prevent software maker Oracle from buying rival PeopleSoft. But you can find a monopoly anywhere if you define the industry narrowly enough. DOJ defined the industry here to include just the particular type of software that those two companies make. Yet there are thousands of software makers in general, and the sector is very dynamic.

The American economy is so dynamic that government "solutions" are usually obsolete by the time they are imposed. Consider the antitrust case against Xerox Corporation in the 1970s.[9] After inventing the photocopier in 1960, Xerox led the industry that it created. It still held a large market share in the early 1970s, which prompted the FTC to charge the company with monopoly. Xerox had a two-year struggle with the FTC that cost millions of dollars and ended in a settlement. As it turned out, government intervention was wholly unneeded as IBM, Eastman-Kodak, Canon, Minolta, and Ricoh surged into the market in the mid-1970s with copiers that were often superior to Xerox's. Xerox's market share eroded rapidly under the competition.

Government intervention was also a big waste of time and energy in the infamous IBM antitrust case that lasted from 1969 to 1982. IBM was charged with monopolizing the mainframe computer business. During the long legal battle, the industry evolved rapidly. In 1982 the government finally dropped its case and conceded that it was without merit. The case cost hundreds of millions of dollars in legal expenses, generated 66 million pages of evidence, and diverted IBM's time and energy from more productive business endeavors.[10] Business efforts to fend off the government antitrust wolves in Washington cost the whole economy billions of dollars a year in lawyers' fees.[11]

Despite decades of such failed interventions, the antitrust bureaucrats still do not understand the dynamic nature of modern markets. In one recent example, the FTC shot down a bid by the Blockbuster movie rental chain to acquire Hollywood Entertainment. These are the two biggest rental companies, but as the *Wall Street Journal* noted, brick-and-mortar rental chains are under serious financial pressure as online competitors such as Netflix grow.[12] The most efficient result might be for the remaining brick-and-mortar chains to merge as online sales squeeze their business. There is no way for the FTC to know what the future of an industry such as video rentals will or should look like.

When one considers the antitrust and antidumping laws together, it is clear that the federal government follows no consistent economic policy. If prices are "too low," businesses are charged with "dumping" or "predatory pricing." If prices are too high, businesses are charged with monopoly price gouging. If businesses keep prices at the same level as others, they are charged with collusion. That confusion is a long-running folly. In the early New Deal, the Roosevelt administration imposed a host of new regulations that created industry cartels to keep prices high. But a few years later, the administration went on an antitrust enforcement binge against supposed monopolies for charging prices that they claimed were too high.[13]

The broader lesson from antitrust and antidumping laws is that federal policymakers need to be far more humble about their ability to successfully intervene in the economy. The data the government would need to outguess dynamic markets is simply not available.

Government policymakers are usually just stumbling around in the dark, and they typically do more harm than good. Besides, even if the government had all the information it needed, its economic machinery is often hijacked by private interests to the detriment of average families.

Loss of Freedom

There are thousands of federal rules and regulations that restrict personal freedom. They range from limits on free speech in broadcasting to limits on the flush volume of toilets. About 75,000 pages of new federal regulations are published by the government each year.[14] Some rules are enacted with the public interest in mind, but many are the result of special interest lobbying. Either way, the private and voluntary sphere of society shrinks as government control expands.

The continual stream of regulations coming out of Washington might be thought of as just affecting "the economy." But regulations are restrictions on our individual freedom. Consider prescription drug approval by the Food and Drug Administration. The drug approval process has been widely criticized for being too lengthy and costly. The FDA has an institutional bias to be too risk averse, and its officials undervalue free choice by doctors and patients.

The result is that life-improving and life-saving drugs are kept off the market. Henry Miller, a senior fellow at the Hoover Institution and former FDA official, argues that "Americans are literally dying for reform" of FDA regulations.[15] For example, an anti-cancer drug, Erbitux, was withheld from cancer patients for two years while the FDA procrastinated on approval. Some argue that the FDA's dithering on this drug may have cost thousands of lives.[16]

The slowness of drug approvals, and the huge costs that the FDA imposes on new drug development, may have cost the lives of hundreds of thousands of Americans over recent decades.[17] While FDA regulation has saved lives as well, the number of lives lost has apparently been many times higher.[18] The FDA's overzealous regulation of medical devices has also been criticized for increasing the costs of medical innovation, increasing patient suffering, and driving medical technology companies overseas or out of business.[19]

There are a number of reforms that could increase access to life-saving drugs and reduce the costs of drug discovery and development. FDA's bungling on Erbitux led to the creation of a group called Abigail Alliance, which argues that there should be wider access to experimental drugs.[20] This group and other reformers propose that there be greater access to drugs that have passed FDA Phase 1 safety tests during the period that Phase 2 and 3 trials for efficacy are ongoing.[21] A broader reform would be to fully repeal the FDA's requirement that new drugs and medical devices be approved for efficacy. Phase 2 and 3 trials are very costly and take years, and they are activities that markets and independent evaluating bodies could probably perform better than a monopoly government agency.

Another area of excessive federal controls is the restrictions on the usage of approved drugs. These restrictions undervalue free choice and they impose real costs on individuals. As an example, the Bush administration has tried to reduce the availability of prescription painkillers. Some analysts calculate that this policy will result in large economic costs, more Americans living in pain, and greater numbers of deaths from heart attacks and strokes.[22] *USA Today* editorialized that tighter surveillance of doctors who prescribe painkillers would be damaging to the tens of millions of Americans who suffer from chronic pain.[23] No one favors prescription drug abuse, but in cases such as this where there is substantial doubt about the justice and efficacy of government controls, freedom and nonintervention should be the starting point of discussion.

A detailed analysis of the costs and benefits of federal regulations is beyond the scope of this book. But what seems to be missing is a presumption that individual freedom is the highest value. Federal bureaucrats, such as those at the FDA, supposedly balance the costs and benefits of government rules. But bureaucrats cannot realistically put values on the lives and goals of 300 million diverse citizens. Many costs and benefits are simply unknowable, and estimates from experts often differ sharply. Add to this the poor management record at most agencies, and the government's ability to improve on markets seems very doubtful. The onus should be on the government to prove that each program and regulation is truly necessary, not by a preponderance of the evidence, but beyond a reasonable doubt.

Social Damage

Despite what were sometimes the good intentions of policymakers, seven decades of growth in the welfare state have created damaging side effects. It is widely recognized today that traditional unrestricted welfare for the poor creates numerous social pathologies, such as trapping people in dependence and reducing upward mobility. Box 7.1 summarizes the ways that government transfer programs have tended to weaken and undermine society.

Federal housing policy provides a good illustration of the social damage done by federal programs. The construction of high-rise public housing projects in the mid-20th century was perhaps the most infamous government failure in social policy. Those projects became warrens of drugs, crime, and despair for millions of families. The related policy of "slum clearing" or "urban renewal" by the federal government left many American cities with hideous zones of concrete and lifelessness.

Congress has begun to fix some of the worst welfare state policies of prior decades. For example, it enacted welfare reforms in 1996 that have cut the number of Americans on welfare by more than half. The 1996 law put greater emphasis on work and advancement by low-income Americans. Also, high-rise public housing was such a colossal failure that the government has been actively demolishing its apartment projects across the country in recent years.

Nonetheless, much of the welfare state remains unreformed. In housing, Congress began replacing public housing in the 1970s with Section 8 housing vouchers, which are now used by two million beneficiaries. Vouchers, which allow recipients to rent private apartments, were supposed to solve the problem of concentrated poverty that was the bane of public housing. But, in practice, Section 8 vouchers have created similar concentrations of poverty with negative effects that radiate outward to surrounding areas in cities.[24] Vouchers also encourage long-term dependence and single-parent households, as did old-fashioned welfare benefits. The income caps on vouchers create disincentives to work or to seek higher earnings.

Prior to the federal government's large-scale intrusion into housing in the 1930s, private markets provided decent low-cost housing relative to standards of the day. When low-cost housing is private and unsubsidized, it gets transformed and improved over time. Tenants in private housing tend to be temporary, not permanent, because they have every incentive to earn more and move up the ladder to better housing. President Bush has proposed some modest reforms to Section 8, but the best reform would be to terminate federal housing programs altogether.[25] The positive role the government can play is to remove regulatory, zoning, tax, and other hurdles

Box 7.1
10 Harms of Handouts

Government transfer programs, such as Social Security, welfare, and farm subsidies, create more harm than just the tax costs of financing them. Here are 10 additional problems caused by federal handouts.[1]

1. Recipients are dissuaded from working, saving, and other productive activities.
2. Recipients set a bad example for others, such as their children, friends, and neighbors. Whole communities of recipients, such as farmers, adopt a dependence mindset that prevents them from taking the steps they need to in order to become self-sufficient.
3. Transfer programs create demands for more transfer programs. Each new program reinforces the idea that people should look to the government to solve problems in society.
4. As a result of the government's expansion, self-help institutions, voluntary associations, and private charities are undercut and pushed aside.
5. Transfer programs create rivalries between organized groups in society. Society becomes balkanized as each group fights selfishly for its share of government largesse.
6. Transfers need large government bureaucracies to determine eligibility, set payment amounts, file paperwork, and handle complaints.
7. Transfers also create bureaucracies in private groups that feed off the federal largesse. Public and private transfer program bureaucracies add nothing to the nation's GDP.
8. Individuals and businesses dependent on handouts devote time and energy to filling out forms, visiting government offices, and changing their behavior to meet program requirements—all activities that take away from them solving their own problems.

9. Government agencies and private groups that depend on handout programs become institutions that support Big Government in general, and they usually oppose economic and budget reforms.
10. Transfer programs undermine civil liberties by giving the government access to huge databanks of personal information on recipients.

1. This list is based very loosely on Robert Higgs, *Against Leviathan: Government Power and a Free Society* (Oakland, CA: Independent Institute, 2004), chap. 3.

to the private construction of low-cost housing. The best housing policy, and best social policy in general, is laissez faire.

Environmental Damage

Free-market reformers and environmentalists are in agreement in opposing federal activities that damage the environment. Both groups object when private interests use their political clout to steer subsidies to environmentally damaging activities. Here are some examples of programs that should be cut as being both wasteful and anti-environmental:

● The Department of Agriculture pays out more than $20 billion annually in crop subsidies for wheat, corn, soybeans, rice, and cotton. These subsidies cause overproduction, the excessive use of fertilizers, and the overuse of marginal farmland that would otherwise be left as forests and wetlands.
● The Forest Service subsidizes the cutting of the nation's forests by undercharging timber companies in its timber harvest program and by the construction of 380,000 miles of logging roads.[26] The *Washington Post* reported last year that a large area of the Tongass National Forest in Alaska was clear-cut and the trees left to rot because of inept planning by the Forest Service.[27] U.S. taxpayers have apparently lost millions of dollars in Tongass. One environmental group calculated that the agency's costs to aid timber companies in the forest exceeded federal fees collected by about $30 million per year.[28] Critics argue that the

Forest Service continues logging in Tongass only to justify the existence of its 500 employees in the area.

- The federal Power Marketing Administrations and Tennessee Valley Authority sell electricity at substantially below-market rates.[29] This has encouraged overconsumption of energy by homes and the large industrial users of PMA and TVA power.
- The federal government's large engineering and construction projects often damage the environment. The Army Corps of Engineers builds and operates infrastructure, such as dams and harbors and for decades has pushed ahead with uneconomic megaprojects favored by powerful members of Congress. In recent years the Army Corps has been rocked with scandal as it was found to be falsifying data to justify large and unneeded projects.[30]
- Federal loans to exporters have supported environmentally damaging projects in less developed countries. For example, Enron Corporation received $200 million in U.S. government financing to build a 390-mile pipeline from Bolivia to Brazil through a tropical forest area in 2001.[31] The *Washington Post* reported that the Chiquitano Forest pipeline, financed by the federal Overseas Private Investment Corporation, was driven through one of the most valuable and unscathed regions of forest in South America.[32]
- The Bureau of Reclamation runs a vast water empire in the western United States that sells water to farmers and homes at a fraction of the market cost. The resulting overuse could lead to a water crisis as the West's population keeps rising. The solution is to move water into the free market and allow prices to rise to efficient and environmentally sound levels.[33] The bureau's huge water projects have a history of cost overruns and running afoul of good environmental policy. For example, the giant Animas–La Plata dam project in southwestern Colorado has environmental groups up in arms, and the official cost estimate jumped from $338 million in 1999 to $500 million by 2003.[34]

The mismanagement of agencies such as the Bureau of Reclamation and the Army Corps is discussed further in Appendix 2. Taxpayers and environmental groups clearly share some common ground. Pro-green budget cuts would be a great way to start downsizing the federal government.[35]

8. Fiscal Federalism

The federal government was designed to have specific limited powers, with most basic governmental functions left to the states. The Tenth Amendment to the Constitution states this clearly: "The powers not delegated to the United States by the Constitution, nor prohibited by it to the States, are reserved to the States respectively, or to the people." Unfortunately, the federal government largely ignored the Tenth Amendment during the 20th century and undertook a large number of activities that were traditionally and constitutionally reserved to the states.

The primary means that the federal government has used to extend its power are grants to state and local governments ("grants in aid"). Federal granting began during the 19th century, expanded during the 1930s, and ballooned during the 1960s. Some of the earliest federal grant schemes were for agriculture and highways.[1] The Federal Aid Road Act of 1916, for example, provided federal aid to the states for highways on a 50-50 funding basis.

In the last two decades, there have been efforts to revive federalism and devolve activities such education and highways back to the states. Under President Ronald Reagan in the 1980s and the Republican Congress of the mid-1990s, some federalism initiatives were pursued. But those initiatives were modest and short-lived, and the federal government has continued to grow, usurping ever more state and local activities.

Size and Scope of Federal Grants

In 2005 federal grants totaling $426 billion will be paid to lower levels of government for a huge range of activities, including education, health care, highways, and housing.[2] Grants to state and local governments increased from 7.6 percent of total federal spending in 1960 to 17.2 percent in 2005.[3]

The federal grant structure is massive and complex, as detailed in the 1,967-page "Catalog of Federal Domestic Assistance" available

105

at www.cfda.gov. This publication is a comprehensive summary of federal grant programs to lower levels of government and private organizations. The CFDA lists 770 different grant programs aimed at state and local governments.[4] Grant programs range from the giant $186 billion Medicaid to hundreds of more obscure programs that most taxpayers have never heard of. The CFDA lists a $16 million grant program for "Nursing Workforce Diversity" and a $60 million program for "Boating Safety Financial Assistance." One Environmental Protection Agency program hands out $25,000 grants to local governments for projects that "raise awareness" about environmental issues.[5]

The huge size of federal granting activity has created an industry of consulting firms, computer software, and trade publications all geared to helping state and local governments win federal grants. But complexity, high administrative costs, and duplication have long been the bane of federal granting.[6] In recent years, for example, spending for "first responders" such as firefighters has been popular, and there are 16 overlapping federal grant programs that provide such funding.[7]

Federal grant programs not only overlap with each other, they overlap with the activities of state and local governments. The result, as political scientists have observed, is that the three layers of government in the United States resemble, not a tidy layer cake, but a jumbled marble cake. Federal expansion into state areas through grants has proven to be a wasteful way of governing the nation, and the federal grant empire should be radically scaled back.

Ronald Reagan tried to do just that. In his 1983 budget message, Reagan argued that "during the past 20 years, what had been a classic division of functions between the federal government and the states and localities has become a confused mess."[8] Reagan tried to cut federal grants and to sort out the "confused mess" of federal and state activities. He had some success as shown in Figure 8.1, which illustrates trends in health and nonhealth grants in constant 2005 dollars. Between 1980 and 1985, Reagan cut overall grant spending by 15 percent in constant dollars and nonhealth grants by 21 percent. However, the cuts were short-lived, and grant spending increased rapidly during the 1990s.

Figure 8.2 shows the total number of federal grant programs for state and local governments. The effect of Reagan's cuts in the early

Figure 8.1
REAL FEDERAL GRANTS TO STATE AND LOCAL GOVERNMENTS

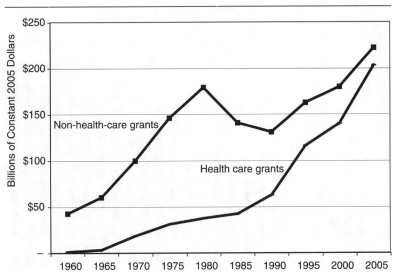

SOURCE: Author's calculations based on *Budget of the United States Government: Fiscal Year 2006, Analytical Perspectives*, p. 131. Fiscal years.

1980s is evident. But since the mid-1980s the number of grant programs has soared, with only a brief retrenchment in the mid-1990s. The number of grant programs increased from 463 in 1990 to 770 in 2004.[9]

The increase in federal grants has occurred because of political logic, not economic logic. Federal grants allow Washington to side-step concerns about expansion of its powers over traditional state activities. By using grants, federal politicians can become activists in areas such as education while overcoming states' concerns about encroachment on their activities by shoveling cash into state coffers. One observer in 1932 noticed that the federal government "bribes the states by federal subsidies to acquiesce in greater federal powers, and the consequent surrender by the states of their reserved powers."[10] The losers are average Americans, who want quality government services at minimum cost but do not get them under the current federal-state structure.

Figure 8.2
NUMBER OF FEDERAL GRANT PROGRAMS FOR STATE/LOCAL
GOVERNMENTS

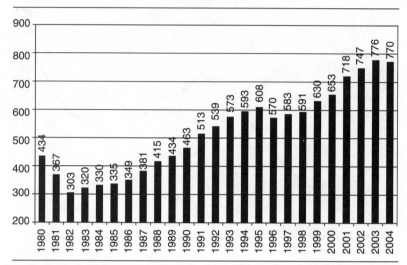

SOURCE: Office of Management and Budget based on the Catalog of Federal Domestic Assistance. The figure for 2002 is estimated. Also note that a revised OMB methodology has boosted the program count somewhat in recent years.

Do Grants Help the Poor?

Much of the support for grants comes from policymakers who think that the federal government should redistribute income from prosperous areas of the country to poor areas. Yet even if that goal is appropriate, it has never been achieved. A major 1981 study on federalism by a government commission concluded, "The record indicates that federal aid programs have never consistently transferred income to the poorest jurisdictions or individuals."[11]

The problem is that politics has undermined such fiscal egalitarianism. The Urban Institute noted a number of years ago: "Political pressures in the design of grant funding formulas considerably limit the design of grants to even out economic disparities among regions, thus undermining one of the major rationales for their use."[12] Even though the initial goal of grant programs might be to aid poor regions, every member of Congress ultimately wants a piece of the action. Grant programs "must sprinkle funds among all jurisdictions to gain acceptance" as each member tries to win votes back home.[13]

Grant money aimed at needy regions gets redirected by powerful members of Congress. A classic case was uncovered in 2005 by the *Washington Post*. A $3 million federal grant that was supposed to help impoverished Indian tribal schools was redirected by Sen. Conrad Burns (R-MT) to the wealthy Saginaw tribe of Indians.[14] The Bureau of Indian Affairs opposed the move by Senator Burns, who oversees funding for the BIA in the Senate. The Saginaws operate a lucrative gambling resort, and each tribe member receives about $70,000 per year in profits. What was in it for the senator? The *Post* revealed that he had important campaign finance ties to the Saginaws.

The $5 billion Community Development Block Grant program also illustrates the political problem of trying to help poor areas with federal money. CDBGs were created in 1974 to channel federal money to low-income urban areas for key services such as fire and police. But today, the program spreads taxpayer largesse widely to some of the wealthiest areas of the country, often for dubious projects. All urban areas with 50,000 or more people are eligible for the program, not just the needy ones. The federal budget noted that the program pays for such projects as the installation of traffic lights in wealthy Newton, Massachusetts.[15]

Federal economic development grants have suffered from this political disease for decades. In the 1960s, the Area Redevelopment Agency was conceived to channel public works grants to about 50 distressed cities. But in order to attract enough support in Congress, the program was expanded to cover 1,000 counties, about one-third of all counties in the country.[16] The ARA's successor agency, the Economic Development Administration, is still with us and has the same problems. After the EDA was founded, the number of jurisdictions qualifying for aid as "depressed" areas was expanded rapidly, with half of all U.S. counties eventually becoming eligible.[17]

The U.S. Department of Education's $13 billion Title I program provides another example of the difficulty of targeting grants to aid poor Americans. A statistical analysis by Nora Gordon of the University of California, San Diego, found that while Title I is supposed to steer money to poor school districts, the actual effect is quite different.[18] She found that within a few years of a grant being given, state and local governments used the federal funds to displace their own funding of poor schools. Thus, poor schools may be no further ahead despite the federal grant money directed to them.

Five Pathologies of Grants

A high-minded purpose may underlie federal grant programs, but grants are an inefficient method of governing America. The money to fund federal grants comes, of course, from taxpayers living in the 50 states. They send their tax money to Washington where it gets reallocated by Capitol Hill horse-trading and routed through layers of departmental bureaucracy. The depleted funds are sent down to state and local agencies, coupled with long lists of complex federal regulations to comply with.

The serious constitutional and practical problems of federal grants to the states have long been recognized. In 1924 Rep. Henry St. George of Virginia stood to oppose a proposed grant to the states for vocational rehabilitation programs. His statement about the irrationality of grants is still true today:

> An examination of the Constitution will show no grant of power to the federal government to legislate on this subject, and therefore it is a question which belongs to the states . . . if it is a federal function, why should not the federal government do it all? If it is a state function, why does not the state do it all? Why should the two governments do the same thing at the same time, when only one can legally do it? . . . The double cost of such a course is not only evident in these respects, but how does the federal government get the money to pay its part? Only by taxation of the people of the states . . . the money collected from the people of the states, brought to Washington, and sent back to the states for purposes like this never gets there; it is eaten up [in bureaucracy].[19]

In 1925 President Calvin Coolidge argued in his message to Congress that grants should be cut because they were "encumbering the National Government beyond its wisdom to comprehend, or its ability to administer" its proper roles.[20] In a 1932 book, *Congress as Santa Claus*, Charles Warren, a constitutional scholar and one-time U.S. assistant attorney general, argued that grants "take money from

110

the National Treasury and spread it among the States for an ostensible National purpose, but in reality for local purposes, often controlled by political reasons. They inevitably tend towards State extravagance."[21]

Expanding on these views, five key pathologies of grants are discussed in turn here. The first pathology of federal grants is that they set off a gold-rush response in state and local governments, producing extravagant overspending, as Warren noted. State and local politicians gold plate their programs and spend wastefully because someone else is paying part of the costs and democratic accountability is more distant. As one extreme example of waste, the head of Maryland's Office of Crime Control and Prevention was indicted in 2004 for diverting federal grant money into a political campaign.[22]

The gold-rush response is particularly acute with federal "matching" grants, under which state politicians can spend an added dollar while charging state taxpayers only a fraction of the cost. If a grant program has a matching rate of 50 percent, state politicians can expand a program by $2 million and taxpayers in their state will pay just $1 million more in taxes. Michael Greve of the American Enterprise Institute concludes that "federal funding has been the principal reason for the stupendous growth of state and local government over the past decades."[23]

Federal grants make program expansion by the states very attractive. With Medicaid, the states have expanded benefits and the number of eligible beneficiaries beyond reasonable levels because of a generous federal match. Indeed, states have abused the federal match by creating essentially fraudulent schemes to maximize federal Medicaid payments.[24] In one scam, some states imposed taxes on health care providers that were at the same time rebated back to the providers. The effect was to increase reported state Medicaid spending and boost federal matching funds. States have continued to operate such schemes despite years of criticism by federal officials.[25] State gamesmanship to maximize federal grants goes back to at least the 1960s.

The second pathology of grants is that they create unfair redistributions of taxpayer money between states. Federal highway grants, which total about $33 billion annually, illustrate the problem. The 50 states receive varying amounts of highway grants for each dollar of gasoline taxes sent to Washington. Some states have been consistent winners, and others losers, for decades. For 2003 the "return

111

Figure 8.3
NUMBER OF EARMARKS IN FEDERAL HIGHWAY BILLS

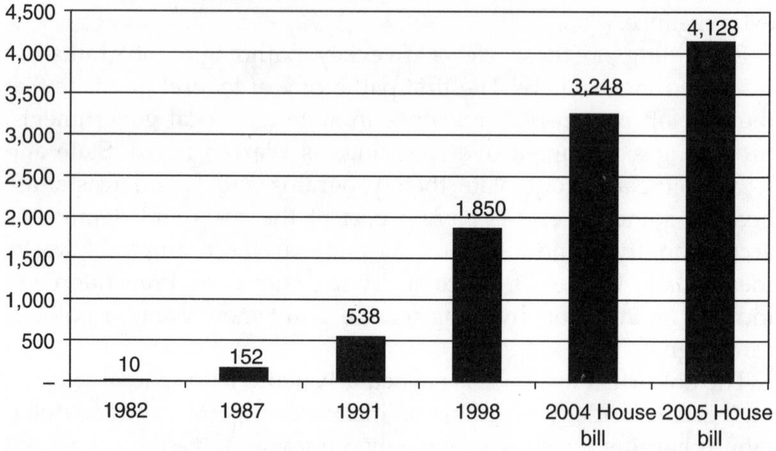

```
4,500                                                        4,128
4,000
3,500                                          3,248
3,000
2,500
2,000                                  1,850
1,500
1,000                        538
 500         10      152
   _
          1982    1987    1991    1998   2004 House 2005 House
                                            bill        bill
```

SOURCE: For the 1982–2004 data, see Gabriel Roth, "Liberating the Roads: Reforming U.S. Highway Policy," Cato Institute Policy Analysis no. 538, March 17, 2005, p. 12. The 2005 figure is from media reports.

ratio" of highway money received to gas tax money paid ranged from 5.2 for lucky Alaska to 0.8 for unlucky Indiana.[26] While some, mainly Southern, states lose out, other states get unneeded "highways to nowhere," often named after champion pork-barrel spenders such as Sen. Robert Byrd (D-WV) and former representative Bud Shuster (R-PA). It is no coincidence that the most massive highway project of recent decades, Boston's "Big Dig," was in the home of the former Democratic Speaker of the House, Tip O'Neill.

Federal highway grants have become increasingly "earmarked," or allotted to important legislators' districts, in recent years. Figure 8.3 shows that the number of earmarks in highway bills has exploded under Republican control of Congress. In the House version of the 2005 highway bill, 4,128 earmarked or pork projects were inserted by legislators. Most members of the House transportation committee secured projects for their districts, such as museums and sideway upgrades, worth tens of millions of dollars.[27] Committee chairman Don Young (R-AK) grabbed $722 million for special projects in Alaska.[28] A final highway bill passed in July with 6,371 earmarks.

112

Note that the executive branch also uses grants as a political tool to buy votes. Leading up to the 2004 election, there was a disgraceful display of Bush administration cabinet secretaries racing around the country to key states and congressional districts to hand out grant money.[29] The energy secretary flew to swing states such as Florida and Pennsylvania handing out $100 million for coal mining here and $235 million for a power plant there. Other administration executives handed out grants for job training, education, and community development. None of those policy areas is a proper function of the federal government.

The third pathology of federal grants is that they reduce state government flexibility and innovation, while increasing state costs. For example, Davis-Bacon labor rules come as a package deal with federal highway dollars. These rules, which mandate the use of high-cost labor, increase highway construction costs by up to 15 percent.[30] The most infamous federal highway regulation was the 55 mph national speed limit. It was enforced between 1974 and 1995 by federal threats of withdrawing state highway grant money.

Medicaid is burdened by perhaps the most inefficient federal regulations of any grant program. The Bush administration argues that the "complex array of Medicaid laws, regulations, and administrative guidance is confusing, overly burdensome, and serves to stifle state innovation and flexibility."[31] But while the administration complains about Medicaid, its own No Child Left Behind education law of 2002 is the source of much state and local anger at top-down federal control. By 2005, 30 state legislatures had passed resolutions attacking NCLB for undermining states' rights.

A fourth pathology of federal grants is the costly federal, state, and local bureaucracies that they require. Complex rules for grant application and administration are needed to keep track of the $426 billion that trickles down through the levels of government. To take one example, the $64 million Weed and Seed anti-drug program for schools has a 74-page application kit that references 1,300 pages of regulations that grant recipients must follow. The Bush administration is right that the federal grant system is "overwhelming," "off-putting," and "intimidating."[32] The administration has also concluded, not surprisingly, that grant programs are even less effective than other federal programs.[33]

Some grant programs involve three levels of bureaucracy—federal, state, and local—before funds are disbursed for a project. For example, the $484 million Safe and Drug Free Schools program sends money to state education bureaucracies, which in turn use complex procedures to send funds down to local school boards. School boards need expert bureaucrats to complete lengthy application forms to get the funds. The Bush administration has concluded that the depleted flow of money from this program that reaches the schools it is often spent wastefully.

Similarly, Community Development Block Grants are handed out to state governments, which in turn hand money out to local governments. The program has terribly complex formulas to determine which areas get funding. The Bush administration finds that this grant program has "an unclear mission, loose targeting requirements, and a lack of focus on results."[34]

To get a sense of the inefficiency of grants, suppose the federal government had a $100 million grant program for reading in disadvantaged schools. Suppose that 5,000 schools applied and received grants and that grant writing and administration at the three levels of government cost $5,000 per school. Bureaucracy would eat up a quarter of the overall funding. You could set up the numbers for this hypothetical in a variety of ways, but this result might not be atypical.

The *Washington Post* recently ran a piece noting that the library system in Fairfax County, Virginia, received a $100,000 federal grant for a literacy program.[35] A substantial share of this relatively small amount of money likely will be consumed by Fairfax administrators because they will need to divide it up and spread it very thinly over the 20 library branches in this county of one million residents. Also note that Fairfax is one of the wealthiest jurisdictions in the country and does not need largesse from taxpayers in the rest of the country to fund its libraries.

A fifth pathology of grants is the time and information "overload" that they create for both citizens and federal politicians. Members of Congress fill their schedules with hearings, meetings, and press conferences on state and local issues. Members and their staff spend much of their time lobbying to steer pork projects from the 770 grant programs to their states and hometowns. House Speaker Dennis Hastert is a king at inserting earmarked projects into legislation for his home state of Illinois. But that results in his time being consumed by such activities as flying back to the state to attend dedication ceremonies for the pork projects he has secured.[36] Hastert's parochial concerns mean that he has less time to deal with national concerns such as fixing mismanagement in the intelligence agencies.

For citizens, the overlapping agendas of federal, state, and local governments make it difficult to understand which politicians are responsible for which issues and programs. All three levels of government play big roles in areas such as transportation and education. That makes political accountability impossible. When programs fail, politicians simply point their fingers at other levels of government. Federal grants are a blight on responsible and transparent democratic government.

Grant Pathologies in Homeland Security

Federal grants for homeland security have been politically popular since 9/11. Tens of billions of dollars have been showered on state and local governments to buy such items as emergency radios. But by most accounts, the money has not been spent effectively, and the effort is bogged down in bureaucracy.[37] A House committee reported in 2004 that $5.2 billion of $6.3 billion in first responder grants since 9/11 remained "stuck in the administrative pipeline at the state, county, and city levels."[38] Some of the grant money has flowed through four levels of bureaucracy—federal, state, county, and city—before being spent.

Much of the first responder money has gone to projects of dubious value. One-third has been allocated to projects without regard to terrorism risk.[39] One rural county in Wyoming of 11,500 people with virtually zero risk of terrorism received $546,000. One county in the state of Washington used a federal grant to buy a $63,000 hazmat unit, but the county has no hazmat team to use it.[40] Some rural states such as Wyoming and South Dakota have received more than $25 per capita in anti-terrorism funding in recent years, but New York has received just $5 per capita.[41] That seems clearly wasteful, but small-state politicians such as Sen. Ted Stevens of Alaska and Sen. Susan Collins of Maine have put their parochial interests ahead of the national interest on homeland security spending.[42]

The waste in federal security grants abounds. In 2004 the inspector general of the Department of Homeland Security lambasted DHS for handing out port security grants to low-value projects.[43] In 2005

115

a *Washington Post* analysis of $324 million given to the D.C. government for security found spending on items such as leather jackets for police, summer jobs programs for teenagers, redundant purchases of emergency vehicles, and "lucrative consulting contracts for political figures."[44]

Security grants have also been subject to another pathology of federal granting—state and local officials spending their time lobbying in Washington rather than solving their own problems at home. A top priority of fire and police chiefs these days is to press their members of Congress to secure federal funding for any local project that is even vaguely related to national security. The large lobbying industry that has developed around federal grants adds nothing to the nation's economy or security.

New Federalism

For higher-quality and lower-cost government, traditional state and local activities should be moved back to the states. That was the goal of the Reagan administration's "New Federalism" policies of the 1980s. Reagan wanted to re-sort federal and state priorities so that each level of government would have full responsibility for financing its own programs. For example, Reagan proposed that welfare and food stamps be fully financed and operated by the states.[45]

Reagan sought to cut grants and terminate spending in areas that were properly state activities. He tried to abolish the Department of Education as an unwarranted boondoggle.[46] Reagan also proposed "turnback" legislation to end federal highway funding and the federal gasoline tax that supports it.[47] Another dimension of Reagan's plan was for the federal government to end funding to local governments and to deal just with state governments.

Reagan's New Federalism was only partly successful. He did manage to cut grant spending and turn some grant programs into block grants. In the Omnibus Budget Reconciliation Act of 1981, 59 grant programs were eliminated, and 80 narrowly focused grants were consolidated into 9 block grants.[48] This consolidation into block grants substantially reduced the regulatory burden for those programs.[49] As noted, real federal grants to the states were cut between 1980 and 1985.[50]

The Republican Congress in the mid-1990s tried to revive Reagan federalism. It sought to abolish the Department of Education but was again unsuccessful. The Republicans did have some success in turning grant programs into block grants, most notably with welfare reform in 1996. However, President Clinton's veto pen was a barrier to many reforms, including the Republican budget plan for 1996 that would have turned Medicaid into a block grant and cut the program by $187 billion over seven years.[51]

Grant spending has soared in recent years, rising from $225 billion in 1995 to $426 billion in 2005. Although Republicans used to seek abolition of the Department of Education, outlays on that department have almost doubled from $36 billion in 2001 to $71 billion in 2005 under the current Republican president.[52]

Under the Republican Congress, the number of "earmarked" local spending projects has exploded.[53] The traditional "public interest" view of government assumed that grants would be allocated by experts to the local areas with the greatest needs. But increasingly, grants for education, university research, health care, highways, and other items are handed out as earmarked political pork to low-priority and wasteful projects.

With the large federal deficit, and with coming cost pressures in programs for the elderly, there is little budget room for spending on state and local activities. State and local governments are in a better position to determine whether residents need more roads, schools, and other projects. Shifting programs down to the states would better allow the diverse preferences of citizens to be realized. When states and localities are free to fashion services such as education independently, it is easier for people to see whether they are receiving value for their money because they can compare their government with the governments of neighboring jurisdictions. Federal policymakers should revive federalism, free the states, and begin cutting and terminating federal grants.

9. Privatization

In recent decades governments on every continent have been busy selling off state-owned assets such as airports, railroads, and energy utilities. The privatization revolution has overthrown the belief widely held in the 20th century that governments should own the most important industries. Privatization has led to reduced production costs, higher service quality, and increased innovation in formerly moribund government industries.

In this country the federal government still owns many assets that could be moved to the private sector. The government should privatize its stand-alone businesses, such as Amtrak, and its infrastructure, such as the air traffic control system. It also has billions of dollars of loan assets and real estate that should be sold off. The budget benefits of privatization would be modest, but the economic benefits would be large as newly private industries such as postal services boosted productivity and improved performance to the benefit of American consumers.

Hurdles and Opportunities

In some industries, the federal government runs a monopoly and has erected barriers that prevent competition. A good example is the U.S. Postal Service's legal monopoly over first class mail. Reforms in other countries make clear that there is no good reason for this restriction. Postal services have been privatized or opened to competition in Belgium, Britain, Denmark, Finland, Germany, the Netherlands, New Zealand, and Sweden.[1] Japan is moving ahead with postal service privatization, and the European Union is taking steps to open postal services to competition in its member countries.

In other industries, the federal government needlessly duplicates services that are already available in the private sector. For example, the USPS operates parcel delivery services that compete with private parcel services. Another example is the federal government's National Zoo in Washington. There is no need for the government to be in the zoo business. Indeed, while the National Zoo has been rocked by scandal in recent years, some of the best zoos in the country, such as the San Diego and Bronx zoos, are private. [2]

There are also industries that businesses are dissuaded from entering because of regulations and unequal competition from the government.[3] For example, private toll highways show promise of helping to reduce congestion, but they face hurdles. One hurdle is that government regulations increase the costs of highway construction. Another is that private highways have to compete against government highways, which have free access and are funded by gas taxes that all drivers must pay.[4] Also, private companies have to pay income taxes, but government enterprises do not.

A former top International Monetary Fund economist, Vito Tanzi, described how difficult it has been for entrepreneurs to compete with governments:

> When in the past the government entered a sector, it introduced laws and regulations that facilitated and justified its own intervention in that sector. It inevitably made it more difficult, or at times even impossible, for the private sector to develop in that sector . . . the only realistic option became, or appeared to be, the government's activity. Public monopolies in electricity, communications, transportation, the provision of pensions, health services, education and several other services prevented the private sector of many countries from developing efficient alternatives to the government.[5]

The presumption that government should have command over industry was challenged by Prime Minister Margaret Thatcher of Britain and other leaders in the 1980s. In this country, some privatization efforts were begun in the 1980s. Ronald Reagan established a President's Commission on Privatization that proposed some reforms, and a few federal entities have been privatized. Conrail, a freight railroad in the Northeast, was privatized in 1987 for $1.7 billion. The Alaska Power Administration was privatized in 1995. The federal helium reserve was privatized in 1996, raising $1.8 billion over a number of years. The Elk Hills Petroleum Reserve was sold in 1997 for $3.7 billion. The U.S. Enrichment Corporation, which provides enriched uranium to the nuclear industry, was privatized in 1998 for $3.1 billion.

Nonetheless, there remain many federal assets that should be privatized. The Bush administration has calculated that about half of all federal employees perform tasks that are also performed in the marketplace and thus are not "inherently governmental."[6] The administration has begun contracting out some of those activities to private firms. The administration estimates that cost savings from such "competitive sourcing" average about 20 percent.[7]

However, competitive sourcing is not privatization. The administration goes astray when it supports competitive sourcing of programs that should instead be fully privatized or terminated. Privatization gets spending off the government's budget entirely, and it provides for greater dynamism, efficiency, and innovation than is possible through government contracting.

Privatization also avoids a serious pitfall of contracting: corruption. A scandal at the Pentagon in 2003 was a textbook example of contracting corruption. Two senior procurement officials were convicted of receiving sexual favors and $1 million in cash for awarding minority set-aside contracts to particular firms.[8] One of the men convicted headed the Pentagon's Office of Small and Disadvantaged Business Utilization, which helps minority firms win contracts. In this case, the best reform is not competitive sourcing but termination of this Pentagon office. In a corruption case at the USPS in 2004, a manager took $800,000 in bribes for handing out USPS printing contracts to favored businesses.[9] Privatizing the USPS would create a profit incentive to minimize such employee theft.

Privatization of federal assets makes a great deal of sense today for a number of reasons. First, sales of federal assets would cut the budget deficit. Second, privatization would reduce the responsibilities of the government so that policymakers could focus on their core responsibilities such as national security. Third, there is vast foreign privatization experience that could be drawn on in pursuing U.S. reforms. Fourth, privatization would spur economic growth by opening new markets to entrepreneurs. For example, privatization of the USPS and repeal of its monopoly would bring major innovation to the mail industry, just as the 1980s breakup of AT&T brought innovation to the telecommunications industry.

Some policymakers think that certain activities, such as air traffic control, are "too important" to leave to the private sector. But the reality is just the opposite. The government has shown itself to be a failure at providing efficient and high-quality air traffic control, passenger rail, and other services, as the following sections document. Those industries are too important to miss out on the innovations and greater safety that private entrepreneurs could bring to them.[10] Even manned space flight is being privatized, as discussed in Box 9.1.

Stand-Alone Businesses

The federal government operates numerous business enterprises that could be converted into publicly traded corporations, including USPS, Amtrak, and a number of electricity utilities.

- **Postal Services.** A report by a presidential commission in 2003 and other studies conclude that the outlook for the mammoth 768,000-person USPS is bleak.[11] The postal service is faced with declining mail volume and rising costs. The way ahead is to privatize the USPS and repeal the mail monopoly that it holds.[12] New Zealand and Germany have implemented bold reforms that Congress should examine. Since 1998 New Zealand's postal market has been open to private competition, with the result that postage rates have fallen and labor productivity at New Zealand Post has risen markedly.[13] Germany's Deutsche Post was partly privatized in 2000. Since then, the company has improved productivity and has expanded into new businesses.[14]
- **Passenger Rail.** Subsidies to Amtrak were supposed to be temporary when it was created in 1970. They haven't been, and Amtrak has provided second-rate rail service for 30 years while consuming about $29 billion in federal subsidies.[15] It has a poor on-time record and its infrastructure is in terrible shape. Reforms elsewhere show that private passenger rail can work. Full or partial rail privatization has occurred in Argentina, Australia, Britain, Germany, Japan, New Zealand, and other countries. Privatization would allow Amtrak greater flexibility in its finances, its capital budget, and the operation of its services—free from costly meddling by Congress.
- **Electricity Utilities.** The U.S. electricity industry is dominated by publicly traded corporations. However, the federal government owns the huge Tennessee Valley Authority and four Power Marketing Administrations, which sell power in 33 states. Those government power companies have become an

Box 9.1
The Sky Is No Limit for Private Enterprise

On June 21, 2004, a small group of engineers in California made history as their SpaceShipOne completed the world's first private manned space flight.[1] The project was the brainchild of Burt Rutan, perhaps the most remarkable inventor of our time, known for his years of innovation in the aircraft industry. Rutan's achievement, and his ambitious plans for the future, suggests that NASA has become obsolete and the dawn of private space travel has arrived.

SpaceShipOne was designed from scratch and financed on a shoestring $20 million budget funded by Microsoft cofounder Paul Allen. By contrast, the cost of each NASA space shuttle flight has been variously estimated at between $500 million and more than $1 billion.[2] The shuttle is larger and does more than SpaceShipOne, but NASA's cost structure is infinitely greater than it ought to be. The shuttle's cost per flight is more than 10 times what NASA originally promised. NASA has failed to deliver on the original promise of a low-cost, reusable spaceship.

It will be up to entrepreneurs like Rutan to make low-cost space flight happen. Rutan's spaceship is based on simpler and more reliable systems than NASA uses. One innovation was "care-free reentry" under which SpaceShipOne automatically aligns to the correct angle upon returning to Earth. Rutan frequently chides NASA for its lack of innovation and its hugely expensive space vehicles.[3] He argues that NASA and its contractors do not focus on making space flight safer or cheaper. Instead, they just make complex, expensive, and bulky versions of past vehicles.

Rutan's critique of the Federal Aviation Administration, which regulates his activities, is also worth noting. He says that the FAA's "license process for our program actually decreased safety and it involved an enormous amount of monitoring. It

(continued next page)

Box 9.1 *continued*

forced our people to defend the product where our safety policy is never to defend it, but always question the safety."[4] When government intervenes to challenge the safety of new technologies, it changes the mindset of innovators. Innovators naturally want to improve their designs, which they do by trying to find flaws in their own work. But they won't do that if they have a government regulator looking over their shoulder. A related problem is that when the government starts imposing design standards on products, it tends to preclude safer approaches from developing. Regulatory intervention tends to slow or freeze progress on safety and other areas of innovation.

The FAA and Congress are trying to be friendly to the new space industry, and Rutan is offering them advice on sensible regulatory approaches. But policymakers need to understand that safety is something that only entrepreneurs can deliver. Rutan stresses that improved safety is the key to making the private space industry grow and become profitable. He is proud of his record in developing 39 different aircraft in 30 years with no major accidents. The government needs to realize that if it starts loading onerous rules on this infant industry, space entrepreneurs will simply move offshore to the many countries that would be eager to host them.

If Washington's regulatory zeal is held at bay, the future of private space travel looks bright. Numerous different teams of investors and entrepreneurs hope to launch private spaceships in coming years. Aside from Rutan, other space ventures are being pursued by PayPal's Elon Musk, Amazon's Jeff Bezos, and hotel developer Robert Bigelow.[5] Still other manned space ventures are California's SpaceDev, Oklahoma's Rocketplane Limited, New Mexico's AERA Corp., and Canada's Canadian Arrow.[6] Perhaps the boldest effort is being pursued by Virgin Group's Richard Branson and his Virgin Galactic. He plans to license Rutan's technology and invest $100 million in a venture

---

to bring tourists to space for about $200,000 each.[7] Further
down the road, he wants to build a space hotel. Branson is
known for his oversize ambitions, but there is nothing wrong
with big dreams if the dreamers are paying the bills.

---

1. William Booth, "Starship Private Enterprise," *Washington Post*, June 22,
2004, p. A1.
2. For the $1 billion estimate, see Leonard David, "Total Tally of Shuttle
Fleet Costs Exceeds Initial Estimates," *space.com news*, February 11, 2005,
www.space.com/news/shuttle_cost_050211.html.
3. Ted Balaker, "It's Mainly Just for Fun," Interview with Burt Rutan, *Reason*,
March 31, 2005.
4. Ibid.
5. John Schwartz, "Thrillionaires: The New Space Capitalists," *New York
Times*, June 14, 2005, p. D1.
6. A good source of news on private space ventures is www.xprizenews.org.
7. William Booth, "Civilian Craft Rises Above," *Washington Post*, October
5, 2004, p. A1.

anachronism as utility privatization has been pursued across
the globe from Britain to Brazil and Argentina to Australia.
Privatization of TVA and the PMAs would eliminate artificially
low power rates that cause overconsumption and increase efficiency in utility operations and capital investment.[16] President
Clinton proposed selling off the four PMAs in his 1996 budget.
It is time to dust off those plans and move ahead with reform.

Infrastructure

Before the 20th century, transportation infrastructure was often
financed and built by the private sector. For example, there were
more than 2,000 companies that built and operated private toll roads
in America in the 18th and 19th centuries.[17] Most of those roads were
put out of business by the spread of the railroads. Then, during the
20th century, roads and other infrastructure became thought of as
a government function. By the 1980s that started to change, and
governments around the world began selling off, or letting private
firms build, airports, highways, bridges, and other facilities.

Any service that can be supported by consumer fees can be privatized. A big advantage of privatized airports, air traffic control, highways, and other items is that private companies can freely tap debt

and equity markets for capital expansion to meet rising demand and reduce congestion. By contrast, upgrades and modernization of government infrastructure are subject to the politics and uncertainties of the budgeting process. As a consequence, government infrastructure often uses old technology and is highly congested.

- **Air Traffic Control.** The Federal Aviation Administration has been mismanaged for decades and provides Americans with second-rate air traffic control (ATC). The FAA has struggled to modernize its technology to maintain safety and expand capacity, but those efforts have fallen behind schedule and gone overbudget. The GAO found that one FAA upgrade begun in 1983 was to be completed by 1996 for $2.5 billion.[18] But the completion date was pushed back to 2003 and the project ended up costing $7.6 billion, with $1.5 billion wasted on activities that were ultimately scrapped. The GAO has had the FAA on its watch list of wasteful agencies for years.[19] Air traffic control is far too important for such government mismanagement. As Holman Jenkins of the *Wall Street Journal* noted regarding our backward ATC, "The cost in delays, inefficient routing and perpetual gridlock is huge."[20] Privatization is long overdue.

    The good news is that a number of countries have partly or fully privatized their ATC and provide good models for U.S. reforms. Canada privatized its system in 1996. It set up a fully private, nonprofit ATC corporation, Nav Canada, which is self-supporting from charges on aviation users. The Canadian system has received rave reviews for investing in the latest technology and reducing air congestion.[21]

- **Highways.** A number of states are experimenting with privately financed and operated highways. The Dulles Greenway in northern Virginia is a 14-mile private highway opened in 1995. It was financed through private bond and equity issues, and it uses an electronic toll system to maximize efficiency for drivers. In Richmond the 895 Connector project is being financed by private capital and will be operated by a nonprofit firm. Fluor, a leading engineering company, signed a deal with Virginia in 2005 to privately fund and build High Occupancy Toll lanes on a 14-mile stretch of the Capital Beltway.[22] Drivers will pay for using the lanes with electronic tolling, which will recoup

Fluor's $900 million investment in the project. The company also has a $1 billion plan to build toll lanes running 56 miles south from Washington along an existing interstate.[23] Similar private highway projects are being pursued in California, Maryland, Texas, North Carolina, and South Carolina.[24] HOT lanes have recently opened in Minneapolis and are under construction in Denver and Houston. California's Route 91 HOT lanes have been open a decade, and there has been very high demand for them.[25] With a strong private-sector interest in funding and building highways, policymakers should pave the way for entrepreneurs to help reduce the nation's traffic congestion.

- **Airports.** Most major airports in the United States are owned by municipal governments, but the federal government helps fund airport renovation and expansion. The United States lags behind airport reforms that are taking place abroad. Airports have been fully or partially privatized in Athens, Auckland, Brussels, Copenhagen, Frankfurt, London, Melbourne, Naples, Rome, Sydney, Vienna, and other cities. The British led the way with the 1987 privatization of the British Airports Authority, which owns London's Heathrow and other airports. Congress needs to take the lead on U.S. airport privatization because there are numerous federal roadblocks that make cities hesitant to proceed.[26] For example, government-owned airports can issue tax-exempt debt, which gives them a financial advantage over private airports.

On a related note, virtually all seaports in the United States are owned by state and local government entities. Many operate below world standards because of inflexible union work rules and other factors. Meanwhile, dozens of countries around the world have privatized their seaports. One Hong Kong company, Hutchinson Whampoa, owns 30 ports in 15 countries. Because of the vital economic role played by seaports in international trade, this should be a high-priority reform area in the United States.

Loans and Other Financial Schemes

The federal government runs a large array of loan and loan guarantee programs for farmers, students, small businesses, utilities, shipbuilders, weapons purchasers, exporters, fishermen, and other groups. There are at least 59 federal loan programs and 70 loan guarantee programs.[27] Loan guarantees are promises to private creditors, such as banks, that the government will cover borrower defaults. At the end of 2004, there was $250 billion in outstanding federal loans and $1.2 trillion in loan guarantees.[28]

In the 1970s federal loans grew rapidly as policymakers discovered that loans could be used to aid favored special interests and that the budget impact was less visible than regular spending. Reforms were passed in 1990 to treat loans more transparently in the budget, but taxpayers are still stuck with all the loan programs that were added in prior decades. Unfortunately, an "iron triangle" of interests stands against reducing loans. Groups that oppose cuts include loan beneficiaries, financial institutions, federal administrators, and the congressional committees that oversee loans. In the 1980s the Reagan administration tried to cut loan programs but did not have much success.

Two types of borrowers take advantage of federal loans. The first is borrowers who are creditworthy and eligible for private financing. In those cases, there is no need for government loans because they simply displace private loans. The second type is those who cannot secure private financing. In these cases, federal loans support debtors who are probably poor credit risks, and taxpayer money is likely to be wasted when loans go into default.

A *Washington Post* story provided an example of the first type of borrower.[29] It profiled the chief executive of a construction consulting firm that is successfully winning projects. The company has good prospects and is owned by an experienced accountant who apparently would have no trouble obtaining regular bank loans. But the company received a Small Business Administration 7(a) loan guarantee from the government. In addition, because this owner is a minority, she is applying to the SBA 8(a) program for "disadvantaged" businesses to obtain subsidies and favored access to federal contracts. (Many federal programs have such "disadvantaged" provisions, which often confer benefits on well-off members of identifiable groups.) [30]

The second type of borrower is those that cannot get private loans. As one example, Farm Service Agency loans go to farmers who are unable to obtain private credit at market interest rates. But such farmers are likely to be bad credit risks with poor prospects. Indeed, default rates on Farm Service Agency loans are higher than on comparable private loans, although the loss rate has fallen in recent years.[31] Taxpayers lose about half a billion dollars each year because of defaults on farm loans.[32]

The federal budget says that government loans are needed because markets suffer from "imperfections," such as lenders' not having perfect information about borrowers.[33] For example, banks are more hesitant to lend to start-up businesses because they do not have long credit histories. But it is appropriate that start-ups face more credit scrutiny and pay higher interest rates because of their higher risk of failure. Failure creates economic waste; thus it is good that creditors are more hesitant to lend to risky businesses. There is no market failure here. Instead, it is government intervention that is a failure when it extends loans to borrowers with excessively risky and low-value projects.

Market allocation of credit is far from perfect, but markets have developed mechanisms for funding risky endeavors. For example, venture capital and angel investment pump tens of billions of dollars into new businesses every year. There is no need for the government to compete with such private finance mechanisms. Yet the federal government runs a failing Small Business Investment Company venture capital program. Taxpayers will be out $2 billion this year because of recent investment losses in this program.[34]

Another failed loan program is the SBA's Participating Securities program. This program was launched in the 1990s to guarantee loans to venture capital companies. The SBA recently admitted that the program has lost $2.7 billion and expects that more losses are on the way.[35] Indeed, the program has been such a disaster that the SBA administrator in charge recommended in 2005 that it be killed altogether, which is a rare move for a turf-protecting bureaucrat.

The failure of the Los Angeles Community Development Bank in 2004 revealed all the typical failings of government loan schemes. The bank received $435 million of federal grants and loan guarantees to spur urban renewal in Los Angeles following the 1992 riots.[36] The bank's mission was to direct loans to applicants who had been rejected by private lenders, a clear recipe for financial instability. To compound the problem, bank managers failed to adequately monitor their loans. But the biggest problems were classic government failings: the bank focused on lending to politically connected people and was pressured to lend to excessively risky and ill-conceived projects for political reasons.[37] With all this baggage, it is not surprising that the bank went bankrupt.

Education loans also illustrate the waste and abuse of federal loan programs. The Department of Education has $7 billion in student loans that are delinquent.[38] Lax enforcement of student loan repayments has led to large losses from defaults, which cost taxpayers $28 billion during the 1990s.[39] Individuals, financial institutions, and college administrators all face incentives to make false claims to maximize student loans.[40] In 2004 it was discovered that financial institutions were swindling the taxpayer out of $1 billion per year through a loophole in student loan rules.[41] Apparently, officials knew about the problem but had ignored it until reporters starting asking questions.

Federal taxpayers are also exposed to losses from a variety of government financial schemes other than loans. The Pension Benefit Guaranty Corporation is a federal entity designed to bail out workers in failed private pension plans. Currently, the PBGC is in financial distress, having reported the largest loss in its history.[42] Airlines, steel companies, and other businesses with traditional defined-benefit pension plans are failing, and they are pushing their pension costs onto the public through the PBGC. The solution is to move Americans away from company pensions and toward individual savings in expanded individual retirement accounts and other vehicles.[43]

Federal taxpayers also face financial exposure from the mortgage giants Fannie Mae and Freddie Mac. Those government-sponsored enterprises (GSEs) are private firms, but taxpayers might become responsible for their debts because of their close ties to the government. The value of those ties created an implicit federal subsidy of $23 billion in 2003.[44] The large size of GSEs threatens to create a major financial crisis should they run into trouble. Balance sheet liabilities of the housing GSEs grew from $374 billion in 1992 to $2.5 trillion by 2003.[45]

A benefit of fully privatizing the GSEs would be to end the corrupting ties that those entities have with the federal establishment. Fannie Mae's expansive executive suites are filled with political cronies receiving excessive salaries. They spend their time handing out campaign contributions to protect the agency's subsidies. As the *Washington Post* noted, "Fannie Mae . . . has become over the years a place where former government officials and others with good political connections can go to make millions of dollars."[46] House hearings in 2004 revealed that 21 Fannie Mae executives earned more than $1 million per year.[47] Fannie Mae has also been in the headlines for a series of accounting scandals. In 2004 the Securities and Exchange Commission found that Fannie had overstated profits in recent years by $9 billion.[48]

Federal Reserve chairman Alan Greenspan and others have argued that Fannie and Freddie need to be subject to more regulatory control because they pose a threat to financial market stability. But a better solution is to make those and other GSEs play by the same rules as other businesses and to end the distortions caused by federal subsidies. The federal government should completely sever its ties with Fannie, Freddie, and the other GSEs.[49]

Federal Assets

At the end of fiscal 2004, the federal government held $1.1 trillion in buildings and equipment, $249 billion in inventory, $601 billion in land, and $801 billion in mineral rights.[50] The federal government owns about one-fourth of the land in the United States and continues to accumulate more holdings.[51] Much of this huge treasure trove of assets is neglected and abused; it would be better cared for in the private sector.

It is common to see government property that is in poor shape. Public housing is perhaps the most infamous federal eyesore. The GAO finds that "many assets are in an alarming state of deterioration" and has put federal property holdings on its high-risk waste list.[52] In a March 2005 performance assessment, the president's budget office gave flunking grades to 12 major departments on their real property management.[53]

The solution is to sell federal assets that are in excess of public needs and to better manage the smaller set of remaining holdings. For example, there are widely reported maintenance backlogs on lands controlled by the Forest Service, Park Service, and Fish and Wildlife Service. The solution is, not a larger maintenance budget, but trimming holdings to fit limited taxpayer resources. Another part of the solution is to scrap the Davis-Bacon rules, which require that excessively high wages be paid on federal contracts, such as maintenance contracts. As the CBO has noted, Davis-Bacon rules push up maintenance costs, resulting in less maintenance being done.[54]

The ongoing process of federalizing the nation's land should be reversed and low-priority holdings sold back to the states and citizens. Unfortunately, bureaucrats do not like to give up their land holdings, even when they have no use for them. As one example, the *Washington Post* reported that the Bureau of Land Management owns 23 acres of land in southern Maryland that have sat idle since 1994 when a radio telescope installation was closed down.[55] But BLM has been vainly trying to find other government uses for the land instead of transferring it back to the private sector.

The government also owns billions of dollars worth of excess buildings. The GAO finds that the government has "many assets it does not need," including 30 vacant Veterans Affairs buildings and 1,200 excess Department of Energy facilities.[56] The Pentagon owns excess supply depots, training facilities, medical facilities, research labs, and other installations. The agency estimates that it spends up to $4 billion each year maintaining its excess facilities.[57] Federal asset sales would help reduce the deficit, allow improved maintenance of remaining assets, and improve economic efficiency by putting assets into more productive private hands.

10. Structural Reforms and Outlook

This book has examined federal programs that should be cut to balance the budget and avert a fiscal crisis. But how can the proposed cuts be achieved, given the political hurdles to reform? There are no simple solutions or silver bullets. But this chapter discusses ways that tax, budget, and electoral institutions could be changed to reduce Washington's pro-spending bias. It also suggests roles that Republican and Democratic politicians and the public can play in the needed reforms. The chapter concludes that there are reasons to be optimistic that budget downsizing can be achieved.

Congressional Term Limits

The Twenty-Second Amendment to the Constitution was added in 1951 to limit presidents to two terms in office. Prompted by uneasiness that Franklin Roosevelt had broken the two-term tradition of prior presidents, the amendment was quickly ratified by the states. Term limits are used for many elected positions across the nation. Governors in 36 states and state legislators in 15 states are subject to term limits.[1]

Term limits should be also applied to members of Congress. Many members stay in office far too long. They put personal power and prestige ahead of the nation's interests, and they deny other citizens a chance to serve. Some members treat Congress like an exclusive private club, and they secure their hold on power by use of the gerrymander and various advantages of incumbency.

In the early 1990s a reform drive swept the country that resulted in placing term limits on congressional delegations from 23 states. Most of those states limited representatives to 6 years in Congress, and all limited their senators to 12 years.[2] Americans in those states voted in favor of term limits by large margins. Now as then, polls show that about two-thirds of the public support term limits. Unfortunately, the Supreme Court undercut these popular reforms. In a

133

1995 ruling, the Court determined that states could not limit the terms of their representatives in Congress.[3]

Yet the problem of entrenched incumbency seems to have grown even worse in the past decade. In recent elections, the House reelection rate has been about 98 percent and the Senate reelection rate about 80 to 90 percent. Those high rates are not the result of strong public approval. A May 2005 Gallup poll found that "only 35 percent of Americans approve of the way Congress is handling its job, the lowest such rating in eight years. Almost 4 in 10 Americans say most Republicans and, separately, most Democrats in Congress are unethical. Overall, the public's low esteem of congressional members appears to hold about equally for both Republicans and Democrats."[4] High reelection rates occur because incumbents have rigged the system in their favor. Only about 40 House districts have been even competitive in recent elections.

The Supreme Court barred states from enacting congressional term limits, but voters themselves can start asking candidates to self-limit their terms. A number of House members limited their own terms in the 1990s, and they had more fiscally conservative records than others.[5] Voters should consider that candidates who are willing to limit their terms are more likely to resist pressures from party leaders and special interests to spend money wastefully.

A permanent solution is a constitutional amendment to set maximum terms for the House and Senate. The House voted on various versions of a constitutional amendment in 1995, but the Republican and Democratic leaderships were not supportive, and these efforts fell short of the votes needed for passage.[6] To their credit, the Republicans have stuck with their 1995 reform that limits House committee chairs to three terms.

Americans should pressure Congress to take another crack at a term limits amendment. Term limits would help solve the federal overspending problem. When elected officials stay in Washington too long they come to view government as the solution for every problem in society. They come to see themselves as philanthropists. With term limits, legislators would be closer to the realities of average people who pay taxes to support all that involuntary federal philanthropy.

Former representative Joe Scarborough (R-FL) argues that, in the 1990s, term-limited members had the independence to stand up to

Newt Gingrich and other GOP leaders who pushed wasteful spending proposals.[7] Without term limits, it is very difficult for a member to take a reform position in opposition to party leaders. And leaders themselves, who have spent years climbing party hierarchies, have little incentive to reform the system that gives them power.

Reform-minded newcomers to Congress face deeply entrenched opposition from the old-timers. They must "play or pay," that is, go along with the system or suffer.[8] To get good committee assignments, to get floor time in debates, or to get cash to campaign for reelection, members have to curry favor with party leaders and power brokers. Members are pressured to overspend on programs that their leaders are pushing.[9] Appropriations committee pork spending is a key tool that incumbents of both parties use to get reelected.[10]

Term limits help solve these problems. If term limited, a member does not need to fill a war chest with cash for reelection, is less interested in climbing party hierarchies, is freer from party discipline, and can easily oppose special interests. For people concerned about money in politics, term limits would help reduce campaign contributions because it would make less sense for lobbying groups to "invest" in politicians if they were only in office for a short time.

Sen. Tom Coburn's (R-OK) book about his experience in the House in the 1990s identified "careerism" as the central corrupting force that causes Congress to overspend.[11] He concludes that term limits would be the most important reform that could be made in Washington. It is not the only needed reform, but it would remove a key systematic bias that promotes continual government growth.

Tax Reforms

The structure of the tax system plays an important role in determining the size of the government. Different tax structures lead to different fiscal outcomes. For example, the introduction of income tax withholding in 1943 made paying taxes less visible and less painful, which helped to fuel government growth in subsequent decades. Reforms are needed to create a tax code that gives citizens a better appreciation of the full cost of government.

Federal taxation should be made simple and transparent. Consumers at the grocery store or gas station like to see prices clearly displayed before making a purchase. The government should be just as transparent about its costs. Unfortunately, the current tax system does not allow an easy way for citizens to gauge the cost of government. The income tax has many different rates, deductions, and credits, making it difficult for people to perceive what share of their earnings is being taxed.

Another problem is that multiple tax bases obscure the overall cost of the government. In the 19th century the federal government had just two main tax sources—excise taxes and customs duties—and it remained small.[12] In the 20th century the individual income tax, corporate income tax, and payroll tax were added, which fueled a rapid growth in federal spending.

Perhaps the most important tax code feature that promotes government growth is the invisibility of a large part of the burden to voters. The employer half of the payroll tax that funds Social Security and Medicare is not reported on paystubs, but the $372 billion annual burden from it ultimately falls on workers. The cost of the $230 billion corporate income tax is ultimately passed through to individuals in the form of higher prices, lower wages, or reduced investment returns. Other hidden federal taxes include tariffs and excise taxes. All in all, 37 percent of federal taxes are hidden.[13] As a consequence, voters perceive the "price" of government to be artificially low, causing the "demand" for government services to be too high.

To help restrain the government's size, the tax burden should be made more transparent. The payroll tax should be made fully visible on paystubs, and the corporate income tax should be repealed. The individual income tax should be converted to a low, flat-rate system on a consumption base.[14] Burdens should be proportional in order to create greater "solidarity" among taxpayers.

H. L. Mencken said, "Democracy is the theory that the common people know what they want, and deserve to get it good and hard."[15] Many people demand government spending to meet their real and perceived needs, but that must be balanced by a tax system under which the people feel the cost of spending "good and hard."

Budget Process Reforms

Just as different tax structures create different fiscal outcomes, so do different federal budgeting structures. There are many pro-spending biases built into the current budget system, as discussed in prior chapters. Congress has a bias to spend on narrow constituencies and hide the costs in the form of deficits. Congress inserts pork projects into large omnibus bills to avoid more visible stand-alone votes. Official budget "baselines" build routine spending increases into projections. "Entitlement" programs grow automatically unless Congress takes steps to limit them.

The large deficits and uncontrolled spending growth of recent years indicate that the current budget process is broken. The Budget Act of 1974 empowered House and Senate budget committees to create an annual blueprint for overall tax and spending levels. But deficits continued, and further temporary mechanisms were created in the 1980s and 1990s to reduce deficits and control discretionary and entitlement spending. Those mechanisms contributed only modestly to fiscal restraint, and they have now expired.

To restrain the budget in the years ahead, two types of approaches should be tried. The first is to create stricter budget rules. To this end, policymakers can look to the states for ideas because they generally have tighter budget rules than the federal government.[16] All the states except Vermont have statutory or constitutional requirements to balance their budgets. Most state governors have line-item vetos to cut special interest giveaways. More than 20 states have some form of overall tax or expenditure limitation.[17] For example, Colorado caps annual state revenue growth at the growth in state population plus inflation. Colorado law also requires voter approval of all tax increases. A number of such caps and controls could be enacted federally. A toolbox of reforms has been proposed by fiscal conservatives in the House, as summarized in Box 10.1.[18]

In recent decades, effort has gone into passing a constitutional amendment to require a balanced budget and create a supermajority requirement for tax increases. In 1995 such an amendment passed the House by a 300-to-132 margin but fell one vote short of passage in the Senate.[19] After the budget went into surplus in 1998, momentum for a balanced budget amendment dissipated. But with the return of high deficits and record spending in recent years, the public should urge Congress to reconsider such an amendment.

With or without a balanced budget requirement, a constitutional amendment to require a supermajority for tax increases makes sense. With the unprecedented cost increases that are projected for entitlement programs for the elderly, taxpayers need new protections. A

Box 10.1
Reforming the Federal Budget Process

Some members of Congress are able to resist the culture of overspending and make serious efforts to reduce the budget. Unfortunately, they are stymied by congressional rules that stack the deck in favor of spending growth. Thus, a reform priority is to change the underlying budget rules to give more weight to taxpayers' interests and spending restraint. Some budget process reform ideas have been packaged in the Family Budget Protection Act introduced in the 109th Congress by Reps. Jeb Hensarling (R-TX), Paul Ryan (R-WI), and Chris Chocola (R-IN).[1] The following is a summary of their reform ideas.

Cap Federal Spending

- Limit growth in entitlement spending to inflation plus population growth.
- Limit growth in discretionary spending to inflation.
- Create special budget accounts for tax relief that particular spending cuts would fund.
- Expand the list of programs that are eligible for a sequester or forced reduction.
- Freeze "advance appropriations," which allow Congress to shift spending into the future to avoid restraint.

Cut Wasteful Programs

- "Sunset" virtually all federal programs (except Social Security, Medicare, and a few others) every 10 years to allow for a thorough analysis to see whether they merit further funding.
- Freeze funding for programs for which the authorization has lapsed.
- Initiate "enhanced rescission" to give the president a tool to eliminate wasteful spending.
- Set up a commission to root out waste, fraud, and abuse in the budget. The commission would provide recommen-

---

dations to Congress, which would have to approve or reject them as a single package without amendments.

Create Transparency in Federal Accounting

- Eliminate "baseline budgeting," by which automatic spending increases are assumed for all programs every year.
- Require the costs of federal pensions and health benefits to be funded up-front as the benefits are accruing.
- Budget for the long-term liabilities of business-related federal insurance programs through risk-assumed budgeting.

Make the Budget Blueprint Simple and Binding

- Convert the annual budget blueprint ("budget resolution") into a legally binding agreement between the president and Congress.
- Simplify the budget blueprint by replacing the 20 budget functions with a one-page budget with just four broad spending categories.
- Abolish the practice of designating spending as "emergency" to get around spending safeguards. True emergencies should be covered by a rainy day fund.
- Allow for a two-year budget cycle rather than the current annual cycle.
- Provide an automatic "continuing resolution" for spending if the budget is not finished by the legal deadline. That would reduce the pressure to pass massive pork-loaded bills at the end of the year under threat of a government shutdown.
- Require a two-thirds supermajority vote, in both the House and the Senate, to sanction spending that is over-budget and in violation of budget caps.

---

1. Available at http://johnshadegg.house.gov/rsc/word/Hensarling—FBPA.doc.

higher voting hurdle for tax increases would help prevent Congress from trying to "solve" its mistake of promising the elderly excessive benefits by crushing young workers with rising tax burdens.

A second approach to restraining the budget is to create countervailing pressures to the pro-spending influences that dominate Washington. One idea is to establish a "sunset commission" and to terminate, or sunset, all programs every 10 years. Such a commission would critically examine each program before termination, and Congress would need to take a stand-alone vote if it wanted to renew funding.[20]

Reformers in the executive branch should put more effort into drawing attention to failed programs, rather than allow agencies to just churn out one-sided propaganda. Offices should be created within every department that would be tasked with identifying low-value programs that could be terminated.

Reformers in Congress should try to rebalance hearings and other public interactions to make sure that policymakers engage with experts who think that programs should be canceled. Members of Congress need to do more "due diligence" of programs, rather than wait for failures to happen and then point their fingers at administration officials after taxpayer money has already been wasted.

Outside Congress, advocates of spending need to be countered by challenging the justice and efficacy of each wasteful program. Reformers often just focus on broad-brush ways to restrain the overall budget. Yet on the other side, advocates of spending promote the merits of each of hundreds of particular programs individually. To counterbalance that narrow focus, reformers have to undermine each program separately. Program failures need to be highlighted, and the morality of taking the public's money for private purposes needs to be questioned. Not only is government too large in general, but many of its programs are unjust in particular.

The Republicans Need Reform Leadership

Fiscally conservative Republicans can make progress on spending reform, but they need more consistent and principled party leadership. President Ronald Reagan called for spending cuts, but many of his cabinet secretaries and top advisers pushed for increases on programs that they personally favored. It was the same under President George H. W. Bush. His budget director, Richard Darman, recounts, "Well-known deficit hawks from both parties pleaded for seriousness about deficit reduction in public, and privately pleaded even more to fund their special interests."[21] Darman says that "the most adamant of the big spenders were the supposed conservatives" such as cabinet members Jack Kemp and Bill Bennett.[22]

After the 1994 election the new Republican majority in Congress seemed set to make some serious budget cuts. But they were blocked by "old bulls" of their own party in the Senate, such as Bob Dole and Pete Domenici, who had little interest in reform. Joe Scarborough notes that "for Dole, the entire Republican Revolution was a noisy distraction from his upcoming 1996 presidential campaign."[23]

Supposed conservatives, such as House Speaker Newt Gingrich (R-GA), regularly undercut budget restraint. Gingrich and other GOP leaders loudly denounced deficits and wasteful Democratic spending but quietly pushed for spending on home-town pork and their favored interests. Gingrich was a backer of expensive highway bills, science funding, and unneeded defense and agriculture spending in Georgia.[24] Trent Lott (R-MS), Senate Majority Leader in the late 1990s, was also a big-time pork spender.

Unfortunately, little has changed. Current Republican leaders, such as Speaker Dennis Hastert (R-IL), are some of the biggest spenders on parochial pork projects. The lack of principled leadership has a corrosive effect on rank-and-file members who might be willing to support cuts but will not put their necks on the line unless there is sacrifice at the top. As Tom Coburn noted on the 1990s, "When our own generals called a halt to the revolution, many of our troops defected to the ranks of the career politicians."[25] Spending cuts will not happen unless leaders lead.

Republicans interested in reform should insist that party leaders not use their powerful positions for personal or parochial gain. Grassroots Republicans ought to stop supporting leaders who call themselves conservatives just because they favor tax cuts. Tax cuts are easy. The real litmus test for fiscal conservatism is a willingness to cut spending even for programs that affect your interests and your state.

Leadership on budget restraint needs to be principled and forthright. Budget cuts should be defended with candor, not evasive justifications. Republican restraint proposals are often put forward timidly, and a retreat is begun as soon as program supporters start complaining. Quick retreats make reformers look guilty of something, and they embolden the special interests. This timidly in restraint efforts is one of the sad fiscal legacies of the current Bush administration. A typical example occurred in early 2005 when the administration proposed some very limited reforms to farm subsidies. Almost as soon as the farm lobby started carping, the administration backed down and farm reform was dead for another year.

Budget cuts also need to be fair-minded. The top priorities for cuts should include items such as business subsidies, Pentagon waste, and welfare for wealthy retirees. If Republicans target welfare for the wealthy before welfare for the poor, they have a better chance of building a broad coalition for reform.

A Reform Role for Democrats

Democrats and liberals have traditionally supported expansive programs for the poor. That is unlikely to change, but there is an opportunity for liberals to lead on reforms to cut welfare for the well-to-do. As discussed, most federal spending does not go to the poor. There are plenty of budget areas that liberals should be prepared to cut, such as spending on Amtrak, NASA, energy subsidies, farm subsidies, unneeded weapons systems, and all sorts of corporate giveaways.

There used to be Democrats who fought to cut wasteful spending. Consider Paul Douglas, a senator from Illinois between 1949 and 1967. He was a self-proclaimed liberal and champion of civil rights. But he was also a critic of government waste who often said, "A liberal need not be a wastrel." His 1952 book, *Economy in the National Government*, is chock full of wisdom that today's liberals should consider. He noted that "waste in the government benefits no one. It is a frittering-away of resources which could be used to improve the lives of people."[26] He also concluded that "federal expenditures are swollen not merely by waste and less necessary outlays, but also by open or hidden subsidies to the wealthy."[27] That is still true.

Another anti-waste liberal was William Proxmire, a Democratic senator from Wisconsin from 1957 to 1989. He became famous for his "golden fleece" awards, which highlighted taxpayer rip-offs. Proxmire sent out a monthly report examining areas of federal waste that he thought the media ought to investigate. His 1972 book was titled *Uncle Sam: The Last of the Big Time Spenders.* When was the last time a Democrat wrote a book with a title like that?

The country needs reform-minded Democrats to step up to the plate and push for cuts. Some liberal and centrist think tanks, such as the Brookings Institution, do call for cuts to some programs, but they do not get much support from Democrats in Congress.[28] Because of rising entitlement costs, Democrats should recognize that, if they want to preserve budget room for anti-poverty programs, they must get out in front and support cuts to low-priority programs and middle-class subsidies. Senator Coburn is right when he says, "Too many politicians in the Democratic party today believe their survival depends on fear mongering about the risks of reform to the poor and elderly, even though maintaining the status quo . . . is the surest recipe for disaster for the very groups they purport to defend."[29]

Voters Need to Be Skeptical

In chronicling some of the failures of federal programs, this book adds to numerous such investigations over the years.[30] Indeed, there are stories in the media every week that highlight failures in federal agencies. One would think that there would be greater public skepticism about the value of much of the $2.5 trillion federal government.

Unfortunately, most people put more effort into researching their consumer purchases than researching what their taxes buy in Washington. Economist Gordon Tullock notes that "politicians know this, and hence they attempt to design policies that will attract ill-informed voters."[31] Politicians dream up ways to expand government programs that are appealing in sound bites but have serious flaws. Because people have little information about federal activities, "deception is much more likely to be a worthwhile tactic" than in private markets.[32] The phony Social Security "trust fund" is a prominent example of such a deception. Structural reforms can make government more transparent, and deception more difficult. Thus, Social Security can be reformed to replace the trust fund with real privately funded accounts.

The best antidote for political deception, however, is voter research and skepticism. People should ask political candidates tough questions about the budget: Why is Washington spending $40 billion on schools when I already pay for schools in local property taxes? Why is Congress taking my hard-earned money and giving it to wealthy farmers? Shouldn't wealthy music stars, not federal taxpayers, be funding Cleveland's Rock and Roll Hall of Fame?

Reform Can Happen

It is easy to despair about the entrenched pro-spending environment in Washington. Thomas Jefferson famously stated that "the natural progress of things is for liberty to yield and government to gain ground."[33] But perhaps Jefferson was too pessimistic. Political resistance to reforms can be overcome, and the culture of overspending can be changed.

The federal government remained quite small through the nation's first 150 years or so. Average people and their representatives in Washington generally believed in a frugal, limited, and constitutional government. Beliefs changed during the 20th century. For example, while lawmakers on the appropriations committees today promote higher spending, until the early 20th century they viewed their role as defending taxpayers against bigger budgets.[34] How policymakers perceive their job, and what the public expects from them, does change over time. A culture of restraint can be reestablished in Washington, but it will take some time.

Congress has occasionally cut spending. At the end of the Cold War, defense spending was downsized. Defense spending peaked at $320 billion in 1991 and then was cut to $266 billion by 1996.[35] As a share of gross domestic product, defense spending was cut from more than 6 percent in the mid-1980s to just 3 percent by the late-1990s. Weapons procurement fell from $82 billion in 1991 to $52 billion in 1997.[36]

Those reductions occurred despite the lobbying power of the "military industrial complex." They occurred despite the parochial interests of the members of Congress who have defense contractors and military bases in their districts. Lobbying power and narrow interests do not always determine legislative outcomes. In the 1990s enough members of both parties became convinced that the large defense budget of the 1980s was no longer needed, and they supported dramatic cuts.[37]

The trick now is to convince Congress that many nondefense programs are as unnecessary as Cold War defense spending. One hurdle is that policymakers are legitimately concerned about the dislocations that are caused by government cuts. However, past reforms suggest that people adjust quickly to the withdrawal of government spending. For example, most communities were able to convert former military bases to civilian uses quite quickly after the base closings of the early 1990s.[38] Or consider that after welfare reforms in 1996 the number on welfare fell by more than half, yet poverty did not rise as some predicted; it fell.[39] Or consider that when Congress zeros out programs, those activities may subsequently thrive on private funding, as did NASA's Search for Extraterrestrial Intelligence project.[40]

One interesting story of survival without subsidy is New Zealand farming.[41] In 1984 New Zealand ended its farm subsidies, which was a bold stroke because the country is four times more dependent on farming than is the United States. The changes were initially met with fierce political resistance, but New Zealand farm productivity, profitability, and output have soared since the reforms. The *International Herald Tribune* reported in 2005 that "shorn of subsidies, New Zealand farmers thrive."[42] New Zealand farmers have cut costs, diversified land use, sought nonfarm income, and developed niche products such as kiwi fruit. The country's main farm organization argues that the experience "thoroughly debunked the myth that the farming sector cannot prosper without government subsidies."[43] That myth needs to be debunked in this country as well.

Another myth is that policymakers cannot make budget cuts without a backlash from voters. Yet reform efforts in the 1990s did not lead to a voter rebuke. In 1996 the Republicans were denounced viciously when they were reforming welfare. But they stuck together and succeeded, and today the achievement is widely hailed. Also in the 1990s, the Republicans proposed reductions to many sensitive programs including Medicare, Medicaid, education, housing, and farm subsidies. In their budget plan for 1996, House Republicans voted to abolish more than 200 programs including whole departments and agencies.

The Republicans who led those reforms were not thrown out of office, despite many of them being specifically targeted for defeat in 1996.[44] The most hard-core budget cutters in the 104th Congress were freshmen who were reelected by larger margins than they had received in 1994. They included John Shadegg and Matt Salmon of Arizona, Joe Scarborough of Florida, David McIntosh and Mark

Souder of Indiana, Steve Largent and Tom Coburn of Oklahoma, Mark Sanford of South Carolina, Van Hilleary of Tennessee, and Mark Neumann of Wisconsin.[45] Indeed, many budget-cutting Republican freshmen got reelected in districts that went for Bill Clinton on the presidential ticket in 1996.[46] The high-profile leader of the House budget cutters, John Kasich (R-OH), consistently won reelection throughout the 1990s with two-to-one margins. In sum, cutting the budget can be good politics when done in a serious and upfront manner.

Downsizing and Our Dynamic Society

Surveying government growth in the 20th century, *The Economist* found that "big government is producing ever more disappointing results."[47] But we have yet to cut big government very much because of biases in the political system that create "a kind of democratic failure, akin to the market failures that government intervention is supposed to remedy."[48] The 21st century may be different, however, as globalization, technology, and other forces help to tame the overbearing state.

Globalization is reducing the power of governments to control businesses and the economy. National borders are dissolving because of rising trade, investment, and knowledge flows. As globalization advances, individuals and businesses gain greater freedom to take advantage of foreign opportunities. That increases pressure on countries to cut taxes and make governments more efficient, or capital and labor will flee abroad. Reform ideas such as privatization have spread as countries have adopted "best practices" from elsewhere to avoid falling behind. Some governments have resisted these forces, but as globalization intensifies, the economic risks of not reforming rise.

Another positive trend is that technological and entrepreneurial innovations are allowing markets to work better and solve more problems in society. Vito Tanzi notes: "As markets develop and become more efficient in performing various tasks, and in allowing individuals to satisfy directly various needs, the theoretical justification for government intervention decreases. This should lead to a fall in public spending."[49] For example, as financial markets have grown more sophisticated and savings options have expanded, there is less need for government-run retirement programs.

The continual rise in American living standards also reduces the need for government programs and safety nets. Even modest real economic growth of 2 percent annually would result in U.S. living standards doubling in the next 35 years. As Americans become wealthier, it should be easier to wean them from government handouts for retirement, health care, education, and other items.

A final positive trend is the increasing heterogeneity of American society. Society is becoming not only more demographically diverse but also more diverse in working patterns, business activities, and cultural tastes and values. A national government that tries to impose one-size-fits-all solutions on 300 million people with very different ways of pursuing happiness makes little sense.

So let the federal downsizing begin! The proposals in this study would balance the budget and help defuse the entitlement cost time bomb that is set to explode on young taxpayers. I am hopeful that as entitlement costs rise, budget cuts that now seem radical to some policymakers will become a policy imperative. *New York Times* columnist David Brooks agrees: "As the situation gets worse, the prospects of change get better, because Americans will not slide noiselessly into oblivion."[50]

Making the needed budget cuts will be a challenge. But policymakers should not view budget cutting as taking bad-tasting medicine. Well-crafted cuts would be positive from many perspectives. Downsizing the federal government would expand the economy, enlarge personal freedom, and leave a positive fiscal legacy to the next generation.

Appendix 1: The Government and the Great Depression

A myth that has promoted federal government growth is that capitalism caused the Great Depression of the 1930s. Another myth is that President Franklin Roosevelt's New Deal subsequently helped to revive the economy. The reality is that government policies caused the sharp contraction in the U.S. economy that began in 1929, and government policies prevented the economy from fully recovering for a decade. Monetary blunders by the Federal Reserve system precipitated the crisis. Then the policies of President Herbert Hoover, Roosevelt, and Congress battered the economy on many fronts. The policy schemes of the 1930s were economically arrogant, and they trampled on civil liberties and the Constitution. Much poverty and despair caused by the Depression could have been avoided if policymakers had been more humble about their ability to successfully intervene in markets.

Understanding the policies of the 1930s is important to appreciating why we have such a big federal government today. For one thing, numerous damaging federal programs that are still with us were begun in the 1930s. Another legacy of the 1930s is that many people believe that America needs a big government in order to prevent, or to soften, economic downturns. But the experience of the Depression and the New Deal shows the opposite—that activist governments increase, not decrease, economic instability. Activist policies and regulations reduce the flexibility that market economies need in order to adjust to shocks and return to growth.

There had been sharp recessions before, but the Depression was unique in how long it took the economy to recover to its initial employment and output levels. Real gross domestic product plunged for four years in the early 1930s, before beginning to recover.[1] Real GDP finally reached its 1929 level by 1936, but then the economy contracted again in 1938, before finally recovering during World

Figure A1.1
U.S. UNEMPLOYMENT RATE, 1920s AND 1930s

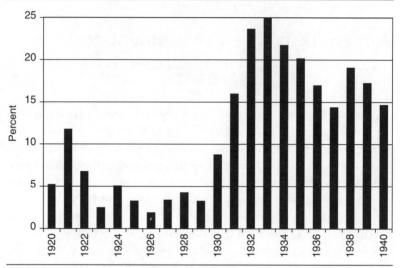

SOURCE: U.S. Bureau of the Census, *Historical Statistics of the United States* (Washington: Government Printing Office, 1975), Part 1, p. 135.

War II.[2] The unemployment rate stayed persistently high throughout the 1930s, as shown in Figure A1.1.[3]

In contrast to the 1930s, the economy recovered rapidly after a sharp contraction in 1921. In that year, real output fell by 9 percent and unemployment rose to 11.7 percent.[4] But the economy bounced back in 1922 and U.S. output recovered all the ground it had lost. The unemployment rate plunged to 6.7 percent in 1922 and 2.4 percent in 1923. The secret to the strong recovery was that the government under President Warren Harding generally stood aside and let the market recover by itself. If market economies are left alone, wages and prices adjust, resources are shifted to promising areas of growth, profits recover, business optimism returns, and investment rises.

Government policies in the 1930s prevented the U.S. economy from making those natural adjustments. The government's multiple failures in economic policy are detailed in historian Jim Powell's book *FDR's Folly*, which is the source of the following information, unless otherwise noted.[5] The following points summarize some of the policy mistakes that put the economy in depression and kept it there:

- **Monetary Contraction.** The initial cause of the Depression was a one-third contraction in the nation's money supply between 1929 and 1933. The contraction was mainly the fault of the Federal Reserve system, the nation's central bank since 1913. The Fed was created partly to bring about greater financial stability, yet its policy errors in the late 1920s and 1930s triggered the greatest economic calamity in U.S. history. After the initial monetary contraction, the Fed made a further error in 1936 and 1937 by hiking bank reserve requirements, a contractionary action that helped shove the economy back into recession in 1938.

  In the years following the stock market crash of 1929, a large number of bank failures occurred, which compounded the shrinkage in the money supply and heightened economic fears. The bank failures were mainly caused by state laws that restricted banks from opening multiple locations, or branches. These laws prevented banks from diversifying their portfolios across jurisdictions. Ninety percent of the banks that failed during the Depression were small one-office banks. By contrast, Canada allowed nationwide branch banking, and as a result did not suffer a single bank failure during the Depression. Policymakers proceeded to further weaken the nation's financial institutions with the Glass-Steagall Act of 1933, which forced the separation of commercial banking from investment banking, thus further reducing diversification possibilities.

- **Tax Hikes.** In the early 1920s Treasury Secretary Andrew Mellon championed a series of income tax cuts that reduced the top individual rate from 73 percent to 25 percent.[6] These tax cuts helped the economy boom during the 1920s. Unfortunately, the lessons of Mellon's successful tax cuts were forgotten as the economy headed downward after 1929. President Hoover signed into law the Revenue Act of 1932, which increased excise taxes, corporate taxes, and individual taxes at all income levels. It was the largest peacetime tax increase in U.S. history. The top income tax rate was increased from 25 percent to 63 percent. After his election in 1932, Roosevelt imposed a series of further tax increases. Under the income tax, personal exemptions were reduced, an earned income credit was eliminated, and the highest marginal tax rate was increased to 79 percent. The corporate income tax rate was greatly increased, and an "undistributed profits tax" was imposed, which penalized firms for retaining earnings for investment. In addition, Roosevelt increased liquor taxes and estate taxes, and he added a new capital stock tax. The new Social Security payroll tax was enacted at a 2 percent rate on wages. State and local governments were also increasing their taxes, with many imposing individual income taxes for the first time during the 1930s. All these tax hikes killed incentives for work, investment, and entrepreneurship that were sorely needed during the Depression. The tax hikes of the 1930s did not even fulfill the stated purpose of balancing the federal budget. Although the budget was balanced throughout the low-tax 1920s, the huge tax increases of the 1930s coincided with higher spending and large federal deficits.[7]

- **International Trade Restrictions**. In 1930 President Hoover signed into law the infamous Smoot-Hawley trade act, which raised import tariffs to an average of 59 percent on more than 25,000 products. More than 60 countries retaliated by slapping new restrictions on imports of U.S. products. As new trade restrictions were imposed around the world, trade plummeted. By 1933 world trade was down to just one-third of the 1929 level. Rising trade protection created economic damage and nationalist anger that helped to sow the seeds of dictatorship in Europe. Although Congress did begin to reverse course with the Reciprocal Trade Agreements Act of 1934, that law resulted in only a 4 percent cut in U.S. tariffs by the end of the decade.

- **Keeping Prices High**. The early centerpiece of the New Deal was the National Industrial Recovery Act of 1933. NIRA created government-directed cartels, which restricted output and kept prices artificially high in hundreds of industries. FDR and his administration thought that government planning of prices, wages, and output should replace "chaotic" market competition. Under NIRA, 550 industrial "codes," or central plans, were instituted by presidential executive order. Businesses were required to cut output and maintain high prices. Price discounters were cajoled by the government, fined, and sometimes arrested. Fortunately, NIRA was struck down by the Supreme Court in 1935.

The Agricultural Adjustment Act of 1933 did to the farm economy what NIRA did to the industrial economy; it restricted production and kept prices high. "Excess" agricultural production was destroyed or dumped abroad by the federal government. It is hard to believe, but while millions of Americans were out of work and going hungry, the federal government plowed under 10 million acres of crops, slaughtered 6 million pigs, and left fruit to rot. In 1937 federal "marketing orders" were begun for a wide variety of products to limit production and raise prices. As production was cut, employment in affected industries was reduced, and families were burdened with higher prices.

At a May 31, 1935, press conference, Roosevelt read letter after letter that he said were from businessmen congratulating him on his policies of industry controls and high prices.[8] With millions out of work and short of money, Roosevelt apparently thought that his job should be to protect high-cost producers from discounters offering cheaper goods to hard-pressed families. The economic ignorance of Roosevelt and his team was a central feature of the New Deal.

- **Raising the Costs of Employment**. Unemployment remained extraordinarily high during the 1930s. The main cause was New Deal policies that raised the costs to employers of hiring workers. NIRA industry codes required artificially high wages. New Social Security taxes increased compensation costs. Minimum wage rules under NIRA in the early 1930s and the Fair Labor Standards Act of 1938 made it uneconomic to hire low-skilled workers. Southern blacks and other vulnerable groups were priced out of the labor market. The National Labor Relations Act of 1935 also kept wages high. The Davis-Bacon Act of 1931 required the payment of high union wages on all federal contracts. These laws and various executive orders encouraged compulsory unionism, which increased hiring costs and convinced businesses to substitute machines for workers. Unions raised wages for the lucky few workers, but that had the effect of reducing employment and output in affected industries. New Deal labor laws also prompted the rise of militant union tactics such as targeting and shutting down plants by force and intimidation. Between 1922 and 1932 there was an average of 980 work stoppages per year in the United States. But during the mid-1930s work stoppages soared, reaching a peak of 4,740 by 1937.

Government was one of the few growth industries in the 1930s. Federal government employment increased from 1 million in 1929 to 5 million in 1936 before leveling off.[9] Meanwhile, private-sector employment fell from 34 million in 1929 to 25 million in 1933. By 1939 private employment had rebounded to 32 million, but that was still short of the peak reached a decade earlier.

- **Raising the Costs of New Investment.** FDR and his administration viewed Wall Street as a key enemy, and they were determined to tie it up in new regulations. The Federal Securities Act of 1933 and the Securities Exchange Act of 1934 created burdensome new rules for the issuance of securities. The new regulations increased the costs of raising new capital and probably reduced new security issues at a time when business expansion was needed more than ever.

- **Demonizing Businesses.** Investment stagnated in the 1930s as a result of falling demand, huge uncertainties in the economy, and the large political risks that business people faced from adverse legislation out of Washington.[10] Roosevelt and others in his administration harassed and demonized American business leaders, investors, and entrepreneurs in speech after speech. FDR called business people "economic royalists" and "privileged princes" who were responsible for a "new despotism" and an "industrial dictatorship." American businesses were hit hard by federal policies during the 1930s. They were taxed to the hilt and buried in piles of new regulations that raised the costs of production. The anti-business drumbeat coming from Washington for years on end made them very pessimistic that expansion would ever arrive.

- **Legal Harassment of Business.** Laws and regulations poured forth from Washington in the 1930s like never before in American history. In his efforts to control the economy from top to bottom, FDR issued more executive orders than all presidents from Harry Truman through Bill Clinton combined. Since Roosevelt, presidents have typically issued just a few hundred executive orders; Roosevelt issued 3,723.[11] His orders ranged from seizing private businesses during strikes to seizing 112,000 U.S. citizens and residents of Japanese descent and putting them into relocation camps.[12]

Roosevelt's antitrust crusade against business was emblematic of his economic policy approach with its accusatory rhetoric that was unhinged from economic reality. Under the Justice Department's Thurman Arnold, hundreds of new lawyers were hired, and a blitzkrieg was begun in 1938 that brought lawsuits against dozens of industries for conspiring to keep prices high. Congress jumped on board with highly publicized hearings over 18 months on the supposed monopoly problem in the U.S. economy.

The irony in the antitrust crusade was that Roosevelt had spent his first term creating industrial cartels, encouraging monopoly unionism, and trying to push up prices of farm products, air travel, oil, manufactured goods, and other items. In the late 1930s, the oil industry was to find itself the target of an antitrust suit for supposedly raising prices during 1935 and 1936—the exact policy that the government had been pushing on the industry at the time.

New Deal interventions were not just bad for workers and the economy; they favored fat cats over average Americans. Farm subsidies went mainly to people who owned lots of land, not to small-time farmers or sharecroppers. The reduction of farm acreage under the New Deal devastated poor sharecroppers. Efforts to keep farm prices high led to the government's destruction of huge stockpiles of food while millions of families went hungry. The New Deal's encouragement of compulsory unionism led to discrimination against blacks because it gave monopoly power to union bosses who often did not want them hired. Union violence was tolerated and encouraged by federal policies. Big business cartels organized by the government prevented entrepreneurs from entering markets and cutting prices for consumers.

Perhaps the most arrogant affront to American liberty in the 1930s was FDR's bullying of the Supreme Court in 1937 with his Court-packing scheme. To knock the remaining believers in economic freedom off the Court, FDR proposed requiring that judges retire at age

70. If they did not, FDR would appoint new judges to serve beside them in an expanded court. Roosevelt claimed that his plan would protect the Constitution.[13] Of course, he was really trying to subvert it, and both his political friends and foes denounced the plan as a power grab by the president.

Politically, FDR's strategies of welfare handouts, government jobs, subsidized loans, and public works projects in politically important states worked well. Similarly, FDR's demonizing of the Supreme Court and American businesses succeeded in polarizing the country and winning him reelection. But economically, Roosevelt and his "brains trust" had no idea what they were doing. Intervention after intervention failed to revive the economy.

The Great Depression was a disaster, and sadly an avoidable disaster. Bad federal policies caused it and sustained it. Since the 1930s, some important policy lessons have been learned by federal lawmakers. Today's policymakers would be unlikely to make monetary and trade policy errors as large as those of the 1930s. There is also a better understanding today of the harm caused by high marginal tax rates. Some damaging interventions put in place in the 1930s have been repealed, such as the Glass-Steagall banking rules. In other areas, however, policymakers have learned little, and they are still too eager to blame economic problems on markets rather than to look to their own counterproductive programs and regulations.

Appendix 2: Discussion of Selected Budget Cuts

This section provides a discussion of selected budget cuts that were itemized in Chapter 4. The text is organized by department. Unless otherwise noted, all spending figures are fiscal year outlays for 2005 from the *Budget of the United States Government: Fiscal Year 2006*.[1] The proposed cuts are not a comprehensive list of possible reforms. Instead, they provide a menu of high-priority targets to help policymakers begin the task of downsizing the federal government.

Department of Agriculture

The U.S. Department of Agriculture has 110,000 employees and 7,400 offices scattered across the country.[2] It provides direct cash subsidies to farmers, as well as indirect subsidies such as marketing support. It imposes an array of legal restrictions on agricultural production and distribution. The USDA also dispenses a variety of general rural subsidies.

Farm programs damage the economy and unfairly redistribute wealth from taxpayers and consumers to farm businesses. For example, sugar prices are more than twice as high in the United States as in the rest of the world because of federal controls. The effect is to burden consumers and damage U.S. food companies that rely on sugar. Agriculture subsidies and controls are also an impediment to world trade negotiations, which are designed to bring greater prosperity to all countries. All farm and rural subsidy programs should be abolished, which would save taxpayers $38 billion annually.

Crop Subsidies

Direct crop subsidies distributed by USDA's Farm Service Agency will cost taxpayers $26 billion in 2005. More than 90 percent of these subsidies go to farmers of just five crops—wheat, corn, soybeans, rice, and cotton.[3] Commodities that are eligible for federal payments account for 36 percent of U.S. farm production, while commodities that survive without federal subsidies, such as fruits and vegetables, account for 64 percent of U.S. production.

It has long been recognized that agriculture controls and subsidies cause distortions such as overproduction of crops and inflated land prices. In 1932 one policymaker noted that the Agriculture Department spent "hundreds of millions a year to stimulate the production of farm products by every method, from irrigating waste lands to loaning and even giving money to the farmers, and simultaneously advising them that there is no adequate market for their crops, and that they should restrict production."[4] The folly is the same seven decades later, except that the dollars handed out have increased from "hundreds of millions" to tens of billions.

Farm subsidies were greatly expanded during the 1930s and subsequent decades until Congress enacted cuts under the Freedom to Farm law of 1996. However, the cuts did not last long as Congress passed a series of large supplemental subsidy bills in the late 1990s. In 2002 Congress passed new farm legislation with the support of the Bush administration that reversed many of the 1996 reforms and increased projected subsidy payments by 74 percent.[5]

Aside from damaging the economy, farm subsidies unfairly redistribute wealth. Although politicians love to discuss the plight of the family farm, the bulk of farm subsidies goes to the largest farms. For example, the largest 7 percent of farms receive about 45 percent of all direct farm subsidy payments.[6] USDA figures show that the average income of farm households is consistently higher than the national average.[7]

In 2005 the Bush administration tried to impose very modest limits on subsidies. The plan would have capped annual payments to farmers at $250,000, down from $360,000 under current law. New rules would have also prevented farmers from skirting the current limits, as some do to collect more than $1 million per year. The administration did not push its proposal very hard, and it was dropped by Congress.

Commercial Services for Farmers

In addition to direct crop subsidies, the USDA provides an array of commercial services to farmers, including loans, marketing services, and research. Those programs should be ended and farmers should purchase such services in the marketplace, as do businesses in other industries. USDA commercial services are generally poorly run. For example, the General Accounting Office found that more than $2 billion in Farm Service Agency loans was delinquent.[8]

One particularly egregious subsidy is the $125 million Market Access Program, which was discussed in Chapter 6. This program received a doubling of funds under the farm subsidy law of 2002. A similar program is the Foreign Market Development Cooperator program, which hands out $35 million annually to groups such as the American Peanut Council, the Cotton Council International, and the Mohair Council of America.[9]

Rural Subsidy Programs

In addition to giving aid to farmers, the USDA operates a range of rural subsidy programs out of more than 800 offices across the country.[10] For example, the Rural Community Advancement program funds everything from fire protection to waste disposal services under a complex grant scheme. The Rural Business-Cooperative Service provides grants and loans for projects such as the National Sheep Industry Improvement Center.[11] The Rural Utilities Service provides subsidized loans to electricity, telephone, and water utilities in rural areas. The RUS has about $28 billion in outstanding loans.

These agencies are sustained by intense lobbying efforts, not by economic logic. The forerunner agency to RUS was founded in the 1930s to electrify rural America. But that job was complete by 1990, and today the RUS subsidizes services such as broadband telecommunications. The RUS is supported by a lobbying group called the Rural Electric Cooperative Association headed by a savvy former congressman.[12] It gives about $1.2 million annually in political contributions that are split evenly between Democrats and Republicans.[13] The lobbying group scored big in 2004 when President Bush announced $3 billion of new loan money for a RUS-connected rural bank just three days before the November election.[14]

Many studies have found that USDA rural subsidy programs are inefficient and mismanaged.[15] More important, these subsidies are unjust redistributions of wealth, especially given that rural dwellers are better off than other Americans in many ways. For example, the home ownership rate in rural America is 10 percent higher than the national average, yet the USDA continues to subsidize rural home loans.[16] Americans who live in rural areas should not be a privileged class deemed more important than other Americans. USDA rural subsidies should be ended.

Department of Commerce

This $6.3 billion department operates numerous "corporate welfare" programs that reformers have long targeted for termination. In the mid-1990s House Republicans proposed that the entire department be closed, although their plan would have moved some Commerce functions to other departments. Given the large federal deficit today, this is a good time for policymakers to reconsider downsizing Commerce, starting with the $1.6 billion in cuts itemized in Table 4.2.

Economic Development Administration

This $392 million agency provides grants and loans to state and local governments, nonprofit groups, and private businesses in regions with high unemployment. The GAO has found that EDA grants do not significantly affect private-sector employment, despite claims by EDA that it creates jobs.[17] Government handouts are not a solution for underperforming regions of the country. Instead, any area can become more prosperous by unleashing entrepreneurs by cutting taxes, reducing regulations, reforming tort laws, enacting right-to-work laws, and reducing burdens on businesses in other ways.

International Trade Administration

This $370 million agency is supposed to promote exports and work with companies to develop strategies to sell abroad. But the GAO has reported that the ITA has been unable to show success in helping businesses enter foreign markets.[18] It makes little sense that career bureaucrats—who may have never worked in private industry—could provide essential help to exporters. Besides, the vast majority of U.S. exporters are successful without government help. All producers should foot the bill for their own trade activities. After all, if they are successful in foreign markets, the profits reaped will be theirs to keep.

Federal Technology and Industry Programs

A number of subsidy programs try to create technological advances in U.S. industry. The $144 million Advanced Technology

Program is supposed to give grants to companies that could not find private funding. However, a study by the GAO found that most companies that applied for ATP grants never even looked for private capital.[19] The ATP is obsolete today because of the large amounts of private financing available for technology firms, including "angel" investment and venture capital. Those two sources of private financing pump roughly $100 billion into small and growing businesses each year.[20]

The Small Business Innovative Research program is also supposed to "stimulate technological innovation" by handing out grants to businesses.[21] But this federal program simply displaces private research money that firms would have spent anyway. One study found that for every dollar of SBIR money received, firms reduce their own research funding by a dollar.[22]

The $117 million Manufacturing Extension Partnership provides grants to extension centers that are supposed to assist small and medium-sized firms in making use of new production technologies. However, the regular workings of the market help disseminate new production knowledge. For example, skilled engineers often move back and forth between firms, which spreads knowledge of the latest techniques. Federal subsidies for this normal market activity are not needed.

Experience in the United States, Japan, and Europe has shown that government subsidization of technology does not work.[23] In the 1980s many naïve pundits thought that the wave of the future was central planning of technology through agencies such as Japan's MITI. But MITI turned out to be a big failure. Its computer ventures were a flop, and it infamously provided bad business advice to Honda and Sony.[24] Japan's industrial success until the 1980s was explained by high levels of domestic competition, not government planning. The most successful Japanese industries, including automobiles, motorcycles, steel, robotics, and consumer electronics, have high numbers of firms that compete intensely.

A number of U.S. states have tried to create technology planning agencies with similarly little success. For example, Virginia has spent more than $100 million on a Center for Innovative Technology, which has a fancy office tower near Dulles airport.[25] But there is an effort to cut off subsidies to CIT because it has accomplished little.[26] Similarly, federal technology subsidies have accomplished little and should be ended.

Fisheries Subsidies

The National Oceanic and Atmospheric Administration funds a variety of subsidies for the fishing industry. NOAA's National Marine Fisheries Service provides industry data, promotes exports, and gives operating assistance. Those activities should be paid for by the industry itself, not the taxpayer.

Department of Defense

The $444 billion Department of Defense has some of the most wasteful spending practices in the government.[27] Eight of 25 federal activities labeled "high-risk" for waste by GAO are in this department.[28] The head of GAO, David Walker, says that Pentagon waste is "unacceptable and should not be tolerated."[29] The secretary of defense estimates that about $22 billion could be saved annually just by improving the department's management of finances and contracting.[30]

Another problem is that the U.S. military is still partly trapped inside a Cold War structure. It has too many troops stationed in Europe and Asia, and it funds unneeded weapons systems that were designed to fight yesterday's wars. Some analysts suggest that the defense budget could be cut by up to half with a major reorganization of U.S. security policy.[31] However, the proposals here take incremental steps that have been widely recommended, including reducing foreign troop strength, cutting the procurement budget, and proceeding with domestic base closings. Those steps would save taxpayers an estimated $41 billion annually.

Reduce Foreign Troop Strength

The United States should make large cuts to the number of troops stationed in Europe and Asia. While U.S. foreign troop levels have been reduced since the 1980s, the large contingents still abroad are a holdover from the Cold War.

At the end of 2004 there were 1.4 million active duty military personnel, of whom 258,000 were ashore in foreign countries (not including the 220,000 deployed in Iraq and Afghanistan at the time).[32] Of those, 110,000 were in Germany, Britain, Italy, and other countries in Europe; 36,000 were in Japan; 36,000 were in Korea; and 76,000 were elsewhere. Germany, Britain, Italy, Japan, and Korea are wealthy countries with substantial military budgets. They have every ability and incentive to defend themselves against possible foreign aggressors. Rather than subsidize the defense of those countries, the United States should simply retain enough of an operational shell abroad to contribute to its own defensive capabilities.

The Bush administration has proposed recalling 70,000 to 100,000 troops from Europe and Asia to be redeployed in the United States. Extending that basic strategy further, the proposal here would cut foreign troop strength in half and reduce the overall number of active duty troops by the same amount. That would mean downsizing active duty troops by 129,000 (about 9 percent) to create annual savings of roughly $20 billion. That figure is calculated as a 9 percent cut in the Pentagon's 2005 personnel budget ($93 billion) and operation and maintenance budget ($133 billion) for active duty troops.[33]

Cut Weapons Purchases

To find savings in the Pentagon budget, defense experts often point to a dozen or so low-priority weapons programs that could be reduced or terminated. The weapons are in various stages of development and production. Many were conceived during the Cold War for different sorts of missions and wars than the nation is now likely to face.

Savings from aircraft procurement could come from reducing purchases of the V-22 helicopter, the C-130J cargo plane, the F/A-22 fighter, the F-35 Joint Strike Fighter, and the F/A-18 fighter. The Bush administration proposed reducing purchases of the C-130J and the F/A-22.[34]

Savings from ship procurement could come from reducing purchases of Virginia Class submarines and DD(X) destroyers. Savings could also come from reducing the number of aircraft carriers in the U.S. fleet. All three options have been proposed by the Bush administration.

Table 4.2 includes savings of $10 billion annually from reduced weapons purchases. This estimate is based on data in CBO's "Budget Options" report, which lists various defense reform alternatives.[35] The following reforms would together create annual savings of about $10 billion: reduce the number of Virginia Class submarines (CBO option no. 050-07), cancel the DD(X) (no. 050-08), cut the number of aircraft carriers from 12 to 11 (no. 050-10), cancel the V-22 (no. 050-14), reduce the number of F-35s (no. 050-16), terminate the airborne laser program (no. 050-18), and cancel the C-130J cargo plane.

While experts often agree as to which programs ought to be cut, every program has congressional defenders who work against savings plans initiated by the administration. Defense bills are usually stuffed with billions of dollars of spending that Pentagon experts do not want. Recognizing the problem, a recent memo by the acting deputy secretary of defense, Gordon England, said that there is "growing and deep concern within Congress and the Pentagon about how weapons systems are purchased."[36] Ultimately, there needs to be an institutional change to end political micromanaging of the defense budget. Something akin to a military base closing commission should be considered for cutting the defense procurement budget so that taxpayers pay for just the weapons that are really needed.

Base Closings

Even before the end of the Cold War, it was apparent that the nation had a large excess of military bases. Many members of Congress thought that closing excess bases was a good idea, but they were not willing to vote for bills that would close just the base in their district. The solution was the Base Realignment and Closure Commission, which undertook four rounds of base closings between 1988 and 1995. Under BRAC, an expert commission draws up a list of excess bases, and Congress votes up-or-down on the overall list. The result is that the political pain is spread broadly to many congressional districts. As it has turned out, the sites of former bases have been redeveloped for uses such as industrial parks more successfully than people initially thought they would be.

The nation still has about 20 percent too many bases, and another BRAC round is currently under way. The Pentagon supports BRAC, but states across the country are lobbying against it.[37] Virginia has spent $1.7 million lobbying to defend its 31 bases. In California, Gov. Arnold Schwarzenegger spent $500,000 to advise communities on how to prevent possible cuts to the state's 62 bases.[38] Members of Congress have been trying to insert language into various bills to protect bases in their states. Nonetheless, BRAC is moving forward, and, if successful, the current round of base closings will save taxpayers about $6 billion annually.

Foreign Military Financing and Sales

The Foreign Military Financing program spends about $5 billion annually to fund weapons purchases by foreign governments. That seems contrary to weapons nonproliferation policy and runs a risk if weapon buyers are not U.S. allies in the future. The program supports grants and loans to more than two dozen countries. The Foreign Military Sales program supports government-to-government sales of arms with the Pentagon acting as a broker, negotiating deals and collecting payments for arms contractors. As a result of these two programs, more than half of U.S. arms sales are facilitated by U.S. taxpayers.[39] Private lenders and defense producers should handle foreign military sales on their own. The U.S. government should get out of the arms exporting business.

Contracting Out

One way to save taxpayer money while improving Pentagon effectiveness is to contract out to private firms support functions that were traditionally done in-house. The Bush administration has moved ahead with contracting out for such activities as military housing. This has worked well because much government-owned military housing was in poor shape and needed to be upgraded.[40] Some lessons might be learned from Britain, which has contracted out all or part of its military airfields, dockyards, bases, recruitment, financial accounting, transport, research, and other functions.

Department of Education

While campaigning for president in 1980, Ronald Reagan called the Department of Education "President Carter's new bureaucratic boondoggle" and proposed eliminating it.[41] The Republican House budget for 1996 also proposed eliminating the department. But instead of being cut, the department has grown by leaps and bounds in the past two decades. By 2005 the department had become President Bush's $71 billion boondoggle after he doubled spending on it in his first term.

The Department of Education is essentially a complex agglomeration of 118 different federal grant programs for state and local governments. It has grant programs for just about everything including distributing television programs to schools, teaching "character education," funding native Hawaiian community centers, funding literacy programs in libraries, funding physical education classes, helping seasonal farm workers to go to college, and helping schools integrate technology into the classroom.[42] The federal government

165

should end its meddling in these properly local and private activities and start cutting this department.

Elementary and Secondary Education

The federal government spends about $40 billion annually on grants for K-12 education.[43] There are grants for "reading first," "arts in education," "improving teacher quality," and many other things. The aims of many grant programs are laudable, but there is no reason that local governments could not handle these activities by themselves.

Chapter 8 discussed the general pathologies of federal grants, and these certainly apply to education grants. The Safe and Drug-Free Schools and Communities program funds grants to reduce substance abuse by youth. That sounds beneficial, but the president's Office of Management and Budget has concluded that the program is "fundamentally flawed."[44] The TRIO program is supposed to increase college enrollment rates of low-income students, but the OMB concludes that the program "has not been effective in increasing college preparation and enrollment."[45] The Even Start program funds educational services for low-income families. The OMB rates the program "ineffective" because it has no measurable impact on the children it is supposed to help.[46]

In such programs, federal money supports expensive bureaucracies at the federal, state, and local levels, with only a depleted flow of funds making it to individual schools. Michigan's former governor John Engler has noted that state administration of federal grant programs required so much staff that only 48 cents of every federal education dollar actually reached the classroom in Michigan.[47]

Federal grants also discourage innovation and diversity in educational approaches because funds are usually tied to restrictive regulations. Governor Engler has said that federal programs "cause schools to set false priorities and waste time going after grants, and they encourage faddish and short-lived reforms . . . federal categorical education programs do worse than nothing. They divert and distract schools from their ultimate mission: educating children."[48] Other state officials have noted that grants foster a mindset of complying with rules rather than improving instructional quality.[49]

From a broad perspective, it is clear that the large increases in spending on education of recent decades at all levels of government have not purchased better results. In constant 2002 dollars, total U.S. K-12 spending increased from $4,505 per pupil in 1970 to $9,553 in 2002.[50] Despite that increase, student performance has not improved. The average SAT score fell from 1049 in 1970 to 1026 in 2003.[51] National Assessment of Education Progress scores are also unimpressive. In national studies for 2001 and 2002, the share of 12th graders scoring "below basic" on writing, history, and geography was 26 percent, 57 percent, and 29 percent, respectively.[52]

Cross-sectional data also do not support the view that greater spending improves performance. Statistical studies have not found a relationship between public school spending levels across the states and educational achievement.[53] The experiment of federal control over the nation's schools and large spending increases has failed. K-12 education should be left to local governments and the private sector.[54]

Student Grants and Loans

Federal student aid for postsecondary education costs taxpayers $26 billion annually. Student aid programs have long been rife with waste, fraud, and abuse. About $22 billion of student loans is in default.[55] Individuals, financial institutions, and administrators at shady institutions have pocketed billions of dollars from false claims for federal aid.[56] Another problem with federal student loans is that they tend to make college more expensive because they fuel tuition inflation.[57]

College students should rely on the private sector to finance their higher education. After all, the students themselves are the ones who gain from the higher salaries and better jobs that follow from a college degree. Indeed, those with a college education will earn, on average, 75 percent more during their lifetimes than those with just high school diplomas.[58]

Department of Energy

To the detriment of taxpayers and the economy, the energy industry has been both coddled and overregulated by this $22 billion department for decades. DoE is a large source of federal business subsidies, and it performs billions of dollars worth of research that should be left to the private sector. Eliminating energy research and business subsidies would save taxpayers more than $6 billion annually.

The DoE has a history of poor management. One problem is that energy projects are often subject to large cost overruns, as documented by the GAO.[59] Another problem has been the poor security at the DoE's energy laboratories, which has led to numerous scandals. Classified nuclear weapons information from Los Alamos National Laboratory may have been acquired by the People's Republic of China.[60] A recent string of security breaches involving missing computers and disks containing nuclear secrets also occurred at Los Alamos. A congressional report a few years ago concluded, "Despite repeated PRC thefts of the most sophisticated U.S. nuclear weapons technology, security at our national nuclear weapons laboratories does not meet even minimal standards."[61] One government report condemned the department as a "dysfunctional bureaucracy" where "organizational disarray, managerial neglect, and a culture of arrogance . . . conspired to create an espionage scandal waiting to happen."[62]

Congress and the Bush administration have taken some steps to fix management problems in the department, such as putting the operation of the national laboratories out for competitive bid. But policymakers cannot seem to quench their thirst for wasteful energy subsidies. The energy bill working its way through Congress in 2005 is stuffed with tens of billions of dollars of subsidies for producers of coal, ethanol, and other products.[63]

Energy Supply

This $820 million program aims to improve energy technologies by funding research by universities, the national laboratories, and private industry. Research areas include solar, wind, and nuclear energy, plus the administration's hydrogen fuel initiative, which will cost taxpayers $94 million in 2005. The hydrogen initiative promises to be a long-term drain on taxpayer wallets, given that the National Academy of Sciences found that hydrogen vehicles may not replace traditional ones until 2050.[64] Hydrogen might become like wind and solar power and receive taxpayer subsidies for decades. It is time that alternative fuels survived on their own in the marketplace. The private sector is wholly capable of funding new technologies when there is a reasonable chance of commercial success.

Fossil Energy Research and Clean Coal

This $615 million program similarly aims to develop energy technologies by funding research in universities, the national laboratories, and private industry. Research is conducted on coal, oil, and natural gas technologies. Federal fossil energy research has a poor record. The CBO concluded: "Federal programs have had a long history of funding fossil-fuel technologies that, although interesting technically, had little chance of commercial implementation. As a result, much of the federal spending has not been productive."[65] That is a polite way of saying that these programs have been a waste of taxpayer money.

The "clean coal" program funds projects that burn coal in an environmentally friendly way. But this program is not taxpayer friendly, and environmental groups do not like it either.[66] The GAO found that many clean coal projects have "experienced delays, cost overruns, bankruptcies, and performance problems."[67] The GAO examined 13 projects and found that "8 had serious delays or financial problems, 6 were behind their original schedules by 2 to 7 years, and 2 projects were bankrupt."[68]

One clean coal project in Alaska gobbled up $117 million of federal taxpayer money during the 1990s.[69] But the project never worked as planned; it cost too much to operate, and it was finally closed down as a failure. But project failure is not a problem in Washington because, as noted, costs are benefits to politicians. The *Washington Post* reported in 2005 that Republican legislators inserted $125 million of taxpayer money into an energy bill to revive the failed Alaska project.[70]

Energy Conservation

Numerous special interest handouts and state grant programs are funded in the $874 million energy conservation budget. One large consumer of taxpayer dollars is the Bush administration's Freedom-Car and fuel cell subsidy program, which will cost $243 million in 2005. Those schemes replaced the Clinton administration's Partnership for a New Generation of Vehicles subsidy program. The PNGV handed out $1.5 billion over eight years to U.S. automakers for development of hybrid cars.[71] Despite the subsidies, U.S. automakers were years behind unsubsidized Honda and Toyota, which introduced the Insight and Prius hybrids, respectively. The Bush administration promises that its new program will work better. The president's 2003 budget said that while PNGV had a "misguided focus," FreedomCar will have "clear goals" and an "accountable manager."[72] That is doubtful. Neither federal managers nor supporters in

Congress were held accountable for wasting $1.5 billion of taxpayer money on PNGV.

Energy Information Administration

The EIA collects data on energy sources, prices, supply and demand, and related items. With an $83 million budget, the EIA is really just a bloated "jobs program" for economists. The agency should be terminated. To the extent that EIA information is valuable to users, private firms should be able to collect it and charge fees for its distribution in private markets.

Power Marketing Administrations

The four PMAs—Bonneville, Southeastern, Southwestern, and Western—market power that is generated by more than 120 federal hydroelectric dams. The dams are owned and operated by the Bureau of Reclamation and the Army Corps of Engineers. The PMAs sell their power to utilities and cooperatives in 33 states, generally at far below market prices.[73] Those low prices distort the economy and encourage overconsumption by consumers and industry. A government analysis found that the artificially low prices had the effect of subsidizing PMA power customers by more than $1 billion annually.[74]

President Clinton proposed selling off Southeastern, Southwestern, and Western in his 1996 budget. Those plans should be revived. CBO estimates that the sale of the Southeastern Power Administration alone would raise about $1.5 billion.[75] Privatization would eliminate artificially low power rates and increase efficiency in utility capital investment.[76] A fifth PMA, the Alaska Power Administration, was privatized in 1995.

Department of Health and Human Services

HHS is the largest federal department and operates Medicare, Medicaid, and hundreds of smaller programs. The department's budget almost doubled during the last decade from $303 billion in 1995 to $586 billion in 2005. HHS is expected to grow explosively in coming years unless major health care reforms are pursued.

Medicare

With a 2005 budget of $325 billion, Medicare is the third largest federal program after Social Security and national defense.[77] But its

170

financial troubles loom even larger than Social Security's. Medicare spending is expected to increase at 9 percent annually during the next decade, compared to 6 percent for Social Security.[78] Medicare's 75-year imbalance in present value terms is $28 trillion, including $8 trillion for the prescription drug benefit added in 2003.[79] By contrast, Social Security's 75-year imbalance is $4 trillion. These imbalances indicate that young Americans face huge tax increases unless those programs are reformed and benefits are cut.

Like Social Security, Medicare costs are expected to rise quickly because of the growing numbers of elderly beneficiaries. But Medicare costs are also growing as a result of rapid health care inflation and the addition of new benefits. Health care inflation is driven by expensive medical technologies and by unconstrained demand for health care services. The low deductibles for Medicare services are one factor that drives high demand.

Another factor pushing up Medicare costs is the huge amount of waste, fraud, and abuse in the program. Medicare pays out erroneous or fraudulent claims of at least $20 billion a year.[80] The GAO has noted that "the sheer size and complexity of the Medicare program make it highly vulnerable to fraud, waste, and abuse."[81] Indeed, the system deals with about 900 million claims each year within a complex structure that has 110,000 pages of regulations and imposes price controls on 7,000 services.[82]

Medicare Part A (Hospital Insurance) is financed by a payroll tax of 2.9 percent on all wages. Part A costs are expected to rise from 3.1 percent of wages in 2005 to 7.1 percent by 2040.[83] The combined costs of Part A and Social Security are expected to rise from 14.2 percent of wages today to 24.6 percent by 2040.[84]

Medicare Part B (Supplemental Medical Insurance) is financed 25 percent by user premiums and 75 percent by general federal revenues. Medicare Part D is the prescription drug benefit added in 2003. By 2015 the shares of total Medicare spending represented by Parts A, B, and D will be 41 percent, 36 percent, and 23 percent, respectively.[85] Thus, the 2003 drug benefit law increased Medicare costs by almost one-third and is one of the most fiscally irresponsible laws ever passed by Congress.

Medicare is financed on a pay-as-you-go basis, as is Social Security, which creates large transfers of resources from the young to the old. Reforms should move both programs away from pay-as-you-go structures to prefunded benefits based on personal savings. Individuals should build up savings during their working years to pay for their own expenses during retirement. Medicare is currently based on unfunded defined benefits that expose taxpayers to whatever uncontrolled cost explosion occurs in the program. By switching to a defined-contribution savings system, taxpayer exposure would be limited.

Under a prefunded Medicare system, a portion of worker payroll taxes would be deposited into savings accounts invested in financial securities. Upon retirement, balances in such Medicare savings accounts would be used to purchase health care insurance. Seniors would choose between competing insurance providers with various coverage options, including options with high deductibles. Any leftover balances in Medicare savings accounts would go toward out-of-pocket health expenses.

Harvard University's Martin Feldstein has calculated that Medicare savings accounts financed by worker deposits averaging 1.4 percent of wages would be enough to make up the future funding shortfall in the program.[86] (However, his estimates were made before Part D was added.) Feldstein concludes that such savings accounts "would eliminate the need for massive taxes that would otherwise reduce the disposable income of low and middle income workers."[87] Savings accounts could be funded by diverting a portion of Medicare payroll taxes, with the resulting budget losses offset by spending cuts in Medicare and other parts of the budget. However, financing the transition to a savings-based Medicare system at the same time as moving to a savings-based Social Security system does present a big fiscal challenge.

Congress took steps toward a savings-based health care system with the creation of health savings accounts (HSAs) in 2003. HSAs provide a model for possible Medicare savings accounts. HSAs combine tax-free savings with high-deductible health insurance plans. HSA funds may be withdrawn for medical expenses, and unused balances can grow indefinitely. This structure will make individuals more cost-conscious users of health care because money not spent is accumulated tax-free.

HSAs should be liberalized to make them larger and more flexible, and individuals should be encouraged to build them up for medical expenses during retirement. Annual contribution limits should be increased, the requirement that HSA holders obtain health insurance should be eliminated, and HSA withdrawals should be allowed for both health insurance premiums and out-of-pocket health expenses.[88]

Liberalized HSAs, and possible Medicare savings accounts, can move health care away from a system dominated by the government and insurance companies. A system based on personal savings, out-of-pocket spending, and high-deductible insurance would reduce health care costs. Competition between providers would be increased and health consumers would be more cost conscious. Administrative costs would be reduced because many payments would be made upon treatment rather than through third-party billing. In Medicare, price controls and top-down planning would give way to choice and competition.

These ideas are long-term reform directions, but there are many Medicare cost savings that could be enacted right away. Numerous cost-cutting ideas are presented in CBO's "Budget Options" report.[89] In the Chapter 4 budget plan, I included two Medicare reforms that were based on CBO options. Both reforms would require the elderly to pay more of their own health care costs, which is reasonable, given that they currently pay only a fraction of costs. One estimate found that transfers from the young finance 75 percent of the health care consumption of the elderly.[90]

The first short-term reform is to increase Medicare Part B premiums. In 2005 Medicare Part B enrollees paid a fairly modest monthly premium of $78.[91] Premiums were originally supposed to cover 50 percent of Part B costs, but they cover just 25 percent today, with taxpayers covering the other 75 percent.[92] Raising Part B premiums to cover 50 percent of costs would create growing savings to federal taxpayers, reaching about $59 billion annually by 2015.[93] Note that this reform would not create an added burden on the poor because their Part B premiums are paid by Medicaid.

The second short-term reform is to increase and conform deductibles and cost sharing for Medicare services and for supplemental medigap policies. CBO notes that the deductibles for Medicare Part B are typically very low, leading to overconsumption of services.[94] Similarly, medigap policies cause overconsumption by often providing first-dollar coverage of expenses not covered by Medicare. Indeed, medigap policyholders consume 25 percent more services than those without this extra coverage.[95]

CBO provides an estimate of the taxpayer savings of an option to increase and conform deductibles for Medicare Part A and B and medigap policies.[96] This option would save taxpayers growing amounts reaching $18 billion annually by 2015. This reform would help reduce overconsumption of health care services. Beneficiaries would pay higher out-of-pocket costs, but CBO believes that that expense would be partly offset by reductions in medigap premiums.

In sum, Medicare reform involves enacting both short-term taxpayer savings and long-term structural changes to reduce health care system costs. Increasing out-of-pocket expenses for retirees, moving younger generations to a savings-based system with HSAs and Medicare savings accounts, and greater use of high-deductible insurance plans are all good directions for health care reform.

Medicaid

Medicaid spending is out of control—federal outlays on the program increased from $118 billion in 2000 to $186 billion in 2005, a 58 percent jump in just five years.[97] The program is expected to more than double in cost to $392 billion by 2015.[98] Medicaid enrollment has increased 40 percent in just the past five years.[99]

Like Medicare, Medicaid is rife with waste, fraud, and abuse. The GAO has warned that "Medicaid is at risk for billions of dollars in improper payments."[100] An investigation found that there is $1 billion of fraud in California's portion of Medicaid alone.[101] The *New York Times* reported in 2005 that from 10 to 40 percent of New York State's annual Medicaid budget of $45 billion may be lost to fraud and abuse.[102] Medicaid is in a financial crisis and major cost-cutting reforms are needed.

One basic cause of Medicaid's overspending is the federal-state structure of the program. The federal government matches state Medicaid spending by between 50 and 83 percent.[103] The federal match provides states a big incentive to expand their programs beyond reasonable levels because only part of the cost falls on state taxpayers. States have even concocted abusive schemes to inappropriately boost their federal match by billions of dollars a year.[104] For example, some states instituted "taxes" on health care providers that were rebated back to the providers. The effect was to increase reported state Medicaid spending and boost federal matching funds.[105] States continue to operate such schemes despite a decade of criticism by the federal government.[106]

Another problem with Medicaid, which is common to all federal handout programs, is that people find ways to game the system to gain unjustified benefits. For example, millions of higher-income retirees use Medicaid to pay for their long-term care, a benefit that is supposed to be for lower-income seniors only. A cottage industry of lawyers has sprung up to help seniors get around Medicaid income limits in order to receive improper benefits.[107] As a consequence, Medicare pays for 43 percent of long-term care costs in the nation, of which the federal taxpayer share in 2005 was $51 billion.[108]

A good first reform step is to turn Medicaid into a block grant and close off the uncontrolled growth in federal costs. Block grants were successfully implemented with welfare reforms in 1996. The idea is to give states federal funding in a lump sum and allow them greater flexibility to enact cost-cutting reforms.

The downsizing plan in Chapter 4 includes a proposal to convert Medicaid to a block grant and limit annual growth to inflation, as measured by the consumer price index. That would limit growth in federal Medicaid spending to about 2.2 percent annually over the next decade. By comparison, Medicaid spending is expected to grow at 7.7 percent annually under current law. Under the proposed reform, federal taxpayer savings would accumulate over time compared with current projections. By 2015 federal taxpayers would be saving $160 billion per year from this reform.[109]

Turning Medicaid into a block grant program was proposed in 1981 by the Reagan administration. That plan would have put 25 different health care grants into one big block grant and capped growth at 5 percent annually.[110] House Republicans proposed similar reforms in their 1996 budget plan. That proposal would have turned Medicaid into a block grant and capped annual growth at 4 percent to cut costs by $182 billion over seven years.[111]

More recently, President Bush has proposed some limited Medicaid block grant reforms. Also, the CBO examined turning Medicaid acute care into a block grant.[112] Acute care includes hospital care, doctor visits, and drug costs, which together account for about two-thirds of Medicaid spending. This option would save federal taxpayers $68 billion annually by 2015 and $292 billion over 10 years.[113]

If Medicaid were block granted, states would have an incentive to control program costs. The states should focus on creating more consumer-driven health coverage. As with Medicare, Medicaid's defined-benefit structure could be replaced by a defined-contribution structure. Funding would flow to individuals in the form of tax credits or vouchers, which would be used to pay for health insurance in private markets. Under such a structure, federal costs would be controlled and much of Medicaid's huge regulatory apparatus could be eliminated.

National Institutes for Health

NIH's budget doubled from $13 billion in 1998 to $26 billion in 2005.[114] NIH funds both basic and applied medical research. Private industry also performs basic and applied research, but it is the former that is considered to have the better argument for taxpayer support. Funding for NIH's applied research should be ended, which would generate taxpayer savings of $12.7 billion annually.[115] Applied research creates direct benefits to businesses such as pharmaceutical firms; thus companies should fund this research themselves without taxpayer help.

Department of Homeland Security

After the terrorist attacks in 2001, legislation was passed to let the federal government take over screening of passengers and baggage at nearly all U.S. commercial airports. That policy, which created 45,000 new federal bureaucrats in the Transportation Security Administration, was a big mistake. Analyses by the GAO and the DHS inspector general (IG) have found that TSA is excessively bureaucratic and unresponsive.[116] The *Washington Post* reported in 2005 that "TSA has been plagued by operational missteps, public relations blunders, and criticism of its performance from both the public and legislators."[117] In 2004 the DHS IG assailed the agency for handing out excessive employee bonuses, throwing a fancy employee awards ceremony that cost $500,000, and other wasteful spending.[118] A report by the IG in 2005 found that excessive TSA spending continued, and it raised concerns about "unethical and illegal activities" at the agency.[119] A government audit in 2005 found that $303 million of the $741 million TSA spent to hire government screeners after 9/11 went for dubious or wasteful expenditures.[120]

More important, government-run airport screening has been no better, and perhaps worse, than private screening. In April 2004 the IG found that U.S. airports with federal screeners and the five U.S. airports that still have private screeners do an equally poor job.[121]

176

In 2005 the GAO found that the five airports with private screeners did a better job than airports with TSA screeners.[122] An important advantage of private airport security firms is that, if they do a poor job, they can be fired. By contrast, individual airports are not allowed to "fire" the TSA. Yet the TSA's performance has been poor, and it is already showing classic signs of bureaucratic inflexibility. As one example, the *Washington Post* reported that when airports need to fill open screener slots, local TSA managers cannot make hiring decisions locally. They must get clearance from Washington, which can often take weeks.[123] For reasons such as this, many airports are lobbying to bring back private screening companies.

The United States nationalized its airport screening, but other countries have moved in the opposite direction. Nearly all large airports in Europe use private security firms for some or all aspects of their baggage screening and airport security. The United States should not be a laggard in commercial aviation. It should privatize its airports, air traffic control, and airport security so that businesses can compete to provide the safest and best-quality services to air travelers.

Department of Housing and Urban Development

A central problem of the dozens of programs in the $43 billion HUD budget is that they deal with properly local and private concerns. There is little evidence that hundreds of billions of dollars of HUD subsidies over the years and related federal regulations have helped urban America on net. Indeed, many federal programs have been destructive to cities, neighborhoods, and private housing markets. HUD programs should be variously terminated, privatized, or devolved to state and local governments.

Housing Programs

Decades of government interference in housing markets through rent controls, zoning regulations, public housing, urban renewal, import barriers on lumber, and other interventions have distorted markets and pushed up housing costs. Federal, state, and local governments have created many of the housing problems that HUD tries to fix.

Federal housing policy is a history of blunders that have been "profoundly destructive," according to Howard Husock, a housing expert at Harvard's Kennedy School of Government.[124] Most infamously, the mass construction of high-rise public housing in the mid-20th century and related "urban renewal" programs were disastrous. Public housing was poorly built and maintained, and it created concentrated and sustained pockets of poverty and hopelessness in America's cities.

HUD programs continue to create social problems. The department spends $23 billion annually for low-income housing assistance. This means-tested assistance has no time limits and thus has encouraged long-term dependence and discouraged participants from improving their positions in life.[125] The system has also promoted the neighborhood concentration of low-income families.

Aside from pursuing damaging policies, HUD has a history of mismanagement. In the 1980s HUD was rocked by scandals caused by influence peddling, pay-offs, and fraud involving billions of dollars.[126] But the scandals go back further. In 1971 *Time* magazine discussed a scandal at the Federal Housing Administration in which "real estate speculators used the program to make huge profits at the expense of the poor through what amounts to sheer fraud."[127] The fraud was apparently widespread in 10 cities that a congressional panel examined.

The *Time* article discussed a scandal from even further back, from the 1950s, in which "builders pocketed millions of dollars of unearned profit from mortgage loans that exceeded the cost of construction" under a HUD program.[128] The magazine concluded, "Whenever the government writes a blank check to the housing industry, some sort of scandal is likely to result."[129]

Mismanagement and fraud still plague HUD. Some HUD programs have been on the GAO high-risk list for waste, fraud, and abuse since 1994.[130] In 2003 the GAO found that HUD makes overpayments of $2 billion every year on its rental subsidies due to error and fraud.[131] The 2006 federal budget boasts that errors and fraud on rental subsidies have been cut to *only* $1.6 billion per year.[132] One scandal erupted at the Newark Housing Authority in 2005. The agency was caught misusing millions of dollars of federal rental subsidies for items such as a $3.9 million land purchase for a New Jersey Devils hockey arena.[133]

With freer housing markets, HUD's programs, including its programs for the poor, would be redundant. Husock argues that it is a myth started by a Lyndon Johnson housing commission that private markets cannot provide decent housing for the poor.[134] The surest way to meet the housing needs of Americans is to deregulate housing markets and to allow entrepreneurs to provide housing for people of all income levels. After all, private businesses provide food, clothing, and thousands of other products for people of all incomes and tastes. Housing programs should be terminated and the public housing stock privatized.

Community Development Block Grants

The $5 billion CDBG program would be perhaps the single best cut to make in the budget. The activities it supports are purely local and private concerns. Some grants go directly to local governments, while others trickle down through the states to local governments. CDBG spending subsidizes private businesses and pays for niceties that ought to be paid for locally, such as shopping malls, parking lots, art museums, colleges, theaters, swimming pools, civic celebrations, and memorials.

The CDBG program was instituted to aid low-income areas, but today a substantial share of its money goes to wealthy jurisdictions. In one year, Greenwich, Connecticut, received five times more funding per low-income resident than Camden, New Jersey.[135] Yet Greenwich has a per capita income six times higher than Camden's. CDBG spending has been shifted from poorer to wealthier communities in recent years.[136] The CDBG program has been rated "ineffective" by the president's budget office due to its "lack of clarity" and "weak targeting of funds."[137] The president's 2006 budget proposed to shift CDBG funding to the Department of Commerce. Instead, the program should be zeroed out.

Department of the Interior

This $9 billion department carries out a wide range of activities, including managing millions of acres of land, building dams, and overseeing programs for Native Americans. Many activities are poorly managed, and many could be privatized or devolved to the states. The president's budget office has generally given the department poor grades on management performance.[138]

Bureau of Reclamation

This $1.2 billion agency constructs and operates water projects to provide power, irrigation, and flood control in 17 western states.

The agency is the largest wholesale seller of water in the country. Its water sales to cities and to one-fifth of all western farmers for irrigation are subsidized in numerous ways, which has encouraged wasteful overconsumption.[139] The bureau is also the second largest producer of hydroelectric power in the country and owns 58 generation plants.

There have been complaints for decades that many of its taxpayer-subsidized power and water projects make little economic or environmental sense. For example, environmentalists have complained about the giant Animas–La Plata project in southwestern Colorado, which redirects the flow of the Animas River to irrigate low-value crops.[140] The project is a budget buster as well: the official cost estimate jumped from $338 million in 1999 to $500 million by 2003.[141]

The bureau's dams, water pipelines, and other infrastructure should be privatized. Water and power should not be subsidized. They should be treated like other commodities and priced by supply and demand to ensure efficient and environmentally friendly usage.

Bureau of Indian Affairs

The $2.4 billion BIA is responsible for the management of land held for Native Americans, which totals about 56 million acres. The BIA operates a wide variety of social, economic, and educational programs, such as running schools for about 48,000 children. But the BIA is one of the worst run agencies in the government. With regard to education, for example, the GAO has concluded that "the academic achievement of many BIA students as measured by their performance on standardized tests and other measures is far below the performance of students in public schools."[142]

The BIA's poor management has been condemned in the ongoing "Indian Enron" scandal, in which the agency mishandled billions of dollars in Indian trust fund money.[143] The government-run trust funds were set up to receive royalty and lease payments for the use of Indian lands. In the 1980s people began noticing that BIA's accounting for the trust funds had been in shambles for decades. In 1996 a class action lawsuit was filed against government officials with U.S. District Court Judge Royce Lamberth overseeing the case. Lamberth concluded that BIA management was "fiscal and governmental irresponsibility in its purest form."[144] He said that the BIA "has served as a gold standard for mismanagement by the federal

180

government for more than a century."[145] Former BIA special trustee Thomas Slonaker testified to Congress that BIA is incapable of reform, unwilling to follow the law, and does not hold managers accountable.[146] Special trustee Paul Homan testified that the "vast majority of upper and middle management at the BIA are incompetent."[147]

The BIA should be terminated and the Indian Enron affair settled. Government subsidies to the tribes should be ended. These days, Native Americans in 30 states earn $19 billion annually in gambling revenues at tribal casinos.[148] That indicates that there should be plenty of private donors within the Indian community willing to support the education and charitable activities that BIA is supposed to perform.

Department of Justice

Like many parts of the federal government, the $21 billion Justice Department has expanded its power over traditionally state and local activities in recent decades. The government has federalized more and more crimes that are properly the responsibility of the states. Between 1994 and 2004, the number of federal criminal laws increased by one-third, from about 3,000 to 4,000.[149]

As in other departments, grants to the states handed out by Justice have been put to low-value uses or squandered. For example, a financial scandal has played out in California recently after auditors discovered widespread abuse in the state office that handles federal justice grants.[150] Hundreds of millions of federal grant dollars were wasted.

To save money in Justice, grants should be terminated, activities that encroach on state law enforcement should be ended, and unneeded statutes such as antitrust laws should be repealed.

Community Oriented Policing Services

The $575 million COPS program funds grants to local governments to put police officers into community patrols. There is no solid evidence that this program has helped reduce crime.[151] Also, grants to local governments make little fiscal sense because the federal government is swimming in red ink while local governments are flush with cash due to rising property taxes. More important, policing is a classic local government responsibility and should remain so. Top-down Washington solutions for policing make no sense because police priorities and tactics vary from city to city. Indeed, top-down control of policing threatens to reduce the local innovation that is needed to fight crime effectively.

Juvenile Justice Grants

These grants are supposed to help states improve juvenile justice systems. But the programs funded by these grants have not led to any measurable reduction in juvenile crime. The OMB has rated this program "ineffective" and asked that its funding be eliminated.[152] Again, this is an area in the justice system that is properly a state and local activity.

Antitrust Enforcement

The Justice Department and the Federal Trade Commission spend more than $200 million per year on antitrust enforcement. But antitrust laws, which are supposed to ensure competitive markets, are a solution in search of a problem. With today's huge flows of international trade and investment, competition is not something that the U.S. economy is short of.

One problem with antitrust, as discussed in Chapter 7, is that the government simply does not know how particular industries should be organized to maximize consumer welfare. It is usually not clear, for example, whether particular business mergers are good or bad for the economy. Yet the antitrust cops pretend to try and make such determinations in our complex and dynamic economy. A study by Brookings Institution scholars found that antitrust enforcement over the decades has had a mixed record at best and the government has often prevented mergers that might have increased consumer welfare.[153] Antitrust laws should be repealed and the antitrust lawyers should find alternative employment that adds to the nation's output, not reduces it.

Department of Labor

Many programs in this $50 billion department are ineffective, actively damaging to the economy, or designed to solve problems that the market solves by itself. Minimum wage laws increase unemployment. Unemployment benefits induce people not to work.[154] Government job training programs are generally ineffective, and they duplicate activities that workers and companies do themselves.[155] The Davis-Bacon Act mandates that high wages be paid on federal construction projects, which wastes taxpayer money and excludes less-skilled workers from federal work. The Service Contract Act imposes various regulations on federal contractors that also push up taxpayer costs.[156]

Employment and Training Administration

The Labor Department's numerous training programs in this $5.2 billion agency have proven to be ineffective.[157] There are no fewer than 44 federal programs run by nine federal agencies for employment and training services, creating much overlap and waste.[158] Federal training programs are unnecessary because workers and companies have incentives to spend their own resources on training. One study found that U.S. businesses spent $373 billion annually of their own money on employee training, including payments for training courses, wages for training time, and other expenses.[159] The government's attempts to train workers have worked poorly, are not needed, and should be ended.

Trade Adjustment Assistance

This $1.1 billion program hands out taxpayer money to workers who have lost their jobs as a result of trade liberalization. The handouts are in the form of extra unemployment insurance, job search and relocation allowances, and subsidized education and training. But it makes no sense that people who lose their jobs to foreign competition should receive special benefits that are not given to those who lose their jobs to domestic competition.

Further, the program does not solve the problem of making American workers and businesses more competitive in the global economy.[160] It would be better to use budget resources to cut corporate tax rates to make sure that businesses are able to create domestic jobs in the first place.

The OMB has labeled this program "ineffective" because it favors a small group of workers who are already eligible for other benefits.[161] But leading up to the 2004 election, the administration put aside its negative critique and supported a costly expansion of trade adjustment assistance.[162]

Community Service for Seniors

This $436 million grant program enrolls older Americans in community service activities. The OMB has rated this program "ineffective" because of it poor accountability, design, and delivery.[163] The basic premise of federal programs for community service makes no sense. If seniors want to volunteer in the community, they can do so without the federal government's help. If seniors add market value to the jobs they are performing, then employers should be able to pay them market wages.

Davis-Bacon Act

This 1931 law requires that companies pay "prevailing wages" for work on federally funded contracts and construction projects, such as highways and transit projects.[164] That generally means higher, union-level wages, which create an added burden on federal taxpayers. The law also unfairly excludes less-skilled workers from a fair chance at gaining employment on federal projects. The Davis-Bacon and the Service Contract Acts should be repealed.

Social Security

Social Security is the largest federal program, accounting for 21 percent of the budget in 2005. The main funding mechanism for Social Security is a 12.4 percent tax on covered wages. Under its pay-as-you-go structure, the program will raise $596 billion in tax revenues this year and pay out benefits of $527 billion.[165] The revenues collected in excess of benefits paid will be spent on other federal programs. As spending rises rapidly in coming years, the excess revenues will disappear and the program will fall deep into deficit unless reformed.[166]

The key to understanding Social Security is to focus on the system's cash flows, not its "trust fund." The existence of the Social Security Trust Fund does not affect the fact that promised benefits are much higher than the taxes that will be available to pay them. By 2040 promised benefits will be 32 percent higher than available taxes.[167] Thus, without cuts in benefits, future workers will be crushed by huge tax increases that will reduce their net earnings and damage the economy.

Looking at Social Security's cash flows, spending will begin exceeding revenues in 2017.[168] But the problem begins before 2017. In 2008 the large baby-boom generation will begin retiring, causing Social Security costs to start increasing quickly. Rising life expectancies will add to the cost pressures. Without reforms, Social Security costs are expected to increase from 11.1 percent of taxable wages today to 17.5 percent by 2040.[169]

184

To defuse this fiscal time bomb, traditional Social Security benefits should be cut. In Chapter 4, I proposed indexing the increases in initial year benefits to prices rather than wages as under current law. Prices are expected to increase at 2.8 percent annually in coming decades, while wages are expected to increase at 3.9 percent, according to the Social Security Trustees.[170] Thus switching to price indexing would slow the growth in initial benefits for future retirees. If implemented now, CBO estimates that price indexing would be saving taxpayers $33 billion annually by 2015.[171]

The effects of price indexing would grow slowly over time, thus allowing future retirees to adjust their plans and increase their private savings. Price indexing is a straightforward reform that could be implemented right away, and it would create permanent long-term solvency in the Social Security system. A more modest reform would be "progressive price indexing," under which future benefits would be reduced for those with middle and higher incomes, but benefits for low-income workers would be unchanged.

Aside from cutting traditional benefits, the other key element of Social Security reform is to allow young workers to fund their own retirement with personal savings accounts. A funded Social Security system would allow each generation to pay for its retirement with accumulated savings. Such a reform would create large pools of private capital in the economy, helping to foster business investment and growth.

There are two good ways of funding the proposed Social Security personal accounts. The first is to "carve out" a portion of the 12.4 percent payroll tax and divert that amount into workers' accounts. That would have the effect of increasing short-term federal budget deficits. However, those deficits could be offset by the budget cuts proposed in this book. Also note that proposed cuts to traditional benefits (through price indexing) would reduce the government's long-term liabilities by an even greater amount.

A second source of funding for private accounts would be additional voluntary savings. Social Security personal accounts could be designed to allow workers to make added voluntary contributions on top of the payroll tax deposits into their accounts. In addition, income tax reforms, such as liberalizing Roth individual retirement accounts (IRAs), could encourage greater savings outside of Social Security.

A Social Security system based on personal accounts has numerous advantages over the current system. A personal account system would provide higher rates of return, create protection against unexpected benefit cuts, encourage the habit of saving, allow bequests to children, and give Americans legal ownership of their retirement funds. Another advantage of personal accounts would be to reduce the economic "deadweight losses" caused by payroll taxes. If payroll taxes were diverted into personal accounts, it would be like a tax cut, which would strengthen work incentives and boost growth.

Numerous plans have been proposed to convert Social Security into a funded system based on personal accounts. The 1997 Social Security Advisory Council report supported moving toward a funded system.[172] The 2001 bipartisan commission appointed by President Bush proposed three options for reform based on personal accounts.[173]

In 2005 the Bush administration proposed personal accounts based on a carve-out of 4 percentage points of the 12.4 percent payroll tax. President Bush's leadership on Social Security has been laudatory, but his proposal for 4 percent accounts is too timid. A number of plans introduced in Congress during the past decade have called for larger carve-outs in the range of 6 to 10 percentage points.[174]

The Cato Institute has proposed a Social Security reform plan based on 6.2 percent personal accounts.[175] A modified version of the Cato plan was introduced in the 109th Congress by Reps. Sam Johnson (R-TX) and Jeff Flake (R-AZ) as H. R. 530. The following is a summary of the Cato plan:

- **Account Funding.** Half of the 12.4 percent Social Security payroll tax would be diverted into the personal retirement accounts of participating workers. Like current Roth IRAs, the accounts would be funded with after-tax dollars, but there would be no taxes on earnings or withdrawals. Individuals could voluntarily deposit added contributions of up to 10 percent of wages in the accounts.
- **Older Workers.** Those aged 55 and older would not be affected by the reforms and would not have their benefits cut.
- **Voluntary Choice.** Workers could stay in the old Social Security system if they chose. They would receive benefits that were less than those currently promised but at a level that is sustainable under projected tax revenues. To effect that change, initial

benefits for future retirees would grow each year on the basis of price indexing rather than wage indexing. Young people would be enrolled in the new personal account system when they started working.

- **Recognition Bonds.** Workers opting for the new system would have 6.2 percent of their wages deposited into personal accounts. They would also receive a "recognition bond" that reflected the accrued value of their past Social Security contributions. The bonds would be redeemable at age 67 to fund a portion of retirement benefits.
- **Investment Options.** Deposits in personal accounts would initially fund a default portfolio of 60 percent equities and 40 percent bonds. Once account assets rose above $10,000, broader investment options would be available.
- **Retirement Benefits.** Upon retirement, individuals would take an annuity or programmed withdrawal of their account assets. Assets in excess of those needed to provide a minimum annuity could be withdrawn. For average workers, retirement benefits (from recognition bonds and personal accounts) would be higher than the benefits that the current system can afford to pay but less than the benefits that are currently promised. The plan would guarantee that no worker's retirement income fell below 120 percent of the poverty level.
- **Solvency.** The Social Security Administration has confirmed that the Johnson-Flake bill (essentially the Cato plan) would create long-run solvency in the system.[176]

The Cato plan would end the looming fiscal crisis in Social Security that threatens young Americans. Transition to the new system would have a budget cost of about $6.5 trillion, but the plan would eliminate the $12.8 trillion unfunded liability of the current system, as measured on a permanent present-value basis.[177] Thus, moving to the new system would essentially save future taxpayers about $6.3 trillion.

The Cato plan would help to create a culture of savings and financial responsibility among younger Americans. It would create an "ownership society," as President Bush has described it. Individuals would enjoy seeing their accounts grow during their working years, and some people who do not currently save would be encouraged to save additional amounts in the new tax-favored retirement accounts.

Americans are more ready than ever for the responsibility of personal Social Security accounts. Consider that when President Franklin Roosevelt introduced the current system in the 1930s, only 10 percent of Americans held stocks.[178] Today, the popularity of mutual funds and other savings vehicles has resulted in half of U.S. households owning stocks.[179] It would be an exciting project to introduce the other half of Americans to the growth potential and security of investment accounts. More than 20 other countries have reformed their social security systems and embraced personal accounts.[180] The time is ripe for America to join the worldwide retirement savings revolution.

Department of Transportation

The Department of Transportation employs 59,000 workers and has a budget of $58 billion. The department's main function is to send federal taxpayer dollars to the states for highways, transit systems, airports, and other facilities. The department should be radically downsized with most activities either moved back to the states or privatized.

The federal government is an unneeded middleman in transportation that misallocates resources as a result of political pressures and inefficient top-down planning. Americans do not need "highways to nowhere" in the districts of important members of Congress, and they do not need the large cost overruns common in federal transportation projects. Instead, Americans need a more efficient transportation system based on state, local, and private financing and control.

Air Traffic Control

The Federal Aviation Administration runs a second-rate and mismanaged air traffic control (ATC) system. Operational safety under the current system has worsened in recent years.[181] The FAA has struggled to modernize its technology to maintain safety, but these efforts have fallen behind schedule and gone overbudget. A GAO review of FAA projects to upgrade ATC found that the combined costs of 16 projects had risen from $8.9 billion to $14.6 billion.[182] For example, a computer system called STARS has jumped in cost from $940 million to $2.8 billion and is seven years behind schedule.[183]

The FAA also faces a looming shortage of available controllers, a problem that a more flexible private system could help solve.[184]

Powerful controller unions and lax FAA oversight have led to scandals. In one recent incident in New York, it was discovered that ATC employees work only a few hours a day, and then they abuse the FAA's sick and overtime pay systems to take home excessive salaries.[185]

The Bush administration has proposed making the ATC system more business oriented. But the system should be fully privatized. The United States lags behind other major nations on ATC reform. During the past 15 years, more than a dozen countries have partly or fully privatized their ATC.

Canada has created a private nonprofit corporation for its ATC, which could be a good model for U.S. reforms. Nav Canada was set up in 1996 and is self-supporting from charges paid by aviation users. The Canadian system has received rave reviews for investing in technology and reducing air congestion.[186] The system has one of the best safety records in the world and it has cut Canadian airspace congestion in half.[187]

In Britain, air traffic control has been moved to the National Air Traffic Services company. NATS has a public-private corporate structure with shares owned by airlines, the government, and employees. Like Canada's system, NATS is self-supporting from fees and charges. Germany has created a self-supporting government corporation for ATC.

The United States should be a leader rather than a laggard in air traffic control, especially given the nation's history of aviation innovation. A privatized system would allow for access to private capital for upgrading ATC infrastructure. It would also improve ATC safety and reduce air congestion by speeding the adoption of advanced technologies.

Essential Air Service

EAS was created in 1978 as a "temporary" program to ensure that air service was continued in rural communities after airline deregulation. The program provides $74 million in annual subsidies to air carriers that serve certain rural markets, meaning those rural areas represented by powerful members of Congress. Today, the air travel market is more advanced than it was in the 1970s, with airlines providing service to many more markets. The GAO has found that EAS "program costs have tripled since 1995, and fewer passengers use the subsidized local service. Most choose to drive to their destination or to fly to and from another nearby airport with more service or lower fares."[188] The EAS should be abolished.

Grants in Aid for Airports

This $3 billion program provides grants to airports to fund terminal expansions, improvements, and noise mitigation. This program should be ended and the nation's airports, which are generally owned by state and local governments, should be privatized. As in other areas, the United States lags behind reforms taking place abroad. Airports have been fully or partially privatized in Athens, Auckland, Brussels, Copenhagen, Frankfurt, London, Melbourne, Naples, Rome, Sydney, Vienna, and other cities. Privatized airports can raise revenues from charges on airport users, and they can access funding for expansion in debt and equity markets. Foreign reforms prove that putting the burden of airport costs on taxpayers is both inefficient and unnecessary.

Federal Highway and Transit Administrations

Congress should devolve the government's $33 billion of highway spending and $8 billion of transit spending to the states. The federal gasoline tax that supports this spending should be repealed. The states can balance the costs and benefits of transportation facilities better than politicians and bureaucrats in Washington can. Federal intervention makes some states winners and others losers. The GAO notes that the formula used for highways "allocates funds among the states based on their historic share of funding. This approach reflects antiquated indicators of highway needs, such as postal road miles and the land area of the state."[189] The result is that tax dollars are not efficiently directed to the states with the largest congestion problems.

Another problem is politics. Highway spending is one of the biggest pork-barrel machines in Washington. When gasoline tax dollars go through Congress, powerful politicians steer them to highway projects in their own states rather than the states most in need. For example, former Senate Appropriations Committee chairman Ted Stevens has ensured that his state of Alaska receives five times more in highway money than Alaska residents pay in gas taxes.[190] The number of earmarked "high-priority" projects for particular congressional districts has soared from 152 in the 1987 highway bill to 4,128 in the House version of the 2005 highway bill, as shown in Figure 8.3.

190

Appendix 2: Discussion of Selected Budget Cuts

The *Washington Post* ran a series of stories in 1998 that revealed the corrupt manner in which highway spending is doled out.[191] Then–House Transportation Committee chairman Bud Shuster (R-PA) dished out funding for highway projects in exchange for millions of dollars in campaign donations. Shuster did not soberly analyze the nation's highway needs, ponder the views of experts, and steer resources to the areas with the highest needs. Rather, Shuster lived a jet-setting lifestyle, frequently winging around the country to hand out highway projects in exchange for campaign cash based on raw political calculations.

When such scandals hit the newspapers, there are usually calls for campaign finance reform. But a better reform would be to repeal the federal gasoline tax and terminate federal highway and transit spending. That would end the money flow to corrupt federal politicians. States could fund transportation according to their own local demands, and they would be free to experiment with new alternatives such as privately financed highways.

Maritime Administration

MARAD funds a number of subsidy programs designed to prop up the shipping industry. Like other corporate welfare programs, MARAD's programs create unsavory ties between the government and industry. The GAO has found that MARAD's loan programs are not operated in a businesslike fashion and are vulnerable to fraud, abuse, and mismanagement.[192] As one example, the Title XI loan guarantee program for U.S. shipbuilders has been subject to scandal. American Classic Voyages received a $1.1 billion loan guarantee to buy two cruise ships to be built in Sen. Trent Lott's hometown in Mississippi.[193] But before the ships were completed, the company went bankrupt and left taxpayers with a $200 million tab. Such episodes are apparently not uncommon. In a 2004 report, government auditors found that 25 percent of loans in the Title XI portfolio were at risk of default.[194]

Another subsidy program is MARAD's operating differential program, which was established to sustain a private U.S. merchant fleet. The problem is that, by shielding U.S. shippers from foreign competition, the subsidies allow them to run higher-cost, less-efficient operations. Taxpayers should not have to pick up the tab for this industry's inefficiency. All maritime and shipbuilding subsidies should be ended.

191

Amtrak

Amtrak was created in 1970 to be a self-supporting business with temporary subsidies to be phased out over time. That has not occurred. Amtrak has consumed $29 billion in subsidies over the years, while providing low-quality rail service to Americans.[195] In recent years, Amtrak's debt has been rising, its on-time performance has been falling, and its poorly maintained equipment is putting passenger safety at risk.[196]

Privatization is the way ahead for U.S. passenger rail, as it has been in other countries. Australia and its states privatized much of that nation's freight and passenger rail infrastructure. Japan National Railways was broken up into seven companies in a 1997 privatization, with the government holding a small and declining block of ownership shares. The German government is preparing to privatize Deutsche Bahn in 2005 or 2006. The head of Deutsche Bahn said that he is eager to get rid of the "civil service mentality" in the German rail company.[197] Argentina, Britain, New Zealand, and other countries have also privatized their rail systems.

In this country, Congress created the Amtrak Reform Council in 1997 to study major reform options. The group proposed a plan that would end Amtrak's monopoly on passenger service, spin off its Northeast Corridor infrastructure, and permit states and private entities to bid for Amtrak routes. Congress has not implemented this plan or the reforms proposed by the Bush administration.

Congress needs to update its thinking about passenger rail and study the reforms taking place abroad. Amtrak should probably be privatized as a single unit including operations, stations, rails, and trains. A key advantage of privatization would be to give Amtrak the flexibility to issue debt and equity for capital investment as needed. Today, Amtrak executives have a difficult time planning for the future because of annual budget battles and the need to satisfy the various special interests in Congress.

Private ownership would allow Amtrak to cut unprofitable routes and to restructure its operations to maximize quality and profitability. Currently, a handful of routes with few riders create large losses for the system.[198] The culprits are members of Congress who put their selfish interests ahead of the national interest and fight efforts to cut little-used rail lines in their states. But Amtrak will not be a success until it has the flexibility to drop unneeded routes, cut costs, and maximize profits. The extent of U.S. passenger rail service should be up to consumers and entrepreneurs, not to Congress.

Other Agencies and Programs

Agency for International Development

USAID is the main U.S. foreign aid agency with a 2005 budget of $3.7 billion. In recent years, there has been a growing realization that traditional foreign aid does not work. Much aid from Western countries has simply propped up corrupt regimes and acted to delay economic reforms that are needed for sustained growth. Aid to countries that do not have secure property rights, market economies, or political stability goes into a black hole and does not increase living standards. Another problem with government aid is that much of it gets swallowed up by high-paid consultants and their expenses, including plane flights, hotels, office space, meals, meetings, and reports.

The realization that traditional aid is ineffective led the Bush administration to create the Millennium Challenge Corporation.[199] This new agency is supposed to avoid USAID's ineffective bureaucracy and its conflicting objectives.[200] Unfortunately, the MCC program will be costing taxpayers $2 billion annually by 2006, on top of the costs of existing aid through USAID.[201]

Instead, U.S. foreign aid should be left to private charitable groups. Private charity is large and has a better track record of achieving results. American private aid after the Indian Ocean tsunami of 2004 topped $700 million.[202] More important than charity, however, is private investment capital. Private capital will flow to those countries that follow sensible economic policies, and it is more likely to be invested in productive projects. With internal reforms, every country has the capability of reducing its poverty and achieving growth without government aid from abroad.

Appalachian Regional Commission

This $76 million agency was established in 1965 to encourage economic development in the rural areas of 13 Appalachian states. Congress has more recently created the similar Denali Commission and Delta Regional Authority to hand out subsidies to Alaska and areas along the Mississippi River, respectively.[203] Those programs represent unjust transfers of wealth from some Americans to others who live in politically favored regions. Even if one accepts the dubious claim that these programs create jobs in the targeted regions, jobs are certainly destroyed in the rest of the country from which the tax money is extracted.

Army Corps of Engineers

The Army Corps of Engineers, which has an annual budget of $4.9 billion, builds and operates infrastructure such as dams and harbors. The Army Corps is the largest owner of hydroelectric power plants in the United States, with 75 plants valued at $18 billion.[204] The agency spends about $1 billion annually on construction and maintenance of commercial harbors.[205] Other activities include spending $100 million annually on beach replenishment.[206]

Most Army Corps activities could be easily privatized. Government electricity generation is an outdated idea that has proven to be inefficient and environmentally unfriendly. Army Corps power plants should be sold to investor-owned utilities. Other Army Corps activities, such as beach replenishment, should be left to state and local governments. The rest of the Army Corps could be turned into a private engineering and construction company that charges fees to customers such as ports and harbors and their users.

Under government ownership, the Army Corps has for decades been used as a political tool for powerful politicians. In recent years, it has been rocked by scandal for falsifying data to justify large and unneeded projects.[207] In 2000 it was discovered that the agency's top managers manipulated economic studies to provide support for a wasteful $1 billion Mississippi River project.[208] A similar scandal erupted over a $311 million project to dredge the Delaware River, and a project analysis for the Chesapeake and Delaware Canal was also rigged.[209] The agency pours billions of dollars into the districts of powerful members of Congress for often environmentally damaging projects.

The Army Corps has a strong pro-spending bias because it does the economic analyses of proposed projects that it later constructs itself. To make matters worse, the *Washington Post* notes that "powerful members of Congress dictate the selection, pace, and price tag for major projects" of the Army Corps.[210] Even after the National Academy of Sciences found that Army Corps studies for projects on the Mississippi River were bogus, "Senator Christopher S. Bond

(R-Mo.) vowed to make sure the projects are funded no matter what the economic studies ultimately conclude," according to the *Post*.[211] To end this sort of corruption and inefficiency, the Army Corps should be privatized.

Cargo Preference Program

The Cargo Preference Act of 1904 requires that certain government-owned or government-financed cargo be shipped only by vessels registered in the United States. The law pushes up shipping costs because it is more expensive to register a ship in the United States than in most foreign countries. The CBO estimates that about $563 million would be saved annually if Congress repealed this wasteful law and the government shipped cargo at market rates.[212]

Corporation for Public Broadcasting

The CPB gives grants to public television and radio stations across the country, which use the funding to pay fees to PBS and National Public Radio. Government-owned broadcasting is a hallmark of unfree societies with controlled media. There is an unavoidable problem with government broadcasting, such as PBS and NPR: that political bias will treat certain parties or policy viewpoints unfairly. Conservatives have long criticized CPB, PBS, and NPR for liberal bias. More recently, liberals are crying foul that conservatives are gaining influence at CPB.

The solution is privatization. Taxpayer support represents just 15 percent of public broadcasting's revenues, with most funding coming from individuals, foundations, corporations, and royalties. PBS and NPR would likely survive and even thrive as private entities without subsidies. After all, a number of public TV programs, such as *Sesame Street*, generate millions of dollars in merchandise sales and foreign broadcasting revenue. Broadcasting is a business, and PBS and NPR should be set free from government to innovate and grow.

Export Subsidies

A number of federal agencies provide subsidies to supposedly boost U.S. exports. The Export-Import Bank makes loans to foreign buyers of U.S. goods, guarantees the loans of financial institutions, and provides export credit insurance. But the amount of trade activity underwritten by Ex-Im Bank is very small—only about 1 percent of exports—so it is unlikely that the agency affects the magnitude of U.S. exports.[213] Ex-Im activities duplicate services that private markets already perform. The agency's subsidies go to some of the biggest Fortune 500 companies, who are capable of finding private financing for their exports. When those companies successfully export, they earn profits. There is no reason for taxpayers to fund private, profit-making activities.

The federal Overseas Private Investment Corporation provides direct loans, guaranteed loans, and insurance to U.S. firms that invest in developing countries. During the 1990s, OPIC loaned Enron $750 million and the Ex-Im Bank loaned Enron $650 million for risky and sometimes environmentally damaging projects.[214] For example, the Chiquitano Forest pipeline, financed by OPIC, was driven through one of the most valuable and unscathed regions of forest in South America.[215] This is a glaring example of corporate welfare waste.

The Trade and Development Agency subsidizes exporting businesses in a variety of ways, such as funding export feasibility studies. TDA subsidies go to big companies such as General Electric, foreign governments, and private investors who engage in commerce with American businesses. The TDA, Ex-Im Bank, OPIC, and other similar agencies should be terminated.

National Aeronautics and Space Administration

NASA is a poorly managed and obsolete agency that will burn through $16 billion in taxpayer money in 2005. The good news is that Americans do not need NASA in order to advance the space age. Space is being opened up by private entrepreneurs, who are planning all kinds of manned spaceflight ventures, as discussed in Box 9.1. NASA's time has passed, and the agency should be closed down.

The official report on the *Columbia* disaster in 2003 found that NASA management had ineffective leadership, flawed analysis, and a safety culture that was reactive and complacent.[216] It noted that the mistakes on *Columbia* were "not isolated failures, but are indicative of systematic flaws" in the agency.[217] The 1986 *Challenger* disaster was also traced to failed NASA management. The Mars Polar Lander failure was caused by one NASA project team using metric and another NASA team using English measurements.[218]

One manifestation of NASA's poor management is that its large projects go far overbudget and fall far behind schedule. The GAO has concluded that NASA has "debilitating weaknesses" in management of large projects.[219] For example, the construction costs of the International Space Station have skyrocketed from $17 billion in 1995 to $30 billion today and it is years behind schedule.[220] Scrapping this project and the space shuttle would save taxpayers $55 billion over the next decade.[221]

Congress shares the blame for NASA's waste because it appropriates the money to fund NASA's white elephant projects such as the space station. Unfortunately, NASA is in the early stages of another white elephant—the Bush administration's plan to send a manned spacecraft to Mars. Former representative Joe Scarborough (R-FL) calls Bush's plan to fund a manned mission to Mars "loopy."[222] He is right. Such a project would take tens or hundreds of billions of dollars in coming decades when the government will be facing massive deficits in entitlement programs for the elderly. Unfortunately, NASA costs are benefits to politicians who have space facilities in their districts. Supporters of this scheme, such as Majority Leader Tom DeLay (R-TX), probably do not care if it is loopy; they just want the money spent on their constituents.

Small Business Administration

The $3 billion SBA provides loans and other services to small businesses. But such loans and subsidies make little economic sense. If a small business has a sound business plan with good prospects, it should be able to raise private debt and equity and pay for its own business services. If a small business has shaky finances and poor prospects, it will be denied private capital, which would be a good result. As it turns out, SBA has a history of high delinquency rates on its loans, suggesting that companies with shaky finances are the ones lining up for aid. The default rate on 7(a) preferred lender loans has averaged about 14 percent in recent years.[223]

Aside from the dubious economics of SBA programs, the agency is poorly managed. The GAO noted that "ineffective lines of communication; confusion over the mission of district offices; complicated, overlapping organizational relationships; and a field structure not consistently matched with mission requirements combine to impede the effective delivery of services."[224]

Most of the nation's 25 million small businesses are funded and grown without government subsidies. Entrepreneurship is definitely one thing that Americans know how to do without government help. The SBA should be terminated.

Tennessee Valley Authority

The federally owned TVA is the largest electricity producer in the United States. It is mismanaged, has made poor investment choices, and has built up a gigantic load of debt. Like other bloated monopolies, TVA overspends on luxuries such as lavish employee parties.[225] TVA's policies have resulted in economic distortions similar to those in the four Power Marketing Administrations, including pricing power too low and encouraging overconsumption.

In the 20th century it was thought that government utilities such as TVA were needed because private companies would not find it profitable to electrify rural America. That is irrelevant today because rural areas have been thoroughly electrified. Indeed, 60 percent of rural America is serviced by investor-owned utilities.

TVA should be moved into the 21st century and privatized. Many other countries including Australia, Britain, Canada, and Germany have privatized their electric utilities. TVA privatization would likely improve utility efficiency, and it would reduce overconsumption by allowing prices to be set by supply and demand.

U.S. Postal Service

Fast, reliable, and cost-efficient communication is vital to the business world and today's lifestyles. The government postal service does not provide such communications, nor is it ever likely to. In fact, service at the $69 billion, 768,000-worker USPS has been deteriorating. The average delivery time today for a first-class letter is 1.9 days, up from 1.6 days in 1981, despite all the new technology that is available to the USPS.[226] The GAO has concluded that USPS "has an outdated and inflexible business model amid a rapidly changing postal landscape."[227] The watchdog has put USPS on its high-risk list because of its growing financial and operational difficulties.

Americans have turned to e-mail and private package carriers for their important communications. However, the USPS still holds a legal monopoly on first-class letters, which is an economically damaging restriction and completely unnecessary. Other countries, including Finland, Germany, the Netherlands, New Zealand, and

Sweden, have opened their postal services to competition or privatized their national mail companies.[228] America should be a leader in postal reform, not a laggard. It is time to privatize the USPS and repeal the government monopoly on mail.

Notes

Chapter 1

1. *Budget of the United States Government: Fiscal Year 2006, Historical Tables* (Washington: Government Printing Office, February 2005), p. 76.

2. Congressional Budget Office, "The Budget and Economic Outlook: Fiscal Years 2006 to 2015," January 2005, p. 3.

3. Total federal outlays and nondefense discretionary outlays both increased 16 percent between fiscal years 1989 and 1991. See *Budget of the United States Government: Fiscal Year 2006, Historical Tables*, p. 125.

4. This is my take on Richard Darman's history of the period in Richard Darman, *Who's in Control? Polar Politics and the Sensible Center* (New York: Simon & Schuster, 1996), pp. 200–205, 233–35, 259. Darman expresses concern about deficits and rising entitlement costs, but he seems very uninterested in cutting any particular programs. Leading up to the budget summit, he thought that cuts would be politically unfeasible, so he put little effort into exploring the option.

5. Ibid.

6. For a discussion of budget summits prior to 1990, see Paul Merski, "A Decade of Budget Summitry," Tax Foundation, June 1990.

7. Darman, p. 272.

8. The discretionary budget savings from the summit came mainly from reduced defense spending, but it was phantom savings because the baseline was artificially inflated. That is, everyone expected that defense spending would be cut because of the end of the Cold War regardless of the outcome of the 1990 budget deal. See Allan Schick, "Deficit Budgeting in the Age of Divided Government," in *Fiscal Politics and the Budget Enforcement Act*, ed. Marvin Kosters (Washington: American Enterprise Institute, 1992), p. 25.

9. Nondefense discretionary outlays rose from $214 billion in FY91 to $247 billion in FY93. Spending measured by budget authority rose at the same rate as outlays. See *Budget of the United States Government: Fiscal Year 2006, Historical Tables*, pp. 104, 125. The 1990 budget deal scheduled most of its reductions from baseline in the last two years of the five-year agreement. Defense and nondefense spending were actually boosted in the first year in order to get summit support from big spenders such as Sen. Robert Byrd (D-WV). That said, the discretionary caps, entitlement pay-go rules, and federal credit reforms were useful innovations of the 1990 budget law. For background, see Marvin Kosters, ed., *Fiscal Politics and the Budget Enforcement Act* (Washington: American Enterprise Institute, 1992), pp. xii, 1, 8, 25, 26, 27, 51. See also Martin Feldstein, "Bush's Budget Deal Made the Deficit Bigger," *Wall Street Journal*, November 29, 1990, p. A12.

10. Alice Rivlin and Isabel Sawhill, eds., *Restoring Fiscal Sanity: How to Balance the Budget* (Washington: Brookings Institution, January 2004), p. 7. Brookings updated this study in 2005.

11. This is the value in 2005. The value of the cuts would be $450 billion annually by 2015, based on the growth rate of CBO's baseline discretionary spending.
12. The National Academy of Sciences released a report in February 2004 that found failures "at all levels" in National Zoo management leading to animal deaths, crumbling facilities, and other problems. See Karlyn Barker and James V. Grimaldi, "National Zoo Director Quits over Lapses," *Washington Post*, February 26, 2004, p. A1.
13. Fred Thompson, Preface to "Government at the Brink," by Senate Committee on Government Affairs, vol. 1, p. 1, June 2001, www.senate.gov/~gov_affairs/vol1.pdf.
14. For an introduction to public choice, see Gordon Tullock, Arthur Seldon, and Gordon Brady, *Government Failure: A Primer in Public Choice* (Washington: Cato Institute, 2002).
15. For a brief summary of the issue, see Jonathan Yardley, "Razed in the City," *Washington Post*, June 10, 2004, p. C3.
16. James M. Beck, *Our Wonderland of Bureaucracy* (New York: Macmillan, 1932), p. xiv.

Chapter 2

1. Author's calculations based on data from the *Budget of the United States Government: Fiscal Year 2006, Historical Tables* (Washington: Government Printing Office, February 2005); and U.S. Bureau of the Census, *Historical Statistics of the United States* (Washington: Government Printing Office, 1975). I have used the average of 1949–1951 to represent federal and state/local spending for 1950 because the annual data were quite volatile during that time period.
2. James M. Beck, *Our Wonderland of Bureaucracy* (New York: Macmillan, 1932), pp. 136–46.
3. Sara Kehaulani Goo, "Air Security Agency Faces Reduced Role," *Washington Post*, April 8, 2005, p. A1.
4. Scott Higham and Robert O'Harrow Jr., "The High Cost of a Rush to Security," *Washington Post*, June 20, 2005, p. A1.
5. Associated Press, "Report: Private Airport Screeners Better," April 20, 2005. The story summarizes a GAO report that found that the five airports that use private screeners did a better job of detecting dangerous objects than TSA screeners.
6. *Budget of the United States Government: Fiscal Year 2006, Historical Tables*, p. 76.
7. Data from Congressional Budget Office (CBO), "An Analysis of the President's Budgetary Proposals for Fiscal Year 2006," March 2005. See also CBO, "The Budget and Economic Outlook: Fiscal Years 2006 to 2015," January 2005, www.cbo.gov. Note that all 2005 budget data in this report are estimated, not final.
8. Government Accountability Office, "Fiscal Year 2004 U.S. Government Financial Statements," GAO-05-284T, February 9, 2005.
9. In Figure 2.3, the data for "Transfer Payments and Subsidies" and "Government Purchases" are FY2005 figures from the National Income and Product Accounts. See Bureau of Economic Analysis, *Survey of Current Business* (Washington: Government Printing Office, March 2005), p. 14. The data for regulations are from Clyde Wayne Crews Jr., "Ten Thousand Commandments: An Annual Snapshot of the Federal Regulatory State, 2005 Edition," Competitive Enterprise Institute, July 2005, p. 1. The number of pages of tax rules is the length of the CCH Inc. *Standard Federal Tax Reporter*. All other data in Figure 2.3 are from the *Budget of the United States Government: Fiscal Year 2006*.

10. What I call tentacles, the Urban Institute has called government "tools." See Lester M. Salamon, ed., *Beyond Privatization: The Tools of Government Action* (Washington: Urban Institute Press, 1989). Other tools not discussed here include vouchers, franchises, licenses, control of real estate, publicity, threats of action, and the Federal Reserve Board. Each tool can have subtools. For example, regulation can include price controls, trade restrictions, and other restraints.

11. Based on the page count of the CCH Inc. *Standard Federal Tax Reporter*, which includes the tax code, regulations, and IRS rulings. The page count has risen from 19,500 in 1974 to 61,224 in 2005.

12. Susan Dudley and Melinda Warren, "Upward Trend in Regulation Continues: An Analysis of the U.S. Budget for Fiscal Years 2005 and 2006," Mercatus Center and Weidenbaum Center, June 2005.

13. Lester M. Salamon, "The Changing Tools of Government Action: An Overview," in *Beyond Privatization: The Tools of Government Action*, ed. Lester M. Salamon (Washington: Urban Institute Press, 1989), p. 17.

14. Paul C. Light, "Fact Sheet on the New True Size of Government," Brookings Institution, September 5, 2003, www.brook.edu/gs/cps/light20030905.htm. See also Paul C. Light, *The True Size of Government* (Washington: Brookings Institution Press, 1999).

15. *Budget of the United States Government: Fiscal Year 2006, Analytical Perspectives*, p. 383.

16. For a detailed discussion, see Chris Edwards and John Samples, eds., *The Republican Revolution 10 Years Later: Smaller Government or Business as Usual?* (Washington: Cato Institute, 2005).

17. Tom A. Coburn, M.D., *Breach of Trust: How Washington Turns Outsiders into Insiders* (Nashville: WND Books, 2003).

18. *Budget of the United States Government: Fiscal Year 2006, Historical Tables*, p. 125.

19. Ibid., p. 76.

20. Demian Brady, "The 108th Congress: Rising Floodwaters or a Change in the Tide?" National Taxpayers Union Policy Paper no. 155, May 5, 2005.

21. National Taxpayers Union analysis summarized in "About Face of the Gingrich Brigade," Week in Review, *New York Times*, February 13, 2005.

22. Hearing testimony available at http://agriculture.senate.gov/Hearings/hearings.cfm?hearingId=1413.

23. Paul H. Douglas, *Economy in the National Government* (Chicago: University of Chicago Press, 1952), p. 59.

24. Note that a simple solution to this problem would be random assignment of members to committees. Thus, for example, House and Senate agriculture committees would end up with a mix of members from both urban and rural regions, which would bring balance to the deliberations.

25. Quoted in Robert Novak, "A Bill Full of Pork," April 5, 2004, www.townhall.com/columnists/robertnovak/rn20040405.shtml.

26. Jeffrey Birnbaum, "Boeing Has a Powerful Ally with Hastert," *Washington Post*, July 18, 2004, p. A10.

27. Ibid.

28. Robert Novak, "The Speaker Makes a Call," *Washington Post*, June 21, 2004, p. A19.

29. Dan Morgan, "Hastert Directs Millions to Birthplace," *Washington Post*, May 29, 2005, p. A1.

30. One example was the exaggeration in a 2005 report by the head of the Centers for Disease Control regarding the number of obesity-related deaths in the United States, a problem she compared with the plague in the Middle Ages. Subsequent analysis by the CDC found that the number given was four times too high. See Dan Seligman, "Flabby Math," *Forbes*, June 20, 2005, p. 140.

31. Christopher Lee, "Prepackaged News Gets GAO Rebuke," *Washington Post*, February 21, 2005, p. A25.

Chapter 3

1. In *United States v. Lopez*, 514 U.S. 549 (1995), Chief Justice William Rehnquist stated: "We start with first principles. The Constitution establishes a government of enumerated powers."

2. Roger Pilon, "Congress, the Courts, and the Constitution," *Cato Handbook on Policy*, 6th ed. (Washington: Cato Institute, 2005), p. 27.

3. *Lopez*.

4. *Gonzales v. Raich*, 545 U.S. ____ (2005).

5. Pilon, "Congress, the Courts, and the Constitution," p. 26.

6. *Schechter Poultry Corp. v. United States*, 295 U.S. 495 (1935). The case involved the New Deal's National Industrial Recovery Act.

7. *United States v. Butler*, 297 U.S. 1 (1936).

8. Roger Pilon, *The Purpose and Limits of Government*, Cato's Letter no. 13 (Washington: Cato Institute, 1999).

9. Bob Drogin and Greg Miller, "Panel Faults CIA's Spying," *Los Angeles Times*, June 24, 2004, p. 1.

10. Jon Kyl, Republican senator from Arizona, "Visa Reform: For More Controls," *Washington Post*, June 20, 2004, p. A21.

11. Eric Lichtblau, "9/11 Report Cites Many Warnings about Hijackings," *New York Times*, February 10, 2005, p. A1.

12. Dan Eggen, "Computer Woes Hinder FBI's Work, Report Says," *Washington Post*, February 4, 2005, p. A15.

13. This was the report of the bipartisan Advisory Commission on Intergovernmental Relations, cited in Michael Greve, "Big Government Federalism," American Enterprise Institute Federalism Outlook, March 1, 2001.

14. Dana Milbank and Paul Blustein, "White House Aided Enron in Dispute," *Washington Post*, January 19, 2002, p. A1.

15. Ibid. The two federal agencies providing loans were the Export-Import Bank and the Overseas Private Investment Corporation.

16. Dan Eggen, "GAO Criticizes System for Tracking Terrorists," *Washington Post*, April 30, 2003, p. A21.

17. John Mintz, "DHS Blamed for Failure to Combine Watch Lists," *Washington Post*, October 2, 2004, p. A2.

18. See Christopher Lee, "GAO Report Points to Pentagon Waste," *Washington Post*, January 26, 2005, p. A19. See also "Post-9/11 Reforms Haven't Fixed Intelligence Failings," editorial, *USA Today*, April 16, 2004.

19. Dana Priest, "Congressional Oversight of Intelligence Criticized," *Washington Post*, April 27, 2004, p. A1.

20. Victoria Toensing, "Oversee? More Like Overlook," op-ed, *Washington Post*, June 13, 2004.

21. Ibid.

22. Robert J. Samuelson, "Economic Death Spiral," *Washington Post*, April 6, 2005, p. A19.

23. *2005 Annual Report of the Board of Trustees of the Federal Old-Age and Survivors Insurance and Disability Insurance Trust Funds* (Washington: Government Printing Office, April 5, 2005), p. 77. These are the intermediate assumptions.

24. Congressional Budget Office (CBO), "The Budget and Economic Outlook: Fiscal Years 2006 to 2015," January 2005, p. 52.

25. *2005 Annual Report of the Board of Trustees of the Federal Old-Age and Survivors Insurance and Disability Insurance Trust Funds*, p. 166. These are the intermediate assumptions.

26. Martin Feldstein, "Prefunding Medicare," National Bureau of Economic Research (NBER) Working Paper no. 6917, January 1999, p. 4.

27. Government Accountability Office (GAO), "21st Century Challenges: Reexamining the Base of the Federal Government," GAO-05-325SP, February 2005, Figure 2, p. 8.

28. GAO, "Fiscal Year 2004 U.S. Government Financial Statements," GAO-05-284T, February 9, 2005, p. 6.

29. Ibid.

30. For a general discussion, see Chris Edwards, "Economic Benefits of Personal Income Tax Rate Reductions," U.S. Congress, Joint Economic Committee, April 2001. For particular estimates, see Edgar Browning, "On the Marginal Welfare Cost of Taxation," *American Economic Review* 77 (March 1987): 11–23; and Martin Feldstein, "Tax Avoidance and the Deadweight Loss of the Income Tax," NBER Working Paper no. 5055, March 1995.

31. CBO, "Budget Options," February 2001, p. 381. For substantially higher estimates, see William Niskanen, "The Economic Burden of Taxation," paper presented at a conference at the Federal Reserve Bank of Dallas, Dallas, Texas, October 22–23, 2003.

32. Martin Feldstein, "How Big Should Government Be?" *National Tax Journal* 50, no. 2 (June 1997): 197–213.

33. Michael Boskin, "A Framework for the Tax Reform Debate," in *Frontiers of Tax Reform*, ed. Michael Boskin (Stanford: Hoover Institution, 1996), p. 14.

34. For an overview of public goods theory, see Harvey Rosen, *Public Finance*, 6th ed. (New York: McGraw-Hill Irwin, 2002), p. 55.

35. A recent illustration of how politicians like to intervene on sexy issues regards Wi-Fi Internet services. Governments in more than 50 cities, including Philadelphia and Minneapolis, are setting up free-access Wi-Fi. But there is no evidence that any market failure has occurred. Indeed, free Wi-Fi has popped up at private businesses, such as coffee shops, across the country.

36. This quote is from *Compania General de Tabacos de Filipinas v. Collector of Internal Revenue*, 275 U.S. 87 (1927).

Chapter 4

1. For ease of presentation, I've included a few entitlement programs in this total and in Table 4.2. In particular, direct farm subsidies and some housing and education programs are considered entitlement spending.

2. The dollar figures in Table 4.2 are the estimated 2005 outlays from the *Budget of the United States Government: Fiscal Year 2006* (Washington: Government Printing

Office, 2005). However, the figures for defense troop level cuts and cuts to weapons systems are the author's estimates (see Appendix 2). The figure for closing military bases is from various media reports. As explained in the previous endnote, Table 4.2 includes not only discretionary programs but also a few entitlement programs.

3. Stephen Moore and Stephen Slivinski, "The Return of the Living Dead: Federal Programs That Survived the Republican Revolution," Cato Institute Policy Analysis no. 375, July 24, 2000.

4. The budget plan targets Social Security, Medicare, and Medicaid, but there are numerous smaller entitlement programs that should also be reformed.

5. Cost figures for the first three options in Table 4.3 are based on data in Congressional Budget Office (CBO), "Budget Options," February 2005. See options 650-06, 570-13, and 570-17. The fourth option is an estimate by the author.

6. CBO, "The Budget and Economic Outlook: Fiscal Years 2006 to 2015," January 2005, p. 52.

7. Ibid., p. 131.

8. Calculations for the figure incorporate standard adjustments for changed federal interest costs as a result of changes in the budget deficit and debt. Those adjustments are estimated by the author on the basis of federal debt and interest rate data in CBO, "An Analysis of the President's Budgetary Proposals for Fiscal Year 2006," March 2005.

9. Note that the dollar value of these cuts is measured against CBO's baseline, not the business-as-usual projection. The cut value would be larger if measured against the business-as-usual scenario. I have adjusted the CBO baseline to include their January 2005 estimate of continued operations in Iraq.

10. The value of $380 billion in 2005 would grow to $450 billion by 2015, based on the growth rate in CBO's baseline for all discretionary programs. I have phased in the cuts one-tenth, or $45 billion, per year. Thus, spending under the reform plan in 2015 would be the CBO baseline spending of that year, adjusted for Iraq and interest costs, less $450 billion from Table 4.2 cuts, less $270 billion in Table 4.3 cuts, and less interest savings.

11. CBO, "An Analysis of the President's Budgetary Proposals for Fiscal Year 2006." The revenue projection includes extension of current tax cuts, AMT reform, and repeal of the gasoline tax.

12. The projections for "spending: business as usual" and "spending: with proposed cuts" are also adjusted to include CBO's estimates of a phase-down of Iraq war costs that are not included in the baseline. See CBO, "The Budget and Economic Outlook: Fiscal Years 2006 to 2015," p. 8.

13. Again adjusted for Iraq war costs.

Chapter 5

1. Steven Davis and John Haltiwanger, "Gross Job Flows," in *Handbook of Labor Economics*, ed. Orley Ashenfelter and David Card (Amsterdam: Elsevier Science, 1999), vol. 3. See also Chris Edwards, "Sunsetting to Reform and Abolish Federal Agencies," Cato Institute Tax & Budget Bulletin no. 6, May 2003.

2. See, for example, William Spangar Peirce, *Bureaucratic Failure and Public Expenditure* (New York: Academic Press, 1981), chap. 5.

3. Paul H. Douglas, *Economy in the National Government* (Chicago: University of Chicago Press, 1952), p. 74.

4. James M. Beck, *Our Wonderland of Bureaucracy* (New York: Macmillan, 1932), p. 260.

5. Ibid., p. 228.

6. Government Accountability Office (GAO), "High-Risk Series: An Update," GAO-05-207, January 2005.

7. Christopher Lee, "Agencies Getting Heavier on Top," *Washington Post*, July 23, 2004, p. A27.

8. Sean Mussenden, "NASA Pork Feeds Hometown Projects," *Orlando Sentinel*, March 3, 2003.

9. Renae Merle, "Military Jet Faces a Fight to Fit In," *Washington Post*, April 19, 2005, p. E1. Note that it is not true that defense contracts are "economic engines" of the U.S. economy. As discussed in Chapter 3, federal spending simply displaces private spending that would otherwise take place.

10. Shailagh Murray, "$82 Billion Bill Advances with War Funds, Add-Ons," *Washington Post*, May 4, 2005, p. A4.

11. CBS News, "Medicare Claims Errors Cost $20B," December 14, 2004, www.cbsnews.com.

12. Nathan Vardi, "Rx for Fraud," *Forbes*, June 20, 2005, p. 124.

13. GAO, "Federal Budget: Opportunities for Oversight and Improved Use of Taxpayer Funds," GAO-03-922T, June 18, 2003, p. 9.

14. Clifford J. Levy and Michael Luo, "New York Medical Fraud May Reach into Billions," *New York Times*, July 18, 2005, p. A1.

15. Michelle Higgins, "Getting Poor on Purpose," *Wall Street Journal*, February 25, 2003, p. D1. The story noted that up to 22 percent of Medicaid's $47 billion in annual benefits goes illegally to well-heeled seniors.

16. Michael Powell and Michelle Garcia, "Ground Zero Funds Often Drifted Uptown," *Washington Post*, May 22, 2004, p. A1.

17. "FEMA Blamed for Abuse in Air Conditioner Fund," Washington in Brief, *Washington Post*, November 2, 2004, p. A5.

18. GAO, "Federal Budget," p. 22.

19. Cheryl Wetzstein, "Cities Seek Head Start Oversight," *Washington Times*, April 6, 2005, p. A4.

20. "GAO Cites Overpayments on Disability Benefits," Washington in Brief, *Washington Post*, October 19, 2004, p. A2.

21. Brian Faler, "Farm Subsidy Rules Called Too Vague; Money Going to Undeserving, GAO Says," *Washington Post*, July 1, 2004, p. A21.

22. GAO, "Federal Budget," p. 17.

23. Mimi Hall, "Report Faults FEMA on Aid," *USA Today*, May 18, 2005, p. 1A.

24. GAO, "Federal Budget," p. 13.

25. For further examples, see Fred Thompson, Preface to "Government at the Brink," by Senate Committee on Government Affairs, vol. 1, June 2001, pp. 4, 31, www.senate.gov/~gov_affairs/vol1.pdf.

26. Senate Committee on Government Affairs, "Government at the Brink," vol. 2, p. 59.

27. "Living Well off the Poor," editorial, *Washington Post*, April 25, 2004. One-third of United Planning Organization's budget is funded by the federal Community Service Block Grant.

28. *Budget of the United States Government: Fiscal Year 2005, Appendix* (Washington: Government Printing Office, February 2004), p. 858.

29. R. Jeffrey Smith, "E-Mails Detail Air Force Push for Boeing Deal," *Washington Post*, June 7, 2005, p. A1.

30. R. Jeffrey Smith, "U.S. Deal to Lease Tankers Criticized," *Washington Post*, April 1, 2004, p. B1.

31. Chuck Neubauer and Richard T. Cooper, "As Alaska Business Ventures Benefited, So Did Stevens," *Washington Post*, December 19, 2003, p. A35 (originally appeared in the *Los Angeles Times*).

32. Ibid.

33. Robert O'Harrow Jr. and Scott Higham, "Alaska Native Corporations Cash In on Contracting Edge," *Washington Post*, November 25, 2004, p. A1.

34. GAO, "Federal Assistance: Grant System Continues to Be Highly Fragmented," GAO-03-718T, April 29, 2003, pp. 6, 7. See also GAO, "Multiple Employment and Training Programs," GAO-03-589, April 2003, p. 2.

35. Senate Committee on Government Affairs, vol. 1, pp. 54–67.

36. SRI International for the Federal Home Loan Bank of Des Moines, "Capitalizing on Rural America," April 2005, www.fhlbdm.com/Docs/About_Us/PF/SRIReport_FINAL.pdf. The report did a count of programs listed by the Rural Information Center at http://grande.nal.usda.gov/ric/funding.php.

37. *Budget of the United States Government: Fiscal Year 2006, Analytical Perspectives*, p. 181.

38. Steven Radelet, "The Millennium Challenge Account," Testimony to the Senate Foreign Relations Committee, March 4, 2003, p. 5.

39. Ibid.

40. A nice summary of the past failures of foreign aid is found in Fredrik Erixon, "Aid and Development: Will It Work This Time?" International Policy Network, London, June 2005, www.policynetwork.net.

41. Murray, p. A4.

42. *Budget of the United States Government: Fiscal Yeac 2006, Analytical Perspectives*, p. 86.

43. Venture capital barely existed 30 years ago, but the industry blossomed as a result of two key policy changes. First, the rules for pension funds were loosened in 1978 to allow higher-risk investments. Second, the capital gains tax rate was cut from 49 percent to 28 percent in 1978 and to 20 percent in 1981. See Chris Edwards, "Entrepreneurial Dynamism and the Success of U.S. High-Tech," U.S. Congress, Joint Economic Committee, October 1999.

44. Paul Light, "Still Searching for Airport Security," *Washington Post*, April 24, 2005, p. B2.

45. John Stuart Mill, *Representative Government*, 1861, http://books.mirror.org/gb.mill.html.

46. Ariana Eunjung Cha, "Finding Support in the Search for E.T.," *Washington Post*, May 30, 2005, p. A1.

47. Guy Gugliotta, "DeLay's Push Helps Deliver NASA Funds," *Washington Post*, December 6, 2004, p. A1.

48. Ronald Bailey, "The Monopoly That Blocks the Way to Mars," *Wall Street Journal*, January 20, 2004, p. D7.

49. Howard Husock, "Let's End Housing Vouchers," *City Journal*, Autumn 2000, www.city-journal.org.

50. Chris Edwards, "Sunsetting to Reform and Abolish Federal Agencies," Cato Institute Tax & Budget Bulletin no. 6, May 2003.

51. Davis and Haltiwanger.

52. Amy E. Knaup, "Survival and Longevity in the Business Employment Dynamics Data," *Monthly Labor Review* (Bureau of Labor Statistics), May 2005, p. 50.

53. GAO, "Major Management Challenges and Program Risks: Department of Defense," GAO-01-244, January 2001. For a more recent assessment, see GAO, "High-Risk Series: An Update," January 2005.

54. Griff Witte, "Pentagon Wasted Supplies, GAO Finds," *Washington Post*, June 8, 2005, p. D1.

55. GAO, "High-Risk Series: An Update," January 2005. See highlights for "Department of Defense Financial Management."

56. John Mintz, "Probe Faults System for Monitoring U.S. Borders," *Washington Post*, April 11, 2005, p. A1.

57. Ibid.

58. John Mintz "Border Camera System Is Assailed," *Washington Post*, June 17, 2005, p. A29.

59. Eric Lipton, "U.S. to Spend Billions More to Alter Security Systems," *New York Times*, May 8, 2005, p. 1.

60. Ibid. The *Times* cites the Department of Homeland Security's inspector general on this point.

61. John Mintz, "Border Patrol Cited for Inaction on Kickbacks," *Washington Post*, June 1, 2005, p. A2.

62. William E. Odom, "Why the FBI Can't Be Reformed," op-ed, *Washington Post*, June 29, 2005, p. A21.

63. Ibid.

64. See Peter Lance, *1000 Years for Revenge: International Terrorism and the FBI— The Untold Story* (New York: Harper Collins-Regan Books, 2003).

65. Quoted in Dan Eggen, "'Pre-9/11 Missteps by FBI Detailed," *Washington Post*, June 10, 2005, p. A1.

66. House Select Committee on U.S. National Security and Military/Commercial Concerns with the People's Republic of China, House Report 105-851, May 25, 1999, p. v.

67. Ibid., p. x.

68. Cited in Senate Committee on Government Reform, vol. 2, pp. 30, 31.

69. NASA, *Columbia Accident Investigation Board* (Washington: NASA, August 2003), vol. 1, pp. 170, 180, 185, www.caib.us.

70. GAO, "Space Station: Actions Underway to Manage Costs but Significant Challenges Remain," GAO-02-735, July 17, 2002, p. 1.

71. GAO, "NASA: Compliance with Cost Limits," GAO-04-648R, April 2, 2004.

72. The issue regards the *Cobell v. Babbitt* case filed in 1996, which is currently on appeal. For background and documents, see www.indiantrust.com.

73. Thomas Slonaker, Testimony before the Senate Committee on Indian Affairs, September 24, 2002.

74. Paul Homan, Testimony before the Senate Committee on Indian Affairs, September 24, 2002.

75. Carol Leonnig, "Interior Dept. Is Denounced," *Washington Post*, April 7, 2004, p. A7.

76. Eric Pianin and Christopher Lee, "Corps of Engineers Chief Drafts Plan to Reorganize Agency," *Washington Post*, September 24, 2003, p. A27. See also Michael

Grunwald and Mike Allen, "Corps of Engineers' Civilian Chief Ousted," *Washington Post*, March 7, 2002, p. A1.

77. Michael Grunwald, "Army Corps Delays Study over Flawed Forecasts," *Washington Post*, October 5, 2000, p. A33.

78. Michael Grunwald, "Army Corps Suspends Del. River Project," *Washington Post*, April 24, 2002, p. A27.

79. Douglas, p. 105.

80. Chris Edwards, "Government Schemes Cost More Than Promised," Cato Institute Tax & Budget Bulletin no. 17, September 2003.

81. For background, see Alan Altshuler and David Luberoff, *Megaprojects* (Washington: Brookings Institution Press, 2003).

82. Michael Shear, "Springfield Interchange Project Is Defended," *Washington Post*, November 26, 2002, p. B1.

83. Senate Committee on Government Affairs, vol. 2, p. 108.

84. GAO, "Cost and Oversight of Major Highway and Bridge Projects: Issues and Options," GAO-03-764T, May 8, 2003, p. 6.

85. Altshuler and Luberoff, p. 167.

86. See the *Boston Globe*'s "Easy Pass" series of reports by Raphael Lewis and Sean Murphy, www.boston.com/globe/metro/packages/bechtel.

87. Ibid.

88. Reuters, "Cost Increases, Delays Cited in FAA Programs," *Washington Post*, June 1, 2005, p. A17.

89. Ibid.

90. Sara Kehaulani Goo, "DOT Says Air Traffic Overhaul Is Flawed," *Washington Post*, November 20, 2004, p. E5.

91. GAO, "Department of Energy: Status of Contract and Project Management Reforms," GAO-03-570T, March 20, 2003.

92. Cited in Senate Committee on Government Affairs, vol. 2, p. 31.

93. GAO, "Department of Energy."

94. Defense items in the cost overrun table based on author calculations and GAO, "Defense Acquisitions: Assessments of Major Weapon Programs," GAO-03-476, May 15, 2003. For the spy satellite, see Dana Priest, "New Spy Satellite Debated on Hill," *Washington Post*, December 11, 2004, p. A1. For the laser anti-missile system, see Bradley Graham, "Pentagon Laser Project Exceeds Cost Estimates, GAO Says," *Washington Post*, May 19, 2004, p. A9.

95. Senate Committee on Government Affairs, vol. 1, pp. 37–47.

96. Paul de la Garza and Stephen Nohlgren, "VA Yanks Troubled Computer System," *St. Petersburg Times*, July 27, 2004.

97. Stephen Barr, "Federal Diary," *Washington Post*, March 10, 2005, p. B2.

98. Curt Anderson, "FBI Nears Completion of Computer Upgrade," Associated Press, March 26, 2004.

99. Jonathan Krin, "FBI Rejects Its New Case File Software," *Washington Post*, January 14, 2005, p. A5. See also Griff Witte, "FBI Outlines Plans for Computer System," *Washington Post*, June 9, 2005, p. A19.

100. Christopher Lee and Spencer Hsu, "GAO Cites Capitol Facility's Costs, Delays," *Washington Post*, November 30, 2004, p. A1.

101. GAO, "Capitol Visitor Center: Current Status of Schedule and Estimated Cost," GAO-03-1014T, July 15, 2003.

102. Jacqueline Trescott, "GAO Cites Cost Overruns at Kennedy Center," *Washington Post*, April 6, 2005, p. C1.

103. The $614 million is a *Washington Post* estimate. David Nakamura, "New Baseball Cost Study Could Take 5 Months," *Washington Post*, December 5, 2004, p. C1.

104. Stanley Engerman and Kenneth Sokoloff, "Digging the Dirt at Public Expense: Governance in the Building of the Erie Canal and Other Public Works," NBER Working Paper no. 10965, December 2004.

105. Edwards, "Government Schemes Cost More Than Promised."

106. Amy Goldstein, "Official Says He Was Told to Withhold Medicare Data," *Washington Post*, March 13, 2004, p. A1.

107. R. Jeffrey Smith, "E-Mails Detail Air Force Push for Boeing Deal," *Washington Post*, June 7, 2005, p. A1.

108. Bent Flyvbjerg, Mette Skamris Holm, and Søren Buhl, "Underestimating Cost in Public Works Projects: Error or Lie?" *Journal of the American Planning Association* 68, no. 3 (Summer 2002).

109. Ibid., p. 281.

110. Howard Husock, "Let's End Housing Vouchers," *City Journal*, Autumn 2000, www.city-journal.org.

111. Ibid.

112. Quoted in Michael A. Fletcher, "Worry over Public Housing," *Washington Post*, June 26, 2005, p. A3.

113. *Budget of the United States Government: Fiscal Year 2005, Appendix*, p. 147.

114. "Message from the Deputy Administrator," USDA's Economic and Community Systems program, www.reeusda.gov/ecs/ecs.htm.

115. *Budget of the United States Government: Fiscal Year 2005, Analytical Perspectives*, p. 54.

116. *Budget of the United States Government: Fiscal Year 2006, Analytical Perspectives*, p. 12.

117. See "The President's Management Agenda," www.whitehouse.gov/results/agenda/scorecard.html.

118. GAO, "Fiscal Year 2003 U.S. Government Financial Statements," GAO-04-477T, March 3, 2004, p. 13.

119. John Mintz, "Infighting Cited at Homeland Security," *Washington Post*, February 2, 2005, p. A1.

120. Scott Higham and Robert O'Harrow Jr., "Contracting Rush for Security Led to Waste, Abuse," *Washington Post*, May 22, 2005, p. A1.

121. "Homeland Security Oversight," editorial, *Washington Post*, December 28, 2004, p. A18.

122. Quoted in Christopher Shays and Carolyn Maloney, "Congress, Reorganize Yourself," *Washington Post*, December 22, 2004.

123. Christopher Lee and Stephen Barr, "Pentagon to Retool Personnel System," *Washington Post*, February 10, 2005, p. A1.

124. Stephen Barr, "Those Pesky People Issues Just Won't Go Away," *Washington Post*, October 3, 2004, p. C2.

125. Cited in Stephen Barr, "Doubts about Leadership Find an Outlet in Survey," *Washington Post*, May 22, 2005, p. C2.

126. Cited in Christopher Lee, "In Survey, Most Workers Are Critical of Management," *Washington Post*, May 20, 2005, p. A19.

127. Office of Personnel Management, "A Fresh Start for Federal Pay: The Case for Modernization," April 2002, p. 17.

128. Chris Edwards and Tad DeHaven, "Federal Government Should Increase Firing Rate," Cato Institute Tax & Budget Bulletin no. 10, November 2002. Data updated from OPM e-mail to author, July 22, 2005. These firing data come from the Office of Personnel Management's central personnel data file, which includes employee removals for poor performance under Title 5, Code of Federal Regulations, Parts 432 and 752. Reforms in 1978 added Part 432 to make firing easier, but removals continue to be rare.

129. In the early 1950s, Sen. Paul Douglas complained that the federal firing rate was just 0.6 percent. See Douglas, p. 77.

130. Walter Pincus, "Analysts behind Iraq Intelligence Were Rewarded," Washington Post, May 28, 2005, p. A1.

131. Edwards and DeHaven. Involuntary separations include firing and layoffs.

132. Richard Morin, "The Spillover Effect," Washington Post, August 18, 2002, p. B5.

133. Office of Personnel Management, "Poor Performers in Government: A Quest for a True Story," January 1999, p. 28.

134. Ibid., p. 1.

135. Ibid., pp. 3, 11.

136. K. C. Swanson, "No Way Out," GovExec.com, November 1, 1996.

137. Merit Systems Protection Board, "Federal Supervisors and Poor Performers," July 1999, p. 12.

138. Christopher Lee and Hal Straus, "Two-Thirds of Federal Workers Get a Bonus," Washington Post, May 17, 2004, p. A1.

139. Office of Personnel Management, p. 10.

140. Ellen Nakashimu, "BIA Official Fired Amid Probes of Influence Peddling," Washington Post, May 25, 2002, p. A5.

141. Merit Systems Protection Board, p. 8.

142. Brookings Institution survey of federal workers summarized in Ben White, "Poor Work Tolerated, Employees Say," Washington Post, October 30, 2001, p. A19.

143. Josh White and Bardley Graham, "Senators Question Absence of Blame in Abuse Report," Washington Post, March 11, 2005, p. 17.

144. These failures were the conclusions of two U.S. Army reports. See Josh White and Thomas Ricks, "Top Brass Won't Be Charged over Abuse," Washington Post, August 27, 2004, p. A17.

145. "Impunity," editorial, Washington Post, April 26, 2005, p. A14.

Chapter 6

1. Joe Scarborough, Rome Wasn't Burnt in a Day (New York, HarperCollins, 2004), p. 163.

2. Ibid.

3. For a discussion, see Tom A. Coburn, Breach of Trust: How Washington Turns Outsiders into Insiders (Nashville: WND Books, 2003), p. 98.

4. Vito Tanzi, "A Lower Tax Future? The Economic Role of the State in the 21st Century," Politeia (London), 2004, p. 7, www.politeia.co.uk.

5. Ibid.

6. "Democracy at Any Price," Survey on the Future of the State, The Economist, September 18, 1997, www.economist.com/surveys.

7. Mark McClellan and Jonathan Skinner, "The Incidence of Medicare," National Bureau of Economic Research (NBER) Working Paper no. 6013, April 1997, p. 47. The authors temper this conclusion by noting that the insurance value of Medicare is probably higher than the dollar transfers suggest.

8. Julia Lynn Coronado, Don Fullerton, and Thomas Glass, "The Progressivity of Social Security," NBER Working Paper no. 7520, February 2000.

9. See USDA, Economic Research Service, "Farm Income and Costs: Farm Income Forecasts," February 11, 2005, www.ers.usda.gov/Briefing/FarmIncome/Data/Hh_t5.htm.

10. See various reports from the Environmental Working Group at www.ewg.org. This group has constructed a detailed database of farm subsidy recipients.

11. Jennifer Cheeseman Day and Eric C. Newburger, "The Big Payoff: Educational Attainment and Synthetic Estimates of Work-Life Earnings," Special Studies, U.S. Bureau of the Census, July 2002. Also note that government data on average earnings show that those with college degrees earn roughly twice what those with just high school diplomas do.

12. A 1983 book by University of Chicago political scientist Benjamin Page concluded that the federal government as a whole redistributes income much less than usually thought. He noted that numerous transfer programs, such as Medicare, unemployment insurance, and government employee pensions, are not directed at the poor. Also, spending on public goods, such as defense and the environment, is probably proportional in its distributional impact. Benjamin I. Page, *Who Gets What from Government* (Berkeley: University of California Press, 1983).

13. Congressional Budget Office, "Reducing Entitlement Spending," September 1994, p. 28, www.cbo.gov/ftpdocs/48xx/doc4849/doc47.pdf.

14. Chris Edwards and Tad DeHaven, "Corporate Welfare Update," Cato Institute Tax & Budget Bulletin no. 7, May 2002.

15. U.S. Department of Agriculture, "USDA Announces Funds to Promote U.S. Food and Agricultural Products Overseas," news release, June 17, 2004, www.fas.usda.gov/scriptsw/PressRelease/pressrel_dout.asp?Entry=valid&PrNum=0112-04.

16. "What Associations Paid Their Chiefs," *National Journal*, February 21, 2004, p. 533.

17. Risk Management Agency, "About the Risk Management Agency," June 2003, www.rma.usda.gov/aboutrma/.

18. The Export-Import Bank loaned Enron $650 million, and the Overseas Private Investment Corporation loaned Enron $750 million. See Neil King Jr., "Questioning the Books: Senator Urges a Probe of Enron and Ex-Im Bank," *Wall Street Journal*, April 3, 2002, p. C1.

19. North American Development Bank, Community Adjustment and Investment Program, *Newsletter* 3, no. 1 (June 2003), www.dcci.com/caip/.

20. Michael Schroeder, "Sugar Growers Hold Up Push for Free Trade," *Wall Street Journal*, February 3, 2004.

21. Laurent Belsie, "Bitter Reality: Candy Less Likely to Be 'Made in US,'" *Christian Science Monitor*, April 8, 2002.

22. John Porretto, "Lott: Cruise Ship Loss May Top $200M," Associated Press, January 12, 2002.

23. Cited in Jeffrey Ball, "Car Makers Split over Timing of Hydrogen-Powered Vehicles," *Wall Street Journal*, February 26, 2004, p. B1.

Chapter 7

1. Susan Dudley and Melinda Warren, "Upward Trend in Regulation Continues: An Analysis of the U.S. Budget for Fiscal Years 2005 and 2006," Mercatus Center and Weidenbaum Center, June 2005.

2. Clyde Wayne Crews Jr., "Ten Thousand Commandments: An Annual Snapshot of the Federal Regulatory State, 2005 Edition," Competitive Enterprise Institute, July 2005, p. 1.

3. For a summary of the Duke University findings, see Christopher J. Conover, "Health Care Regulation: A $169 Billion Hidden Tax," Cato Institute Policy Analysis no. 527, October 2, 2004. The author is an assistant research professor at Duke.

4. U.S. trade protection is estimated to create annual costs to U.S. consumers of roughly 1 percent of gross domestic product. Some estimates are higher. For example, see Howard Wall, "Using the Gravity Model to Estimate the Costs of Protection," *Federal Reserve Bank of St. Louis Review*, January–February 1999, p. 33.

5. For background on antidumping law, see Brink Lindsey and Dan Ikenson, *Antidumping Exposed: The Devilish Details of Unfair Trade Law* (Washington: Cato Institute, 2003).

6. See Sebastian Mallaby, "A Fishy Approach to Fair Trade," *Washington Post*, March 29, 2004, p. A23.

7. Robert W. Crandall and Clifford Winston, "Does Antitrust Policy Improve Consumer Welfare? Assessing the Evidence," *Journal of Economic Perspectives* 17, no. 4 (Fall 2003): 4.

8. Richard Rahn, "Markets and Monopolies," op-ed, *Washington Times*, January 9, 2004.

9. Discussed in Chris Edwards, "Entrepreneurial Dynamism and the Success of U.S. High-Tech," U.S. Congress, Joint Economic Committee, October 1999, p. 13.

10. Gary Anthes, "What Microsoft Could Learn from U.S. vs. IBM," *Computerworld*, March 2, 1998.

11. This is a guesstimate from Crandall and Winston.

12. "Blocking Blockbuster," editorial, *Wall Street Journal*, March 30, 2005. The *Journal* says that the FTC prodded Blockbuster to drop its planned bid for Hollywood in 2005 and also blocked the same merger back in 1999.

13. Jim Powell, *FDR's Folly: How Roosevelt and His New Deal Prolonged the Great Depression* (New York: Crown Forum, 2003), p. 236.

14. Crews. This is the number of pages in the *Federal Register*.

15. Henry Miller, "Dying for FDA Reform," op-ed, *Washington Times*, March 10, 2004.

16. Dr. David Gratzer, "Wanted: Leadership at the FDA," March 2, 2004, www.nationalreview.com.

17. Doug Bandow summarizes the research in "Demonizing Drugmakers: The Political Assault on the Pharmaceutical Industry," Cato Institute Policy Analysis no. 475, May 8, 2003, pp. 32–35.

18. Conover, p. 15.

19. Robert Higgs, "Wrecking Ball: FDA Regulation of Medical Devices," Cato Institute Policy Analysis no. 235, August 7, 1995. See also Charles Homsy, "How FDA Regulation and Injury Litigation Cripple the Medical Device Industry," Cato Institute Policy Analysis no. 412, August 28, 2001.

20. See www.abigail-alliance.org.

21. For such a reform proposal, see Bartley J. Madden, "Breaking the FDA Monopoly," *Regulation*, Summer 2004, p. 64.

22. Patrick J. Michaels, "A DEA Crackdown That's Going to Hurt Those in Pain," op-ed, *Washington Post*, February 29, 2004, p. B2.

23. "Federal Assault on Painkiller Abuse Makes Patients Suffer," editorial, *USA Today*, March 11, 2004.

24. Howard Husock, "How Public Housing Harms Cities," *City Journal*, Winter 2003, www.city-journal.org. See also Howard Husock, "Let's End Housing Vouchers," *City Journal*, Autumn 2000.

25. In its FY2004 budget, the administration proposed turning Section 8 into a block grant. In its FY2005 budget, the administration proposed bypassing the states and giving lump-sum payments directly to local governments. See Amy Goldstein, "Bush Aims to Localize Rent Aid," *Washington Post*, April 13, 2004, p. A1.

26. The Congressional Budget Office (CBO) finds that the Forest Service spends more on the timber program than it charges to companies harvesting timber, which may cause excessive depletion of timber and destruction of forests that have recreational value. See CBO, "Budget Options," February 2005, p. 97.

27. Blaine Harden, "Reopening Forest Areas Stirs Debate in Alaska," *Washington Post*, August 1, 2004, p. A3.

28. Southeast Alaska Conservation Council, *How Tongass Rainforest Logging Costs Taxpayers Millions* (Juneau: Southeast Alaska Conservation Council, 2003), p. 3.

29. For a discussion of reforms for the PMAs and TVA, see CBO, pp. 84–87.

30. Eric Pianin and Christopher Lee, "Corps of Engineers Chief Drafts Plan to Reorganize Agency," *Washington Post*, September 24, 2003, p. A27. See also Michael Grunwald and Mike Allen, "Corps of Engineers' Civilian Chief Ousted," *Washington Post*, March 7, 2002, p. A1.

31. James V. Grimaldi, "Enron Pipeline Leaves Scar on South America," *Washington Post*, May 6, 2002, p. A1.

32. Ibid.

33. Jim Carlton, "Is Water Too Cheap?" *Wall Street Journal*, March 17, 2004, p. B1. See also Green Scissors Campaign, "Green Scissors 2003: Cutting Wasteful & Environmentally Harmful Spending," May 8, 2003, www.greenscissors.com, pp. 14, 25.

34. U.S. Department of the Interior, Bureau of Reclamation, "Animas–La Plata Project Construction Cost Estimates," November 26, 2003.

35. The Green Scissors Campaign annual report is a good place to find pro-green budget reforms. See www.greenscissors.com.

Chapter 8

1. James M. Beck, *Our Wonderland of Bureaucracy* (New York: Macmillan, 1932), p. 223.

2. *Budget of the United States Government: Fiscal Year 2006, Analytical Perspectives* (Washington: Government Printing Office, February 2005), p. 131. For general background on federal grants, see Government Accountability Office (GAO), "Federal Assistance: Grant System Continues to Be Highly Fragmented," GAO-03-718T, April 29, 2003.

3. Ibid.

4. Office of Management and Budget (OMB), Budget Analysis and Systems Division, "The Number of Federal Grant Programs to State and Local Governments, 1980–2004," April 8, 2005. In addition, the OMB analysis found 298 other grant programs that were aimed at individuals, nonprofits, and businesses, not state and local governments.

5. *Federal Grants and Contracts Weekly* (Arlington, VA), November 17, 2003, p. 3.

6. GAO, "Federal Assistance." The GAO has been pointing out these problems of federal grants since at least 1975.

7. Ibid., p. 9.

8. "Budget Message of the President," in *Budget of the United States Government: Fiscal Year 1983* (Washington: Government Printing Office, February 1982), p. M22.

9. The OMB notes that its count of the number of grant programs is up in recent years partly due to changes in definitions.

10. Beck, p. 213.

11. This was a report from the bipartisan Advisory Commission on Intergovernmental Relations. Cited in Michael Greve, "Big Government Federalism," *Federalism Outlook* (American Enterprise Institute), March 1, 2001.

12. Lester M. Salamon, "The Changing Tools of Government Action: An Overview," in *Beyond Privatization: The Tools of Government Action*, ed. Lester M. Salamon (Washington: Urban Institute Press, 1989), p. 16.

13. Donald Haider, "Grants as a Tool of Public Policy," in ibid., p. 114.

14. Susan Schmidt, "Tribal Grant Is Being Questioned," *Washington Post*, March 1, 2005, p. A3.

15. *Budget of the United States Government: Fiscal Year 2003* (Washington: Government Printing Office, February 2002), p. 175.

16. William Spangar Peirce, *Bureaucratic Failure and Public Expenditure* (New York: Academic Press, 1981), p. 158.

17. Tracey Farrigan and Amy Glasmeier, "Economic Development Administration: Background and History," Pennsylvania State University, One Nation Pulling Apart project, n.d., www.onenation.psu.edu.

18. Nora Gordon, "Do Federal Grants Boost School Spending? Evidence from Title I," Department of Economics, University of California, San Diego, Working Paper, September 2002.

19. Quoted in Beck, p. 217.

20. Quoted in Charles Warren, *Congress as Santa Claus or National Donations and the General Welfare Clause of the Constitution* (New York: Arno, 1978), p. 103 (originally published by the Michie Company, Charlottesville, Virginia, 1932).

21. Ibid., p. 100.

22. Eric Rich, "Crime Agency's Ex-Chief Indicated on Md. Grant Use," *Washington Post*, March 18, 2004, p. B1.

23. Greve.

24. GAO, "Medicaid: HCFA Reversed Its Position and Approved Additional State Financing Schemes," GAO-02-147, October 10, 2001, p. 1.

25. GAO, "Opportunities for Oversight and Improved Use of Taxpayer Funds: Examples from Selected GAO Work," GAO-03-1006, August 2003, p. 146.

26. Gabriel Roth, "Liberating the Roads: Reforming U.S. Highway Policy," Cato Institute Policy Analysis no. 538, March 17, 2005, p. 11.

27. Ibid., p. 12.

28. Shailagh Murray, "Grudgingly, House Accepts $284 Billion Bill," *Washington Post*, March 11, 2005, p. A5.

29. Michael Dobbs, "Run-Up to Vote Is Season for U.S. Largess," *Washington Post*, October 28, 2004, p. A23.

30. Roth, p. 7 and footnote 29.

31. *Budget of the United States Government: Fiscal Year 2005, Analytical Perspectives*, p. 117.

32. White House, "Barriers to Community-Based Organizations and Other Small and Newcomer Organizations," news release, August 16, 2001, www.white house.gov/news/releases/2001/08/.

33. *Budget of the United States Government: Fiscal Year 2005, Analytical Perspectives*, pp. 114, 119.

34. *Budget of the United States Government: Fiscal Year 2005*, p. 181.

35. Diane Mattingly and Stephen Fehr, "Library to Receive Funds for Literacy," *Fairfax Extra, Washington Post*, December 22, 2004.

36. Dan Morgan, "Hastert Directs Millions to Birthplace," *Washington Post*, May 31, 2005, p. A1.

37. For background, see Veronique de Rugy, "What Does Homeland Security Spending Buy?" American Enterprise Institute, October 29, 2004. See also Angie Marek, "Pigging Out," *U.S. News & World Report*, May 30, 2005, p. 22.

38. House Select Committee on Homeland Security, "An Analysis of First Responder Grant Funding," April 27, 2004.

39. Ibid.

40. Ibid., p. 6.

41. John Mintz, "Security Spending Initiates Disputes," *Washington Post*, April 13, 2005, p. A15.

42. Ibid.

43. Sam Hananel, "Report Criticizes Use of Port Security Grants," *Washington Post*, December 28, 2004.

44. Spencer Hsu and Sarah Cohen, "Most Area Terrorism Funding Not Spent," *Washington Post*, April 10, 2005, p. A1.

45. John L. Palmer and Isabel V. Sawhill, "Perspectives on the Reagan Experiment," in *The Reagan Experiment*, ed. John L. Palmer and Isabel V. Sawhill (Washington: Urban Institute, 1982), p. 12.

46. Donald M. Rothberg, "Reagan Urges New Weapon to Overcome U.S.-Soviet Military Gap," Associated Press, May 5, 1980.

47. Roth, p. 16.

48. GAO, "Federal-State-Local Relations: Trends of the Past Decade and Emerging Issues," GAO/HRD-90-34, March 1990, p. 15.

49. Palmer and Sawhill, pp. 12, 16.

50. *Budget of the United States Government: Fiscal Year 2006, Analytical Perspectives*, p. 131.

51. *Congressional Quarterly Almanac 1995*, vol. 51 (1996): 2-22.

52. *Budget of the United States Government: Fiscal Year 2006, Historical Tables*, p. 76. Data are for fiscal years.

53. Dan Morgan and Helen Dewar, "GOP Dishes Out Pork in Growing Portions," *Washington Post*, November 24, 2003, p. A19.

Chapter 9

1. Rick Geddes, "The Structure and Effect of International Postal Reform," American Enterprise Institute Postal Reform Papers, April 29, 2003.

2. Marc Fisher, "Privatizing Zoo Would Rescue It, for a Modest Fee," *Washington Post*, December 9, 2003, p. B1. Fisher notes that about 40 percent of U.S. zoos, including the top-notch San Diego and Bronx zoos, are run by private, nonprofit groups, and he notes that private ownership seems to have a superior record. Many private zoos, however, do receive various government subsidies. Regarding the National Zoo, the National Academy of Sciences reported in 2004 that it found failures "at all levels" in zoo management leading to animal deaths, crumbling facilities, and other problems. See Karlyn Barker and James V. Grimaldi, "National Zoo Director Quits over Lapses," *Washington Post*, February 26, 2004, p. A1.

3. A good survey of the issues is Gabriel Roth, ed., *Competing with the Government* (Stanford, CA: Hoover Institution Press, 2004).

4. Gabriel Roth, "Liberating the Roads: Reforming U.S. Highway Policy," Cato Institute Policy Analysis no. 538, March 17, 2005, pp. 10, 13.

5. Vito Tanzi, "A Lower Tax Future? The Economic Role of the State in the 21st Century," *Politeia* (London), 2004, p. 14, www.politeia.co.uk.

6. *Budget of the United States Government: Fiscal Year 2003* (Washington: Government Printing Office, February 2002), p. 45.

7. Ibid.

8. Jerry Markon, "2 Pentagon Officials Get 24 Years in Fraud," *Washington Post*, December 13, 2003, p. B3.

9. Nicole Fuller, "Ex-Postal Official Admits Taking Nearly $800,000 in Bribes," *Washington Post*, October 8, 2004, p. A20.

10. Private air traffic control would probably be safer because private firms can access capital markets to raise funds for investment in new technologies. Also, current government work rules can reduce the safety consciousness of controllers.

11. For a summary of the issue, see Christopher Lee, "Postal Services Finances Bleak," *Washington Post*, March 23, 2004, p. A17.

12. For a detailed discussion of postal service reform, see Edward L. Hudgins, ed., *Mail @ the Millennium: Will the Postal Service Go Private?* (Washington: Cato Institute, 2000).

13. Geddes.

14. Ibid.

15. Joseph Vranich and Edward Hudgins, "Help Passenger Rail by Privatizing Amtrak," Cato Institute Policy Analysis no. 419, November 1, 2001. I have updated the subsidy costs listed in this report.

16. GAO, "Opportunities for Oversight and Improved Use of Taxpayer Funds: Examples from Selected GAO Work," GAO-03-1006, August 2003, p. 58. The GAO notes that the PMAs have inefficient levels of capital investment because of the unreliability of federal funding.

17. Daniel B. Klein, "Private Highways in America, 1792–1916," *The Freeman: Ideas on Liberty*, February 1994, www.fee.org. State governments did intervene extensively in infrastructure projects such as canals and railroads, but intervention often ended in corruption scandals. See also James Rolph Edwards, "How Nineteenth-Century Americans Responded to Government Corruption," *The Freeman: Ideas on Liberty*, April 2004, p. 24. See also Eduardo Engel, Ron Fischer, and Alexander Galetovic, "A New Approach to Private Roads," *Regulation*, Fall 2002, p. 18.

18. GAO, "Air Traffic Control: Evolution and Status of FAA's Automation Program," GAO/T-RCED/AIMD-98-85, March 5, 1998.

19. GAO, "High-Risk Series: An Update," GAO-05-207, January 2005, p. 5.

20. Holman W. Jenkins Jr., "The Coming Revolution in Air Traffic Control," *Wall Street Journal*, August 18, 2004, p. A11.

21. Joel Bagnole, "How Canada Gets Jets across the Sea," *Wall Street Journal*, May 9, 2002, p. A12.

22. Steven Ginsberg, "Beltway to Get Va. Toll Lanes," *Washington Post*, April 29, 2005, p. A1.

23. Lisa Rein, "Toll Lane Proposals Pick Up Momentum," *Washington Post*, March 17, 2004, p. B1.

24. Fred Bayles, "Toll Lanes: A Freer Ride, for a Price," *USA Today*, April 8, 2004, p. 3A.

25. Amy Argetsinger and Steven Ginsberg, "Lessons of Calif.'s Toll Lanes," *Washington Post*, June 20, 2005, p. A1.

26. See Jerry Ellig, "The $7.7 Billion Mistake: Federal Barriers to State and Local Privatization," U.S. Congress, Joint Economic Committee, February 1996.

27. Author's count of loan programs in *Budget of the United States Government: Fiscal Year 2005, Federal Credit Supplement*, www.gpoaccess.gov/usbudget/fy05/browse.html.

28. *Budget of the United States Government: Fiscal Year 2006, Analytical Perspectives* (Washington: Government Printing Office, February 2005), p. 109. Note that the outlay amounts for loans in the federal budget are the net subsidy amounts, which are the present values of the net taxpayer costs. This treatment, established by the Federal Credit Reform Act of 1990, allows comparison between the costs of loans and other federal programs.

29. Susan Straight, "Women Expand Niche in Owning Construction Firms," *Washington Post*, February 21, 2004, p. F1.

30. For example, Alaska Native Corporations get special access to federal no-bid contracts.

31. *Budget of the United States Government: Fiscal Year 2006, Analytical Perspectives*, p. 99.

32. GAO, "Farm Loan Programs: Improvements in the Loan Portfolio but Continued Monitoring Needed," GAO-01-732T, May 16, 2001, p. 2.

33. *Budget of the United States Government: Fiscal Year 2006, Analytical Perspectives*, p. 85.

34. Ibid., p. 87

35. "Venture Capitol-ism," editorial, *Wall Street Journal*, April 13, 2005, p. 18.

36. Robert Krol and Shirley Svorny, "The Collapse of a Noble Idea," *Regulation* 27, no. 4 (Winter 2004–2005): 30.

37. Ibid.

38. *Budget of the United States Government: Fiscal Year 2006, Analytical Perspectives*, p. 109. See also Charles Lane, "Justices to Review Loan Offsets," *Washington Post*, April 26, 2005, p. A2.

39. GAO, "Federal Budget: Opportunities for Oversight and Improved Use of Taxpayer Funds," GAO-03-922T, June 18, 2003, p. 26.

40. Ibid., p. 16.

41. Anne Applebaum, "Student Loan Swindle," *Washington Post*, September 29, 2004, p. A29.

42. Albert Crenshaw, "U.S. Pension Agency Goes $11 Billion in Red," *Washington Post*, January 31, 2003, p. E1.

43. For a discussion, see Chris Edwards, "Replacing the Scandal-Plagued Corporate Income Tax with a Cash-Flow Tax," Cato Institute Policy Analysis no. 484, August 14, 2003, pp. 28–29.

44. David Hilzenrath, "Lenders' Subsidy Grows, CBO Says," *Washington Post*, April 13, 2004, p. E1.

45. *Budget of the United States Government: Fiscal Year 2006, Analytical Perspectives*, p. 91. This is the debt for Fannie Mae, Freddie Mac, and the Federal Home Loan Banks.

46. Albert Crenshaw, "High Pay at Fannie Mae for the Well-Connected," *Washington Post*, December 23, 2004, p. E3.

47. David Hilzenrath, "Fannie Mae Salaries Rile Hill," *Washington Post*, October 11, 2004, p. E1.

48. David Hilzenrath, "Both Sides Critical at Fannie Hearing," *Washington Post*, October 7, 2004, p. E1.

49. For background, see Lawrence J. White, "Fannie Mae, Freddie Mac, and Housing Finance: Why True Privatization Is Good Public Policy," Cato Institute Policy Analysis no. 528, October 7, 2004.

50. *Budget of the United States Government: Fiscal Year 2006, Analytical Perspectives*, p. 206.

51. GAO, "Federal Budget," p. 30.

52. GAO, "High-Risk Series: An Update," GAO-05-207, January 2005. See highlights for "Managing Federal Real Property."

53. See www.whitehouse.gov/results/agenda/scorecard.htm.

54. CBO, "Budget Options," February 2001, p. 82.

55. Joshua Partlow, "Radio Telescopes' Time in the Sun Has Passed," *Washington Post*, April 12, 2004, p. B3.

56. GAO, "High-Risk Series: Federal Real Property," GAO-03-122, January 1, 2003, pp. 8, 9.

57. Ibid., p. 11.

Chapter 10

1. For background on term limits, see U.S. Term Limits at www.termlimits.org.

2. Edward Crane and Patrick Basham, "Term Limits," *Cato Handbook on Policy*, 6th ed. (Washington: Cato Institute, 2005), p. 161.

3. In a five-to-four ruling in *U.S. Term Limits, Inc. v. Thornton*, 514 U.S. 779 (1995), the Court overturned congressional term limits that had been imposed by 23 states.

4. David W. Moore, "Congress Job Approval at 35%, Lowest in Eight Years," Gallup Organization, May 10, 2005, www.gallup.com.

5. John Berthoud, "Self-Limited Members of Congress: A Continued Commitment to Their Convictions," National Taxpayers Union Issue Brief no. 128, August 29, 2000.

6. Kenneth Cooper, "House Rejects Measures to Require Term Limits," *Washington Post*, March 30, 1995, p. A1. The House voted on four different versions of term limits, a strategy that allowed members to each vote for a particular version but to have none of them pass.

7. Joe Scarborough, *Rome Wasn't Burnt in a Day* (New York: HarperCollins, 2004), p. 178.

8. Ibid., pp. 8, 61.

9. Ibid., pp. 164–69.

10. Tom A. Coburn, *Breach of Trust: How Washington Turns Outsiders into Insiders* (Nashville: WND Books, 2003), p. 39.

11. Ibid., pp. xix, xxiv, 50.

12. In 1900 alcohol excises accounted for 35 percent of federal revenues and customs duties accounted for 45 percent. See Chris Edwards, "The U.S. Economy at the Beginning and End of the 20th Century," U.S. Congress, Joint Economic Committee, December 1999, p. 26.

13. Chris Edwards, "Options for Tax Reform," Cato Institute Policy Analysis no. 536, February 24, 2005.

14. For a discussion of tax reform options, see ibid.

15. H. L. Mencken, *A Little Book in C Major*, 1916, www.bartleby.com/73/423.html.

16. Louis Fisher, "Line Item Veto Act of 1996: Lessons from the States," Congressional Research Service, December 26, 1996.

17. For state experiences with budget limitations, see Michael New, "Proposition 13 and State Budget Limitations: Past Successes and Future Options," Cato Institute Briefing Paper no. 83, June 19, 2003.

18. The House Republican Study Committee has proposed changes to the budget process in the "Family Budget Protection Act," www.house.gov/burton/RSC/word/Hensarling101303tp.pdf.

19. *Congressional Quarterly Almanac, 1995* (Washington: Congressional Quarterly, 1996), p. 2-34.

20. For background, see Chris Edwards, "Sunsetting to Reform and Abolish Federal Agencies," Cato Institute Tax & Budget Bulletin no. 6, May 2002.

21. Richard Darman, *Who's in Control? Polar Politics and the Sensible Center* (New York: Simon & Schuster, 1996), p. 236.

22. Ibid., p. 234.

23. Scarborough, p. 63

24. For example, Gingrich pushed for funding, which was not requested by the Pentagon, for C-130 transport planes. The planes were built in his Georgia district.

25. Coburn, p. xxii.

26. Paul H. Douglas, *Economy in the National Government* (Chicago: University of Chicago Press, 1952), p. 22.

27. Ibid., p. 24.

28. However, there are about 35 "Blue Dog" Democrats in the House, such as Jim Cooper of Tennessee, who support broad budget process reforms to restrain growth in spending. See www.house.gov/cardoza/BlueDogs/bluedogs.shtml. For Brookings Institution proposals, see Alice Rivlin and Isabel Sawhill, eds., *Restoring Fiscal Sanity 2005* (Washington: Brookings Institution, April 2005).

29. Coburn, p. xxvi.

30. Some past general critiques of federal spending that I found useful, but which I have not previously referenced, include: C. Lowell Harriss, ed., *Control of Federal Spending* (New York: Academy of Political Science, 1985); Randall Fitzgerald and Gerald Lipson, *Pork Barrel: The Unexpurgated Grace Commission Story of Congressional Profligacy* (Washington: Cato Institute, 1984); and Lewis Uhler, *Setting Limits* (Washington: Regnery Gateway, 1989). From a liberal perspective, a well-written critique of wasteful federal spending is Mark Zepezauer, *Take the Rich off Welfare* (Cambridge, MA: South End, 2004).

31. Gordon Tullock, Arthur Seldon, and Gordon Brady, *Government Failure: A Primer in Public Choice* (Washington: Cato Institute, 2002), p. 12.

32. Ibid., p. 20.

33. Thomas Jefferson, letter to Edward Carrington, May 27, 1788, in *The Writings of Thomas Jefferson*, ed. Andrew A. Lipscomb and Albert Ellery Bergh (Washington: Issued under the auspices of the Thomas Jefferson Memorial Association of the United States, 1903–04), vol. 7: p. 37.

34. James L. Payne, *The Culture of Spending: Why Congress Lives beyond Our Means* (San Francisco: Institute for Contemporary Studies, 1991), p. 61.

35. *Budget of the United States Government: Fiscal Year 2006, Historical Perspectives* (Washington: Government Printing Office, 2005), p. 125. These figures are current or nominal dollars.

36. Ibid., p. 162.

37. For a discussion of why defense spending was reduced, see Payne, p. 146.

38. Taxpayers for Common Sense and the Center for Defense Information, "New Beginnings: How Base Closures Can Improve Local Economies and Transform America's Military," October 2001.

39. Ron Haskins, "Welfare Reform: The Biggest Accomplishment of the Revolution," in *The Republican Revolution 10 Years Later: Smaller Government or Business as Usual?* ed. Chris Edwards and John Samples (Washington: Cato Institute, 2005).

40. Ariana Eunjung Cha, "Finding Support in the Search for E.T.," *Washington Post*, May 30, 2005, p. A1.

41. Chris Edwards and Tad DeHaven, "Save the Farms—End the Subsidies," op-ed, *Washington Post*, March 3, 2002.

42. Vaudine England, "Shorn of Subsidies, New Zealand Farmers Thrive," *International Herald Tribune*, July 2, 2005, http://iht.com.

43. Federated Farmers of New Zealand, "Life after Subsidies," www.fedfarm.org.nz/homepage.html.

44. Linda Killian, *The Freshman: What Happened to the Republican Revolution* (Boulder, CO: Westview, 1998), pp. 407–13. The Republicans lost a net two seats in the House in 1996. The GOP losers were not so much conservative as simply people who were particularly poor candidates.

45. Ibid., pp. 441–43. Some other hard-line reformers, such as Sue Myrick of North Carolina and Lindsey Graham of South Carolina, did not increase their vote percentage but did well nonetheless. Note that Mark Sanford ran unopposed in 1996.

46. Ibid., p. 412. As one example, President Clinton carried Tom Coburn's district by 7 percentage points, but Coburn won reelection by a 10 percentage point margin. Coburn was perhaps the most hard-core House budget cutter.

47. "The Enigma of Acquiescence, Survey on the Future of the State," *The Economist*, September 18, 1997, www.economist.com/surveys.

48. Ibid.

49. Vito Tanzi, "A Lower Tax Future? The Economic Role of the State in the 21st Century," *Politeia* (London), 2004, p. 13, www.politeia.co.uk.

50. David Brooks, "The Do-Nothing Conspiracy," *New York Times*, March 18, 2005, p. A27.

Appendix 1

1. U.S. Bureau of Economic Analysis, *Survey of Current Business* (Washington: Government Printing Office, April 2000), p. 15.

2. Ibid.

3. U.S. Bureau of the Census, *Historical Statistics of the United States* (Washington: Government Printing Office, 1975), Part 1, p. 135.

4. For the change in real gross national product during the 1920s, see ibid., p. 224. For the unemployment rate, see p. 135.

5. Jim Powell, *FDR's Folly: How Roosevelt and His New Deal Prolonged the Great Depression* (New York: Crown Forum, 2003).

6. Tax information based author's research and Veronique de Rugy, "High Taxes and High Budget Deficits: The Hoover-Roosevelt Tax Increases of the 1930s," Cato Institute Tax & Budget Bulletin no. 14, March 2003.

7. Ibid.

8. http://newdeal.feri.org/court/fdr5_31_35.htm.

9. U.S. Bureau of Economic Analysis, National Income and Product Accounts, Table 6.4A, www.bea.gov/bea/dn/nipaweb.

10. Real gross private domestic investment did not reach its 1929 level until 1936, and then it plummeted again in 1938. U.S. Bureau of Economic Analysis, *Survey of Current Business*, p. 15.

11. William J. Olson and Alan Woll, "Executive Orders and National Emergencies: How Presidents Have Come to 'Run the Country' by Usurping Legislative Power," Cato Institute Policy Analysis no. 358, October 28, 1999, p. 13.

12. Ibid., p. 16.

13. See FDR's fireside chat regarding his Court proposal, March 9, 1937, www.hpol.org/fdr/chat/.

Appendix 2

1. *Budget of the United States Government: Fiscal Year 2006* (Washington: Government Printing Office, February 2005).

2. *Budget of the U.S. Government: Fiscal Year 2005* (Washington: Government Printing Office, February 2004), p. 64.

3. Chris Edwards and Tad DeHaven, "Farm Subsidies at Record Levels As Congress Considers New Farm Bill," Cato Institute Briefing Paper no. 70, October 18, 2001.

4. James M. Beck, *Our Wonderland of Bureaucracy* (New York: Macmillan, 1932), p. viii.

5. *Budget of the United States Government: Fiscal Year 2006*, p. 61.

6. Edwards and DeHaven, p. 7.

7. See U.S. Department of Agriculture, Economic Research Service, "Farm Income and Costs: Farm Income Forecasts," February 11, 2005, www.ers.usda.gov/Briefing/FarmIncome/Data/Hh_t5.htm.

8. General Accounting Office (GAO), "Farm Loan Programs: Improvements in the Loan Portfolio but Continued Monitoring Needed," GAO-01-732T, May 16, 2001, p. 1.

9. U.S. Department of Agriculture, "USDA Announces Funds to Promote U.S. Food and Agricultural Products Overseas," June 17, 2004, www.fas.usda.gov/scriptsw/PressRelease/pressrel_frm.asp.

10. Visit the USDA's rural development site, www.rurdev.usda.gov/rd, to see the huge range of activities funded.

11. See www.rurdev.usda.gov/rbs/coops/cssheep.htm.

12. John J. Fialka, "Lobbying Works for Rural Co-ops," *Wall Street Journal*, December 27, 2004.

13. Ibid.

14. Ibid.

15. For example, see GAO, "Rural Housing Service: Opportunities to Improve Management," GAO-03-911T, June 19, 2003, p. 7.

16. Ibid., p. 2.

17. GAO, "Economic Development: Observations Regarding the Economic Development Administration's May 1998 Final Report on Its Public Works Program," RCED-99-11R, March 23, 1999, p. 2.

18. GAO, "Major Management Challenges and Program Risks: Department of Commerce," GAO-01-243, January 2001, p. 8.

19. GAO, "Measuring Performance: The Advanced Technology Program and Private-Sector Funding," GAO/RECD-96-47, January 1996, p. 3.

20. For background, see Chris Edwards, "Entrepreneurial Dynamism and the Success of U.S. High-Tech," U.S. Congress, Joint Economic Committee, October 1999. For venture capital data, see National Venture Capital Association, "Latest Industry Statistics," n.d., www.nvca.org.

21. Scott J. Wallsten, "The R&D Boondoggle," *Regulation* 23, no. 4 (Winter 2000–2001): 13.

22. Ibid., pp. 14–15.

23. For a discussion, see Chris Edwards, "Entrepreneurs Creating the New Economy," U.S. Congress, Joint Economic Committee, November 2000.

24. Ibid.

25. Ellen McCarthy, "Technology Center Modifies Its Focus to Secure Funding," *Washington Post*, March 18, 2004, p. E1.

26. Part of CIT's mission is to lobby Congress for more federal tax dollars. Its website says: "CIT leads the Commonwealth's efforts to increase the flow of federal research funding into Virginia. CIT's Federal Funding Assistance Program identifies and accelerates opportunities for Virginia's small technology businesses to obtain SBIR, STTR and ATP grants and contracts." See "CIT Programs" at www.cit.org.

27. Note that outlays for the budget function of "national defense," including supplemental costs of Iraq, were $495 billion in FY05, as shown in Figure 2.2.

28. GAO, "High-Risk Series: An Update," GAO-05-207, January 2005.

29. Quoted in Christopher Lee, "GAO Report Points to Pentagon Waste," *Washington Post*, January 26, 2005, p. A19.

30. Cited in GAO, "High-Risk Series: An Update," January 2005. See highlights for "Department of Defense Approach to Business Transformation."

31. Charles V. Peña, "$400 Billion Defense Budget Unnecessary to Fight War on Terrorism," Cato Institute Policy Analysis no. 539, March 29, 2005, p. 14. See also Ivan Eland, *Putting "Defense" Back into U.S. Defense Policy* (Westport, CT: Praeger, 2001).

32. Data from U.S. Department of Defense, "Active Duty Military Personnel Strengths by Regional Area and by Country," December 31, 2004, www.dior.whs.mil/mmid/military/miltop.htm. Figure 2.3 and Table 2.1 list 1.5 million uniformed military, data from the federal budget that include Coast Guard and Commissioned Corps.

33. *Budget of the United States Government: Fiscal Year 2006, Analytical Perspectives*, chap. 28, pp. 31, 34. These are outlays. The O&M amount is the sum of active duty Army, Navy, Marine Corps, and Air Force, plus health program costs.

34. Shailagh Murray, "Pentagon Plans Spark Action," *Wall Street Journal*, February 1, 2005, p. A4. Later in 2005, the administration changed its mind on the C-130Js.

35. Savings are based on annual averages during the next decade from the Congressional Budget Office (CBO), "Budget Options," February 2005. Savings from canceling the C-130J would be about $1 billion annually, according to various news reports.

36. Quoted in Renae Merle, "Tuning Up Weaponry Budgets," *Washington Post*, June 15, 2005, p. D1.

37. Jonathan Finer, "Threat of Closure Gives States Big Case of Base Fever," *Washington Post*, April 10, 2005, p. A3.

38. J. R. Labbe, "The Business of Base Closures," *Fort Worth Star-Telegram*, February 13, 2005.

39. William D. Hartung, "Corporate Welfare for Weapons Makers: The Hidden Costs of Spending on Defense and Foreign Aid," Cato Institute Policy Analysis no. 350, August 12, 1999, p. 5.

40. For a general discussion, see Office of the Deputy Under Secretary of Defense, "Military Housing Privatization," n.d., www.acq.osd.mil/housing/.

41. Donald M. Rothberg, "Reagan Urges New Weapon to Overcome U.S.-Soviet Military Gap," Associated Press, May 5, 1980.

42. U.S. Department of Education, "FY 2006 Program Performance Plan," www.ed.gov/about/reports/annual/2006plan/program.html.

43. *Budget of the United States Government: Fiscal Year 2006, Analytical Perspectives*, p. 123.

44. *Budget of the United States Government: Fiscal Year 2005*, "Program Assessment Rating Tool, Program Summaries," p. 91.

45. Ibid., p. 99.

46. Ibid., p. 74.

47. Cited in Chester E. Finn Jr., Marci Kanstoroom, and Michael J. Petrilli, "Overview," in "New Directions: Federal Education Policy in the Twenty-First Century," Fordham Foundation and the Manhattan Institute, March 1, 1999, www.edexcellence.net/institute/publication/publication.cfm?id = 38.

48. Quoted in ibid.

49. Ibid.

50. U.S. Department of Education, "Digest of Education Statistics 2003," Table 166, http://nces.ed.gov/programs/digest.

51. Ibid., Table 134.

52. U.S. Department of Education, National Center for Education Statistics, "The Nation's Report Card," 2001 and 2002, http://nces.ed.gov/nationsreportcard/.

53. For an analysis of school spending and performance across states, see Andrew LeFevre and Rea Hederman, "Report Card on American Education: A State-by-State Analysis 1976–2001," American Legislative Exchange Council, October 2002.

54. For an overview of federal K-12 spending, see Neal McCluskey, "A Lesson in Waste: Where Does All the Federal Education Money Go?" Cato Institute Policy Analysis no. 518, July 7, 2004.

55. GAO, "Federal Budget: Opportunities for Oversight and Improved Use of Taxpayer Funds," GAO-03-922T, June 18, 2003, p. 17.

56. Fred Thompson, Preface to "Government at the Brink," by Senate Committee on Government Affairs, June 2001, vol. 1, p. 24, www.senate.gov/~gov_affairs/vol1.pdf.

57. Gary Wolfram, "Making College More Expensive: The Unintended Consequences of Federal Tuition Aid," Cato Institute Policy Analysis no. 531, January 25, 2005.

58. Jennifer Cheeseman Day and Eric C. Newburger, "The Big Payoff: Educational Attainment and Synthetic Estimates of Work-Life Earnings," Special Studies, U.S. Bureau of the Census, July 2002.

59. GAO, "National Ignition Facility: Management and Oversight Failures Caused Major Cost Overruns and Schedule Delays," RCED-00-141, August 8, 2000, p. 5.

60. U.S. House of Representatives, Select Committee on U.S. National Security and Military/Commercial Concerns with the People's Republic of China, House Report 105-851, May 25, 1999, p. v.

61. Ibid., p. x.

62. These conclusions are from a White House panel cited in Senate Committee on Government Affairs, "Government at the Brink," vol. 2, pp. 30, 31, www.senate.gov/~gov_affairs/vol2.pdf.

63. See various analyses of the 2005 energy bill by Taxpayers for Common Sense at www.taxpayer.net/energy/energywatch.htm.

64. Cited in Jeffrey Ball, "Car Makers Split over Timing of Hydrogen-Powered Vehicles," *Wall Street Journal*, February 26, 2004, p. B1.

65. CBO, "Budget Options," March 2003, p. 60.

66. For example, see Green Scissors Campaign discussion at www.greenscissors.org/energy/cleancoal.htm.

67. GAO, "Fossil Fuel R&D: Lessons Learned in the Clean Coal Technology Program," GAO-01-854T, June 12, 2001, p. 2.

68. Ibid., pp. 2–4.

69. Justin Blum, "U.S. Loan Proposed to Rescue Alaska Power Plant," *Washington Post*, April 24, 2005, p. A4.

70. Ibid.

71. Chris Edwards and Tad DeHaven, "Corporate Welfare Update," Cato Institute Tax & Budget Bulletin no. 7, May 2002.

72. *Budget of the United States Government: Fiscal Year 2003* (Washington: Government Printing Office, February 2002), p. 132.

73. CBO, "Budget Options," February 2005, p. 84.

74. GAO summary of a study done by the Department of Energy for 1998. See GAO, "National Energy Policy," GAO-05-379, June 2005, p. 61.

75. CBO, "Budget Options," February 2005, p. 85.

76. GAO, "Opportunities for Oversight and Improved Use of Taxpayer Funds: Examples from Selected GAO Work," GAO-03-1006, August 2003, p. 58.

77. This figure is gross of Medicare premiums of $38 billion in 2005. Net of premiums, Medicare spending was $287 billion in 2005.

78. CBO, "The Budget and Economic Outlook: Fiscal Years 2006 to 2015," January 2005, p. 52.

79. GAO, "Fiscal Year 2004 U.S. Government Financial Statements," GAO-05-284T, February 9, 2005.

80. CBS News, "Medicare Claims Errors Cost $20B," December 14, 2004, www.cbsnews.com.

81. GAO, "Federal Budget: Opportunities for Oversight and Improved Use of Taxpayer Funds," p. 7.

82. Robert Moffit, "Improving and Preserving Medicare for Tomorrow's Seniors," in *Priorities for the President* (Washington: Heritage Foundation, January 2001), p. 2.

83. *2005 Report of the Board of Trustees of the Federal Old-Age and Survivors Insurance and Disability Insurance Trust Funds* (Washington: Government Printing Office, April 5, 2005), p. 166. This is the "cost rate" under the intermediate projection.

84. Ibid.

85. *2005 Annual Report of the Boards of Trustees of the Federal Hospital Insurance and Federal Supplemental Medical Insurance Trust Funds* (Washington: Government Printing Office, March 23, 2005), p. 29.

86. Martin Feldstein, "Prefunding Medicare," National Bureau of Economic Research (NBER) Working Paper no. 6917, January 1999, p. 8.

87. Ibid., p. 10.

88. For background, see Michael Cannon, "Combining Tax Reform and Health Care Reform with Large HSAs," Cato Institute Tax & Budget Bulletin no. 23, May 2005.

89. CBO, "Budget Options," February 2005, pp. 191–216.

90. Victor Fuchs, "The Financial Problems of the Elderly: A Holistic Approach," NBER Working Paper no. 8236, April 2001, p. 11.

91. U.S. Department of Health and Human Services, "HHS Announces Medicare Premium, Deductibles for 2005," news release, September 3, 2004.

92. CBO, "Budget Options," February 2005, p. 570.

93. Author's estimate based on CBO data. The CBO does an estimate of the savings from raising premiums to cover 30 percent of costs. CBO, "Budget Options," February 2005, p. 570. I scaled up the savings from their proposal.

94. Ibid., February 2005, p. 208.

95. Ibid., p. 210.

96. For details on the option, see ibid., p. 211.

97. CBO, "The Budget and Fiscal Outlook: Fiscal Years 2006 to 2015," January 2005, pp. 52, 142. Fiscal years.

98. Ibid.

99. "The Medicaid Explosion," editorial, *Washington Post*, June 19, 2006, p. B6.

100. GAO, "Medicaid: State Efforts to Control Improper Payments Vary," GAO-01-662, June 7, 2001, p. 4. See also Medicaid discussion in GAO, "High-Risk Series: An Update," GAO-05-207, January 2005.

101. GAO, "Opportunities for Oversight and Improved Use of Taxpayer Funds," p. 152.

102. Clifford J. Levy and Michael Luo, "New York Medicaid Fraud May Reach into Billions," *New York Times*, July 18, 2005, p. A1.

103. CBO, "Budget Options," February 2005, p. 176.

104. GAO, "Medicaid: HCFA Reversed Its Position and Approved Additional State Financing Schemes," GAO-02-147, October 10, 2001, p. 1.

105. Richard Teske, "Abolishing the Medicaid Ghetto: Putting Patients First," American Legislative Exchange Council, April 2002, p. 4.

106. See Medicaid discussion in GAO, "High-Risk Series: An Update," GAO-05-207, January 2005.

107. Teske, p. 10.

108. CBO, "Budget Options," February 2005, p. 176.

109. Author's estimate based on the CBO baseline projection for Medicaid spending.

110. *Congressional Quarterly Almanac 1995*, vol. 51 (1996): 7–16.

111. Ibid., p. 2-31.

112. CBO, "Budget Options," February 2005, p. 176.

113. Ibid. The estimate for 2015 is the author's based on the CBO projection.

114. *Budget of the United States Government: Fiscal Year 2006, Historical Tables*, p. 180.

115. American Association for the Advancement of Science, "R&D Programs Face Another Rough Year in 2006; Cuts for Many, Gains for Space and Homeland Security," March 22, 2005, Table 1, www.aaas.org/spp/rd/prel06pr.htm.
116. Tom Ramstack, "Airport Screeners Perform Poorly," *Washington Times*, April 23, 2004, p. A1.
117. Sara Kehaulani Goo, "TSA Slated for Dismantling," *Washington Post*, April 7, 2005. Accessed electronically on MSNBC.com.
118. Christopher Lee, "Appointment Runs Out for DHS Inspector General," *Washington Post*, December 17, 2004, p. A31.
119. Sara Kehaulani Goo, "Probe Finds Overspending for TSA Center," *Washington Post*, April 20, 2005, p. A2.
120. Scott Higham and Robert O'Harrow Jr., "The High Cost of a Rush to Security," *Washington Post*, June 20, 2005, p. A1.
121. Ibid. Note that the few private screening companies contract to the TSA, not to the airports as they did prior to 9/11.
122. Associated Press, "Report: Private Airport Screeners Better," April 20, 2005. The story reports on a GAO study that found that the five airports that use private screeners did a better job of detecting dangerous objects than TSA screeners.
123. Sara Kehaulani Goo, "Airport Screeners New Guard," *Washington Post*, July 6, 2004, p. E1.
124. Howard Husock, "We Don't Need Subsidized Housing," *City Journal*, Winter 1997, www.city-journal.org.
125. For background, see Howard Husock, "The Housing Reform That Backfired," *City Journal*, Summer 2004, www.city-journal.org.
126. Guy Gugliotta, "Kemp Helped Agency Recover Self-Respect," *Washington Post*, December 29, 1992, p. A13.
127. "Subsidized Fraud," *Time*, January 18, 1971.
128. Ibid.
129. Ibid.
130. GAO, "High-Risk Series: An Update," GAO-05-207, January 2005, p. 5.
131. GAO, "Opportunities for Oversight and Improved Use of Taxpayer Funds," p. 22.
132. *Budget of the United States Government: Fiscal Year 2006*, p. 178.
133. Jeffery C. Mays, "Housing Authority Makes Management Changes," *New Jersey Star-Ledger*, June 24, 2005, p. 19.
134. Howard Husock, "Let's End Housing Vouchers," *City Journal*, Autumn 2000, www.city-journal.org.
135. GAO, "Opportunities for Oversight and Improved Use of Taxpayer Funds," p. 232
136. CBO, "Budget Options," February 2005, p. 142.
137. *Budget of the United States Government: Fiscal Year 2005*, "Program Assessment Rating Tool, Program Summaries," p. 206.
138. Ibid., pp. 218–47.
139. For background, see GAO, "Bureau of Reclamation," GAO/RCED-96-109, July 1996.
140. For a discussion of this project, see the Green Scissors Campaign at www.greenscissors.org.
141. U.S. Department of the Interior, Bureau of Reclamation, "Animas–La Plata Project Construction Cost Estimates," November 2003, www.usbr.gov/uc/pro gact/animas/.

142. GAO, "BIA and DOD Schools: Student Achievement and Other Characteristics Often Differ from Public Schools," GAO-01-934, September 28, 2001, p. 2.

143. The issue regards the *Cobell v. Babbitt* case, filed in 1996 and currently on appeal. For background and documents, see www.indiantrust.com.

144. The quote is from Lamberth's opinion in the case available at www.dcd.uscourts.gov/96-1285i.pdf.

145. Quoted in Sheryl McCarthy, "U.S.'s Rape of the Indians Continues Still Today," *Newsday*, September 19, 2003.

146. Thomas Slonaker, Testimony before the Senate Committee on Indian Affairs, September 24, 2002.

147. Paul Homan, Testimony before the Senate Committee on Indian Affairs, September 24, 2002.

148. Chris T. Nguyen, "Report: California Tribes Lead Nation in Indian Gaming Revenue," Associated Press, June 15, 2005. See also "Tribal Data" at the National Indian Gaming Commission, www.nigc.gov/nigc.

149. Tim Lynch, "A Smooth Transition: Crime, Federalism, and the GOP," in *The Republican Revolution 10 Years Later: Smaller Government or Business as Usual?* ed. Chris Edwards and John Samples (Washington: Cato Institute, 2005), p. 220.

150. Andy Furillo, "California Agency Misplaced Hundreds of Millions of Dollars," *Budget & Tax News* 3, no. 4 (April 2005): 1.

151. David B. Muhlhausen and Ralph Rector, "Will the Bush Administration Hold the Line on COPS?" Heritage Foundation, May 22, 2002.

152. *Budget of the United States Government: Fiscal Year 2005*, "Program Assessment Rating Tool, Program Summaries," p. 255.

153. Robert W Crandall and Clifford Winston, "Does Antitrust Policy Improve Consumer Welfare? Assessing the Evidence," *Journal of Economic Perspectives* 17, no. 4 (Fall 2003).

154. Martin Feldstein, "Rethinking Social Insurance," NBER Working Paper no. 11250, March 2005.

155. David Muhlhausen and Paul Kersey, "In the Dark on Job Training: Federal Job-Training Programs Have a Record of Failure," Heritage Foundation, July 6, 2004.

156. For cost savings from repealing the Davis-Bacon and the Service Contract Acts, see CBO, "Budget Options," February 2001, pp. 367, 368.

157. Muhlhausen and Kersey.

158. GAO, "Multiple Employment and Training Programs," GAO-03-589, April 2003, p. 2.

159. Anita Hattiangadi, "Upgrading Workplace Skills," Employment Policy Foundation, Issue Backgrounder, April 10, 2000.

160. GAO, "Trade Adjustment Assistance: Improvements Necessary, but Programs Cannot Solve Communities' Long-Term Problems," GAO-01-988T, July 20, 2001, p. 3.

161. *Budget of the United States Government: Fiscal Year 2005*, "Program Assessment Rating Tool, Program Summaries," p. 276.

162. Paul Blustein, "White House Warms Up to Worker Aid," *Washington Post*, March 13, 2004, p. A1.

163. *Budget of the United States Government: Fiscal Year 2005*, "Program Assessment Rating Tool, Program Summaries," p. 267.

164. CBO, "Budget Options," February 2005, p. 258.

165. *2005 Report of the Board of Trustees of the Federal Old-Age and Survivors Insurance and Disability Insurance Trust Funds*, p. 181. Calendar year data. The $527 billion includes administrative expenses.

166. See Cato's Social Security website, www.socialsecurity.org, for an extensive list of books, briefing papers, and other information on Social Security problems and reform options.

167. *2005 Report of the Board of Trustees of the Federal Old-Age and Survivors Insurance and Disability Insurance Trust Funds*, p. 181. The taxes available to fund benefits include payroll taxes and income taxes on Social Security benefits.

168. Ibid., p. 2.

169. Ibid., p. 43.

170. Author's calculations based on inflation and average wage index projections in *2005 Report of the Board of Trustees of the Federal Old-Age and Survivors Insurance and Disability Insurance Trust Funds*, p. 176.

171. CBO, "Budget Options," February 2005, p. 234. Author received a more detailed e-mail from CBO.

172. Social Security Administration, *Report of the 1994–1996 Advisory Council on Social Security*, vol. 1, *Findings and Recommendations*, January 1997, www.ssa.gov/history/reports/adcouncil/.

173. President's Commission to Strengthen Social Security, "Strengthening Social Security and Creating Personal Wealth for All Americans," December 21, 2001, www.csss.gov.

174. For a summary of proposals in the 106th Congress, see Chris Edwards, "Personal Account Options for Social Security Reform," U.S. Congress, Joint Economic Committee, January 2000.

175. For details on the Cato plan, see Michael Tanner, "A Better Deal at Half the Cost: SSA Scoring of the Cato Social Security Reform Plan," Cato Institute Briefing Paper no. 92, April 26, 2005. See also Michael Tanner, "The 6.2 Percent Solution: A Plan for Reforming Social Security," Cato Institute Social Security Paper no. 32, February 17, 2004.

176. The Social Security Administration's Office of the Actuary examined the Johnson-Flake bill and found that it would create permanent "sustainable solvency." See Tanner, "A Better Deal at Half the Cost," for a discussion.

177. Ibid., p. 4.

178. Richard Nadler, "The Rise of Worker Capitalism," Cato Institute Policy Analysis no. 359, November 1, 1999, p. 3.

179. Investment Company Institute and Security Industry Association, "Equity Ownership in America," 2002, www.ici.org/pdf/rpt_02_equity_owners.pdf.

180. A website devoted to social security reforms around the world is www.pensionreform.org.

181. Senate Committee on Government Affairs, vol. 2, p. 106.

182. Reuters, "Cost Increases, Delays Cited in FAA Programs," *Washington Post*, June 1, 2005, p. A17.

183. Ibid.

184. Amy Schatz, "FAA Plans Hiring Spree for Air-Traffic Controllers," *Wall Street Journal*, December 22, 2004, p. A8.

185. Sara Kehaulani Goo, "FAA Faults Air Traffic Controllers," *Washington Post*, June 3, 2005, p. A5.

186. Joel Bagnole, "How Canada Gets Jets across the Sea," *Wall Street Journal*, May 9, 2002, p. A12.

187. The Nav Canada website has background on the system at www.navcanada.ca.

188. GAO, "Commercial Aviation: Issues Regarding Federal Assistance for Enhancing Air Service to Small Communities," GAO-03-540T, March 11, 2003, Executive Summary.

189. GAO, "Opportunities for Oversight and Improved Use of Taxpayer Funds," p. 232.

190. Gabriel Roth, "Liberating the Roads: Reforming U.S. Highway Policy," Cato Institute Policy Analysis no. 538, March 17, 2005, p. 11.

191. Eric Pianin and Charles Babcock, "Easy Street: The Shuster Interchange," *Washington Post Magazine*, April 5, 1998.

192. GAO, "Maritime Administration: Weaknesses Identified in Management of the Title XI Loan Guarantee Program," GAO-03-728T, May 15, 2003, Executive Summary.

193. John Porretto, "Lott: Cruise Ship Loss May Top $200M," Associated Press, January 12, 2002.

194. U.S. Department of Transportation, Office of Inspector General, "Top Management Challenges," Report no. PT-2005-008, November 15, 2004.

195. *Budget of the United States Government: Fiscal Year 2006*, p. 242.

196. Ibid.

197. Anthony O'Connor, "Deutsche Bahn Moves towards Privatisation," August 12, 2003, www.janes.com.

198. CBO, "Budget Options," February 2005, p. 130. Cutting just five routes would save $250 million annually.

199. Steven Radelet, "The Millennium Challenge Account," Testimony to the Senate Foreign Relations Committee, March 4, 2003.

200. Ibid., p. 5.

201. *Budget of the United States Government: Fiscal Year 2006, Appendix*, p. 1007.

202. White House, "Fact Sheet: Continuing Support for Tsunami Relief," February 9, 2005, www.whitehouse.gov/news/index.html.

203. See discussion in CBO, "Budget Options," February 2005, p. 144.

204. GAO, "National Energy Policy," GAO-05-379, June 2005, p. 59.

205. Ibid., p. 79.

206. Ibid., p. 81.

207. Eric Pianin and Christopher Lee, "Corps of Engineers Chief Drafts Plan to Reorganize Agency," *Washington Post*, September 24, 2003, p. A27. See also Michael Grunwald and Mike Allen, "Corps of Engineers' Civilian Chief Ousted," *Washington Post*, March 7, 2002, p. A1.

208. Michael Grunwald, "Army Corps Delays Study over Flawed Forecasts," *Washington Post*, October 5, 2000, p. A33.

209. Michael Grunwald, "Army Corps Suspends Del. River Project," *Washington Post*, April 24, 2002, p. A27.

210. Pianin and Lee. See also Grunwald and Allen.

211. Grunwald, "Army Corps Delays Study."

212. CBO, "Budget Options," February 2005, p. 260. This is the annual average of CBO's 10-year estimate.

213. Aaron Lukas and Ian Vásquez, "Rethinking the Export-Import Bank," Cato Institute Trade Briefing Paper no. 15, March 12, 2002, p. 5.

214. Neil King Jr., "Questioning the Books: Senator Urges a Probe of Enron and Ex-Im Bank," *Wall Street Journal*, April 3, 2002.

215. Ibid.

216. NASA, Columbia Accident Investigation Board, *Final Report*, vol. 1 (Washington: NASA, August 2003), www.caib.us.

217. Ibid., pp. 170, 180, 185.

218. Senate Committee on Government Affairs, vol. 1, p. 4.

219. GAO, "Major Management Challenges and Program Risks: NASA," GAO-03-114, January 2003, p. 16.

220. GAO, "Space Station: Actions Underway to Manage Costs but Significant Challenges Remain," GAO-02-735, July 17, 2002, p. 1.

221. CBO, "Budget Options," February 2005, p. 74.

222. Joe Scarborough, *Rome Wasn't Burnt in a Day* (New York: HarperCollins, 2004), p. 100.

223. GAO, "Opportunities for Oversight and Improved Use of Taxpayer Funds," p. 102.

224. GAO, "Small Business Administration: Current Structure Presents Challenges for Service Delivery," GAO-02-17, October 26, 2001, p. 2.

225. Associated Press, "TVA Utility Spent Millions on Hospitality," *Washington Post*, October 18, 2004, p. A17.

226. Ruth Y. Goldway, Postal Rate Commission, Testimony to the President's Commission of the U.S. Postal Service, February 3, 2003, www.prc.gov/tsp/113/comments.doc.

227. GAO, "U.S. Postal Service: Bold Action Needed to Continue Progress on Postal Transformation," GAO-04-108T, November 5, 2003, Executive Summary.

228. Rick Geddes, "The Structure and Effect of International Postal Reform," American Enterprise Institute, April 29, 2003.

Index

An *n* following a page number denotes an endnote.

PNGV, 94, 169–70
Coburn, Tom, 13, 83, 135, 141, 143
Cochran, Thad, 54, 82
Collins, Susan, 115
Columbia disaster report, 64, 196
Commerce, Department of
budget and problem description, 160
high-priority targets, 160–62
high-priority targets (table), 39–40
Community Adjustment and
Investment Program, 93
Community Development Block Grants
(CDBG), 109, 114
termination, 179
community oriented policing services
(COPS) program, termination,
181–82
community service for seniors
program, termination, 183–84
Congress
1930s policy schemes and, 149–56
agency micromanagement, 53
budget-cutting freshmen reelections,
145–46
campaign promises, 18
constitutional limits and, 23–26
cost overruns and, 69–70
"due diligence" of programs, 140
duplicative programs and, 59
duties of reformers in, 140
energy bill, 168
failed focus on terrorism, 27
financial management and
accountability, 10
fraud and Catch-22 situations, 56
getting along/going along with
system, 21, 135
majority voting and cost benefit
analysis, 79–80
"New Federalism" revival attempt,
117
overspending. *See* overspending
philanthropic fallacy, 18–19
scandals arising from member fraud
and abuse, 57
special interests and. *See* special
interest legislation and spending
term limits, 20, 133–35
time and information overload
regarding grants, 114–15
vote trading, 80–81, 86
voter backlash from federal budget
cuts, 145–46
voting and spending patterns, 16

Congress as Santa Claus, 110–11
Congressional Budget Office (CBO)
"Budget Options" report findings
defense reform alternatives, 163
fossil fuel technology funding, 169
Medicare and Medicaid, 173, 174,
175
Social Security and price indexing,
185
Davis-Bacon rules, 131–32
economic cost of dollar of tax
revenue, 33
projection of federal revenues and
spending, 48–50
transfer program spending analysis,
89–90
congressional district benefits (pork
projects). *See* pork projects; special
interest legislation and spending
congressional hearings
reforms, 140
slanted witness phenomenon, 16,
17–18, 21–22
Congressional Research Service, 83
Conrail, 120
Constitution of the United States
balanced budget amendment, 137
Commerce Clause, 23–24, 25
doctrine of enumerated powers,
25–26
downsizing out of respect for, 23–26
FDR's subversion of, 156
General Welfare Clause, 24, 25
limited powers, 5, 23–26
Tenth Amendment, 25, 105
term limits amendment, 134
construction projects and procurement,
cost overruns, 65–70
"Contract with America," 17
contracting out
Bush administration activities, 121
Defense Department, 165
Coolidge, Calvin, on federal grants, 110
COPS. *See* community oriented policing
services (COPS) program
core government functions/services, 4,
9, 28
Holmes on taxes and civil society, 35
Coronado, Julia Lynn, 89
"corporate welfare" programs, 90–94
agricultural subsidies, 80–81, 90–93
Commerce Department, 90, 160–62
MARAD programs, 93–94, 191
OPIC, 46, 93, 104, 196

235

HUD, 177–79
Labor Department, 182, 183
Senate Committee on Government
Affairs examination, 58

Earned Income Tax Credit (EITC),
fraud, 56
EAS. *See* Essential Air Service (EAS)
Economic Development Administration
(EDA), 109
termination, 160
economic policies
damaging. *See* damaging laws and
programs
death spiral, 28–32
laissez faire, 6, 34, 150
mistakes causing the Depression,
150–55
economies of scale, performance and,
9–10
The Economist, 88, 146
Economy and the National Government,
142
EDA. *See* Economic Development
Administration (EDA)
Education, Department of, 13
abolition, 15, 117
budget and problem description,
165–67
education spending failures, 166–67
high-priority targets, 165–67
high-priority targets (table), 40–41
Title I program, 109–10
EIA. *See* Energy Information
Administration (EIA)
EITC. *See* earned income tax credit
(EITC)
elderly persons
community service for seniors
program termination, 183–84
Medicare reform options affecting,
173–74. *See also* Medicare
spending on, 28–32
electric utilities, privatization, 122, 125
elimination. *See* termination
Elk Hills Petroleum Reserve,
privatization, 120
employment cost increases, the
Depression and, 153–54
Employment Training Administration,
termination, 183
Energy, Department of (DoE), 4
budget and problem description,
167–68

cost overruns, 67
high-priority targets, 168–70
high-priority targets (table), 41
mismanagement, 63–64
subsidies spending, 88
energy conservation programs,
termination, 169–70
Energy Information Administration
(EIA), termination, 170
energy supply program, privatization,
168
England, Gordon, 164
Enron Corporation, 93, 104, 196
entitlement program spending, 1, 9, 137
business-as-usual budget scenario,
30–31
cost overruns, 68–69
reforms and spending cuts, 3, 6, 32,
38, 47, 137, 138
reforms and spending cuts (table),
39–46
see also Medicaid; Medicare; Social
Security
environmentally damaging laws and
programs. *See* damaging laws and
programs
Essential Air Service (EAS),
termination, 189–90
Even Start program, inefficiency, 166
Ex-Im. *See* Export-Import Bank (Ex-Im)
executive branch
duties of reformers in, 140
"enhanced recission" powers for, 138
federal spending increases and, 22
grants as political tools in, 113
presidential term limits, 133
Export-Import Bank (Ex-Im), 45, 195–96
export subsidies
damage from, 104
termination, 195–96

FAA. *See* Federal Aviation
Administration (FAA)
failures
accountability and, 114–15
education programs, 166–67
energy programs, 169
foreign aid system, 58
housing programs, 101, 103, 177–79
involving 9/11. *See* September 11
terrorist attacks (9/11)
NASA, 64, 196–97
noting and doing more "due
diligence" of programs, 140

237

political backing, 107, 108–10
as political tools in executive branch, 113
St. George's comment on irrationality of, 110
size and scope, 105–7
Warren on, 110–11
see also grants to states and local governments; grants, other
Federal Highway and Transit Administration, devolution to states, 190–91
Federal Home Loan Bank of Des Moines, study, 58
Federal Housing Administration (FHA), scandals, 177–79
federal income, size of government and, 35–36
federal loan and loan guarantee programs
as obsolete, 59
privatization, 127–31
federal officials. See bureaucracy; politicians, officials, and administrators
federal programs
"bedtime stories," 6
goal description and obfuscation, 71–72
presumption of government efficacy, 18
sunsetting, 61, 138, 140
see also targets for reform; specific programs
federal regulations. See regulations and regulatory agencies
Federal Reserve system, the Depression and, 149, 151
federal revenue. See federal spending; taxes and taxation
Federal Securities Act of 1933, 154
federal spending
in 2005, 9–11, 157
by agency/department/program, 13, 14. See also specific agencies, departments, and programs
beneficiaries of, 88–90
by budget categories, 13, 15
caps, 138
federal workforce compensation, 11–12
overall, distributional impact of, 89–90
percentage of GDP, 49–50

and the poor, 86–90
projection of federal revenues and spending, 48–50
purchases, 11
salaries portion, 88
scope of government and, 9–12, 57
see also overspending; specific expenditures, e.g., transfer payments/programs
federal spending increases, 1–2, 5, 7–9, 13–14
agency budget defense, 22
"baseline budgeting," 139
bureaucracy and, 22
executive branch and, 22
federal unions and, 22
Federal Trade Commission (FTC), antitrust and, 45, 96, 97–98
federal unions, spending increases, 22
federal workforce
1930s growth in, 154
executive performance, 77–78
"shadow workforce," 12
size and compensation, 11–12
workforce rules, 73–77
federalism
bipartisan report on, 27
1930s and, 7
original concept and modern practices, 105
Republican stance on, 14–15
see also fiscal federalism
Feldstein, Martin, 30, 33, 172
FEMA. See Federal Emergency Management Agency (FEMA)
FHA. See Federal Housing Administration (FHA)
financial crisis, looming, 1, 2, 187
firing poor federal workforce performers, 74–77
fiscal federalism, 105
efficacy of federal grant programs in helping the poor, 108–10
five pathologies of grants, 110–15
grant pathologies in homeland security, 115–16
"New Federalism," 106–7, 108, 116–17
size and scope of federal grants, 105–7
fisheries subsidies, 162
Flake, Jeff, 84
Food and Drug Administration (FDA), drug approval process, 99–100

food stamp programs, fraud, 55
foreign aid
  ineffective programs, 70
  system failures, 58
Foreign Market Development
  Cooperator, 159
foreign military financing and sales,
  program termination, 164–65
Forest Service, damaging subsidies,
  103–4
fossil energy research programs,
  termination, 168
Freddie Mac, 130
freedom, damaging laws and programs
  and, 99–100
FreedomCar and fuel cell subsidy
  program, 94, 169
FSA. *See* Farm Service Agency (FSA)
FTC. *See* Federal Trade Commission
  (FTC)
Fullerton, Don, 89

GAO. *See* Government Accountability
  Office (GAO)
GDP. *See* gross domestic product (GDP)
General Welfare Clause, 24
Gingrich, Newt, 15, 135, 141
Glass, Thomas, 89
Glass-Steagall Act of 1933, 151, 156
globalization, reforms and, 146
Gonzalez v. Raich, 24
Gordon, Nora, 109–10
Gore, Al, "reinventing government," 52
Government Accountability Office
  (GAO)
  BIA findings, 180
  business-as-usual budget scenario,
    30–31, 47–50
  cost overruns in and around
    Washington/Capitol Hill, 68
  DoE program findings, 63–64, 67,
    168, 169
  Essential Air Service program
    findings, 189–90
  FAA project findings, 126, 188
  financial statement certification
    problems, 10
  list of high-risk activities, 53
  MARAD program findings, 191
  NASA findings, 64, 196–97
  program analyses, 38
  terrorist "watch lists" report, 27
  TSA analyses, 176–77

  USPS findings, 122, 198–99
government jobs training programs,
  182, 183–84
government land, 131–32
government policy
  manifest and latent perspectives,
    19–20
  perversions and perverse results, 5,
    70, 101, 102–3
  theories involving key drivers of, 5
government property ownership and
  management, privatization, 121,
  131–32
government-sponsored enterprises
  (GSEs), 130–31
Grace Commission, 82
grants, other
  block grants, 109, 114, 175–76, 179
  Education Department, 165–66
  fraud and abuse in, 55, 56, 115–16
grants to states and local governments
  cuts, 50, 106–7, 108, 116–17, 165–67
  education, 165–67
  efficacy in helping the poor, 108–10
  energy conservation funding, 169–70
  five pathologies of grants, 110–15
  grant pathologies in homeland
    security, 115–16
  higher education, 89, 167
  juvenile justice grants, 182
  K–12 education, 166–67
  "New Federalism" and, 106–7, 108,
    116–17
  privatization of grants in aid for
    airports, 190
  size and scope of federal grants,
    105–7
  undermining states' rights, 113
Great Depression
  business cartels and artificially high
    prices and, 152–53, 155
  demonization of business and
    Supreme Court, 154, 155–56
  employment cost increases and,
    153–54
  FDR's executive orders/regulatory
    harassment and, 154–55
  international trade restrictions and,
    152
  monetary contraction and, 149, 151
  new government powers generated
    by, 7
  new investment cost increases and,
    154

About the Author

Chris Edwards is director of tax policy at the Cato Institute. Before joining Cato in 2001, Edwards was senior economist on the congressional Joint Economic Committee examining tax and budget issues. From 1994 to 1998, he was a consultant and manager with PriceWaterhouseCoopers, where he researched fiscal issues being considered by Congress. From 1992 to 1994, he was an economist with the Tax Foundation. Edwards's articles on the federal budget have appeared in the *Washington Post*, the *Wall Street Journal*, the *Los Angeles Times*, the *Washington Times*, *Investors Business Daily*, and other major papers. He holds a masters degree in economics from George Mason University in Virginia.

Cato Institute

Founded in 1977, the Cato Institute is a public policy research foundation dedicated to broadening the parameters of policy debate to allow consideration of more options that are consistent with the traditional American principles of limited government, individual liberty, and peace. To that end, the Institute strives to achieve greater involvement of the intelligent, concerned lay public in questions of policy and the proper role of government.

The Institute is named for *Cato's Letters*, libertarian pamphlets that were widely read in the American Colonies in the early 18th century and played a major role in laying the philosophical foundation for the American Revolution.

Despite the achievement of the nation's Founders, today virtually no aspect of life is free from government encroachment. A pervasive intolerance for individual rights is shown by government's arbitrary intrusions into private economic transactions and its disregard for civil liberties.

To counter that trend, the Cato Institute undertakes an extensive publications program that addresses the complete spectrum of policy issues. Books, monographs, and shorter studies are commissioned to examine the federal budget, Social Security, regulation, military spending, international trade, and myriad other issues. Major policy conferences are held throughout the year, from which papers are published thrice yearly in the *Cato Journal*. The Institute also publishes the quarterly magazine *Regulation*.

In order to maintain its independence, the Cato Institute accepts no government funding. Contributions are received from foundations, corporations, and individuals, and other revenue is generated from the sale of publications. The Institute is a nonprofit, tax-exempt, educational foundation under Section 501(c)3 of the Internal Revenue Code.

CATO INSTITUTE
1000 Massachusetts Ave., N.W.
Washington, D.C. 20001
www.cato.org